The only monthly magazine serving Lotus Notes & Lotus Domino application developers, managers and users.

SAMS
Teach Yourself

Lotus Notes 4.6

in 24 Hours

Cate Richards
with Stuart Hunter and
Jane Calabria, Dave Hatter,
Rob Kirkland, Susan Trost

SAMS
Teach Yourself

Lotus Notes 4.6

in 24 Hours

SAMS

A Division of Macmillan Computer Publishing
201 West 103rd Street, Indianapolis, Indiana 46290 USA

Sams Teach Yourself Lotus Notes 4.6 in 24 Hours

Library of Congress Catalog No.: 97-81440

ISBN: 0-672-31256-5

01 00 99 98   4 3 2

Interpretation of the printing code: the rightmost double-digit number is the year of the book's printing; the rightmost single-digit number, the number of the book's printing. For example, a printing code of 98-1 shows that the first printing of the book occurred in 1998.

All terms mentioned in this book that are known to be trademarks or service marks have been appropriately capitalized. Que cannot attest to the accuracy of this information. Use of a term in this book should not be regarded as affecting the validity of any trademark or service mark.

Screen reproductions in this book were created using Collage Plus from Inner Media, Inc., Hollis, NH.

President Richard K. Swadley
Publisher Don Fowley
Executive Editor Al Valvano
Managing Editor Sarah Kearns

Development Editor
Ami Frank

Technical Editor
Dave Hatter

Senior Editor
Mike La Bonne

Production Editors
Mike La Bonne
Tom Lamoureux

Editors
Jenny Clark, Pamela Emanoil,
Gayle Johnson, Julie MacLean,
Audra McFarland, Julie
McNamee, San Dee Phillips

Team Coordinator
Lynette Quinn

Brand Marketing VP
Jim Price

Brand Marketing Director
Alan Bower

Cover Designer
Tim Amrhein

Book Designer
Gary Adair

Production Supervisor
Andrew Stone

Production Team
Betsy Deeter, Brad Lenser

Indexer
Tim Tate

Overview

Contents

Hour 24   Working Remotely   333

About the Authors

Cate Richards is the Manager of Consulting & Application Solutions Services for Bay Resources, Inc., a Lotus Business Partner in St. Petersburg, Florida. Her primary responsibility is to manage and work with her team to assist clients in automating and maintaining their business systems by using Lotus Notes as the platform. She also spends a great deal of her time training and mentoring her clients and team in the use of Notes, assisting with reengineering business processes, and working with both to document clients' policies, procedures, and systems. Cate has worked with Lotus Notes for over seven years, and has been a beta test participant since version 2.0 of Notes. Cate holds a master's degree in business administration from the Roy E. Crummer Graduate School of Business at Rollins College in Winter Park, Florida, and a bachelor of arts degree in marketing from the University of South Florida in Tampa, Florida. This is Cate's sixth writing endeavor on Lotus Notes books for Que, and she is currently working on her seventh book—*Special Edition Using Lotus Notes & Domino 4.6*—written for the more advanced Notes user. Cate has also contributed time to Xephon as a technical editor for its *Notes Update* magazine. She is also an L-Team member, selected by Lotus, to assist users in the CompuServe Lotus Notes support forum (GO LOTUSC). You can find her there most days trying to assist other Notes users, and having a little fun at the same time! You can reach Cate via email at **crichards@bay.com**.

Stuart Hunter is a Certified Lotus Notes Engineer and Certified Lotus Notes Instructor working for Global Dynamics Inc., in Miami, Florida. His duties include managing and maintaining the Notes network at client sites and developing tools to help with that process. Originally from Edinburgh, Scotland, Stuart came to Miami by way of Paris, France, where he looked after the European Notes network for Unilever. Stuart lives with his wife, Jan, and their daughter, Alex. Stuart can be reached via email at **shuntera@compuserve.com**.

Jane "JC" Calabria is a Certified Lotus Notes Instructor (CLI), Certified Notes Consultant (CLP), and author of several Que books on Lotus Notes, including *10-Minute Guide to Lotus Notes Mail, Lotus Notes and the Internet 6-in-1*, and *10-Minute Guide to InterNotes Web Navigator*. She teaches classes in Lotus Notes, desktop applications, groupware, and Windows 95 for Rockey & Associates in Malvern, Pennsylvania. As a consultant, she works with Lotus Notes planning and implementation, Notes application development, and develops PC support organization models for large corporations. Jane is also a correspondent for Philadelphia's KYW News Radio 1060 AM where she broadcasts weekly as "JC on PCs" with her computer news and tips. She can be reached on CompuServe at **74754,3360**.

Rob Kirkland is a Certified Lotus Notes Instructor (CLI), a Certified NetWare Engineer (CNE), and a Microsoft Certified Product Specialist (MCPS) for Windows NT. He is a contributing author of several Que books including Using Windows NT Workstation, Intranet Publishing, Running a Perfect Intranet, and Intranet HTML. He teaches Lotus

Notes, Novell NetWare, Windows NT, communications software, numerous application programs, and hardware management. Rob works for Rockey & Associates in Malvern, Pennsylvania, with his wife, Jane. They are featured in two Lotus Notes training videos and CD-ROMs produced by LearnKey Inc., in St. George, Utah, titled *Lotus Notes Application Development I* and *Domino Web Server*. As a consultant, he sets up networks and designs applications, and subdues unruly hardware or software. In his spare time, Rob picked up a law degree. He can be reached on CompuServe at **74754,3360**.

Dave Hatter is a groupware/messaging specialist with Entex Information Services, the largest PC systems integrator in the United States, and is recognized as the leading provider of "Total PC Management" for large organizations. Dave has over five years of programming experience with a variety of tools and has been working with Lotus Notes for nearly three years. He is a Lotus Certified Notes Specialist (LCNS) for Notes R3.x, and a Certified Lotus Professional Developer and Certified Lotus Professional System Administrator for Notes R4.x. He holds a bachelor of science degree in information systems from Northern Kentucky University. Dave lives in Ft. Wright, Kentucky, with his wife, Leslee, and his son, Samuel. Dave can be reached via e-mail at **dhatter@one.net** or visit his Web page at **w3.one.net/~dhatter**.

Susan Trost is an independent Notes consultant and has been working with Notes since early 1992. She has worked internationally for Andersen Consulting and Lotus Development and was one of the first certified engineers for communications products at Lotus. Susan holds a bachelor of science degree from Towson State University in Maryland, and a master's degree in telecommunications from the University of Colorado in Boulder. She can be reached via e-mail on **100102,3500@compuserve.com**.

We'd Like to Hear from You!

As part of our continuing effort to produce books of the highest possible quality, Sams would like to hear your comments. To stay competitive, we really want you, as a computer book reader and user, to let us know what you like or dislike most about this book or other Macmillan products.

You can mail comments, ideas, or suggestions for improving future editions to the address below, or send us a fax at (317) 581-4663. The address of our Internet site is **http://www.mcp.com** (World Wide Web).

Thanks in advance—your comments will help us to continue publishing the best books available on computer topics in today's market.

Al Valvano
Executive Editor
201 W. 103rd Street
Indianapolis, Indiana 46290
USA

Although we cannot provide general technical support, we're happy to help you resolve problems you encounter related to our books, disks, or other products. If you need such assistance, please contact our Tech Support department at 800-545-5914 ext. 3833.

Acknowledgments

My first and foremost thank yous go to the teams of Lotus Notes professionals and Macmillan editors. Not only have I been blessed with wonderful folks who really know what they are doing, but also I have formed some lifetime friendships that span across the oceans! I would also like to give special thanks to **Stuart Hunter** for all of his hard work on this book. There would be no book without his dedicated help in getting so many of the chapters up-to-date. I salute you on your first book! I encourage you to review Stuart's and all of the past authors' biographies and the credits in the preceding pages.

Next in line, but first in my heart, is my family. My parents, **Ann** and **Bill Collins**, and my son, **Robert Richards**, have been my cheerleaders, dietitians, exercise monitors, sounding boards, housekeepers, back massagers, and all-around sanity checkers from day one! Mom and Dad, you are the greatest!! Without you I couldn't have gotten through this! And Robert, what can Mommy say…"You are my life!" Mommy is very proud of you! **Brother Bill** and **Sister Shau Li**, thank you for your support from afar—I promise to come see you at your house soon!

Heartfelt thanks go out to all of the folks at Lotus who have helped throughout the course of the development of this book. Special thanks go to **Landon Hunsucker** and **Sherry Lautenbach**, our Business Partner representatives in Atlanta, who have been fantastic in helping get the information we need for the book—as well as in answering all of those pesky questions we always seem to come up with! Thanks also to **Wizop Ildiko Nagy** for her assistance and trust in the CompuServe LOTUSC forum!

I would be remiss if I did not thank all of the folks at Bay Resources (who are too many to name individually). Special thanks to **Cass Casucci** and **Bob Hamilton** for all of your support. Your overwhelming encouragement in these "book things" is something I've never had before in a company, and it is greatly appreciated!

Thanks to all of the folks at Macmillan who have helped make this book happen. The folks at Macmillan are THE BEST around—even if they do set a deadline that keeps you working all night and through the weekend! Salute!

I have been told that I will be in big trouble if I don't say thanks to all of the folks in the CompuServe Lotus Notes forum (GO LOTUSC) for all of the inspiration, fun, and answers they have provided over the past year! LOTUSC is definitely the best (if not the wackiest) forum going! <CG>

Personal thanks to my mentors—**Linda Metcalf** (and **Doug**, too) and **Gary Strack**—for jump-starting me years ago into "doing what I want to do." —Cate Richards

I first thank my wife, **Jan**, for her support (and suffering!) throughout the long evenings and weekends spent researching and writing for this book. Thanks go too, to daughter, **Alex**, for the well-timed kisses and hugs, the innocent and genuine affection that reminds me what is really important in life.

Next, I thank **Cate Richards** for encouraging me to join her on this book and **Al Valvano** and **Ami Frank** at Macmillan for the sleepless nights and killing my social life. B-)

I owe a debt of gratitude and thanks to **John Haunton** and **Jean-Jacques Meric,** two outstanding Notes professionals from whom I learned a lot while in Paris. I look forward to meeting up with you soon.

Thanks also to the Ryder and IBM Notes teams of **Mike Deggs**, **Anita Morgan**, **Ron Sweat**, **Carol Shandraw**, and **Giorgio Mascagni** for their support and expertise. I think we make a great team.

Finally, thanks go to my parents back home in Edinburgh, **Jim** and **Sheila Hunter**, for their love and understanding and for always encouraging me to pursue my goals, even if it did mean taking their granddaughter to another continent!   —Stuart Hunter

Introduction

Chances are, your company has decided to implement Notes, and now you are trying to learn it. Good for your company and good for you! This book is set up to familiarize you with everything you need to know for your daily activities in just 24 hours.

Who Should Use This Book?

This book is written for the user who is new to Notes and wants to learn how to work with Notes documents and views. Readers of this book will learn how to work with NotesMail, the web browser, calendaring and scheduling, text and document features, and other features that make working with Notes easier and more beneficial. Readers will also learn how to customize their Notes environment to meet their needs and to set up and work remotely with Lotus Notes.

How to Use This Book

This book is set up as a task-based tutorial. Each chapter (as you will notice in the table of contents) focuses on some concept or activity that you need to understand or carry out to effectively use Notes in your everyday work.

Each chapter starts with a brief introduction to the material and a list of what you can expect to learn by the end of the chapter. Then, you'll go through some tasks, which you should read first and then attempt on your own equipment. Sometimes, you won't need to do anything except make sure you understand what's being discussed. At the end of every chapter, there is a workshop section, comprised of a summary, key terms, and common questions. You might find this review helpful when you run into a problem or term with which you are unfamiliar.

Does Each Chapter Take an Hour?

Each chapter should take you approximately one hour. Of course, this depends on your own personal speed and how much you choose to experiment with what you learn. Some chapters might take a little longer, whereas others will take less. That is the nature of the program and of different learners. But don't worry; the most important goal is that you learn! (Note: It will take you less time if you are already familiar with the Windows format.)

Conventions Used in This Book

Macmillian has over a decade of experience developing the most successful computer books available. That experience has taught us which special features help readers the most. Look for these special features throughout the book to enhance your learning experience.

Several type and font conventions are used in this book to help make reading and learning easier:

- ☐ *Italic* type emphasizes the author's points or introduces new terms.
- ☐ Screen messages, code listings, and command samples appear in a monospace typeface.
- ☐ Anything that you are asked to type appears in **boldface**.

Tips give you shortcuts and hints on how to get more productivity from Lotus Notes 4.6.

Notes give you comments and asides about the topic at hand, as well as full explanations.

Cautions tell you how to make your life miserable if you do something wrong. Heed these or suffer.

Sidebar

Longer discussions not integral to the flow of the chapter are set aside as sidebars. Look for these sidebars for additional information.

Hour 1

Understanding the Big Picture

Goals for This Hour

To work proficiently with Lotus Notes, first you need to learn some of the basics. In this hour, you learn to do the following:

- ☐ Start Notes
- ☐ Use the menu bar
- ☐ Use databases and workspace pages
- ☐ Use the SmartStatus strip
- ☐ Understand context-sensitive menus
- ☐ Work with SmartIcons
- ☐ Change the position of SmartIcons
- ☐ Customize SmartIcon Sets
- ☐ Resize SmartIcons

As you work through these lessons, you will gain knowledge of the basic workspace and language of Lotus Notes. This will provide you with a strong foundation for understanding the remaining building blocks of the Lotus Notes application.

Often, the most difficult part of working with Lotus Notes is trying to explain just what it is. You might think of Lotus Notes as simply electronic mail (email), because that is often where you begin your introduction to Notes. Or you might call it a database software package, a workflow product, a document library, groupware, communications software, and so on. In truth, Notes is all of these things and more. Notes consolidates the tools that an organization needs to communicate and collaborate effectively. Notes provides the following tools:

- ☐ Electronic mail (email)
- ☐ Group discussion
- ☐ Workflow
- ☐ Scheduling
- ☐ Document management
- ☐ Application development
- ☐ Web publishing and browsing
- ☐ Database replication
- ☐ Centralized directory services (the address book)

You can use Notes simply as an email package that enables you to send email to other Notes users on your network. Or, by having your Notes administrator install some special software and gateways, he or she can extend your email capabilities so that you can send and receive faxes, communicate with Notes users outside your network, and even send mail over the Internet to non-Notes users. When set up to use the adjunct products available with Notes, your network becomes a user-friendly, single source of access to multiple email and other communications services—essentially making Notes a "universal Inbox" for all your communication needs. You can send and receive mail by using any email package if you have a gateway (another server program that translates information) between the two systems.

Businesses benefit greatly not only from Notes' powerful email capability but also from the capability to redefine and automate their business processes. For example, many businesses using Notes have successfully automated their hiring process, purchase-approval process (to include signature authorizations at each phase), and many other tasks that before now have been so specific to a particular company that they have been too difficult or expensive to automate. Some companies run their entire business communications on Notes, often using Notes as a front-end, data-gathering tool for information that eventually is stored on a mainframe. Likewise, many companies build reporting applications in Notes that import data from mainframe computers to report across a wide range of users in a corporation.

1

There are not many business applications that cannot find a home in Notes. Many applications are simple, easy-to-develop databases that enable you to communicate better with a group of users; other applications might be sophisticated business process "programs" developed with a combination of Lotus Notes and other programming languages and software tools. Someone within your organization or outside consultants can design these applications. As you read this book, you will learn a great deal about the tools, applications, and methods for successfully working with Notes 4.6.

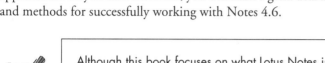

Although this book focuses on what Lotus Notes is, it is prudent to discuss briefly what it isn't. Lotus Notes is *not* a relational database system, in which changes made to one record automatically update all instances of that entry throughout the system.

For example, a bank might use an application that tracks all information about a banking customer for each account held at the bank. If the customer changes his or her phone number, a relational system updates that number throughout every record in the system related to that customer. In Lotus Notes, if the phone number changes in a customer record, you have to create an agent to update all instances of that phone number in subsequent documents related to that client; otherwise, you must edit the records individually to make the change. Careful layout of a database's design can overcome some of these limitations, but companies should keep this limitation in mind when deciding which system they need to address their business problems.

Nor is Lotus Notes meant to be a high-volume, transactional-based system that accesses and creates thousands of documents each day. Although Notes can handle high-volume tasks if you plan and develop the system carefully, the system's responsiveness and capacity might suffer. Companies should consider the transaction volume level when selecting which type of system best meets their business needs.

Task 1.1: Understanding What's New in Release 4.6

If you have worked with Lotus Notes before, you will find changes that further enhance your use of Notes. These changes are in response to the wealth of information provided by users, business partners, and Lotus support desk information collected over the past few years.

This section briefly highlights some of the major features that Lotus has incorporated into Lotus Notes 4.6 to give you a sneak peek at what you will learn in this book. The section covers only the highlights; you will learn more as you progress through this book.

New to Notes 4.6 are the following:

- ☐ *Portfolios*   You can now represent a collection of databases with a single database icon, so managing related databases has become a lot easier. You learn more about this feature in Hour 5, "Working with Databases."

- ☐ *Using Word or WordPro as your email editor*   If you need more powerful editing features in your email messages, you can now edit your email messages with Microsoft Word or Lotus WordPro. You learn more about this feature in Hour 9, "Creating Outgoing Mail."

- ☐ *Using Internet Explorer as your Web browser*   If you have found the browser in Notes to be lacking in some advanced HTML features, you can now use Microsoft's Internet Explorer as your Web browser from within Notes. You learn more about this feature in Hour 13, "Using the Personal Address Book."

- ☐ *Contact Management*   The Person document and People view are gone from the Personal Address Book, replaced by Business Cards that simplify the creation of contact information. You learn more about this feature in Hour 13.

- ☐ *Document Anchors, Background Bitmaps, and Horizontal Rules*   Lotus has not been blind to developments on the World Wide Web, and these useful features have now found themselves integrated into the Notes environment. Document Anchors enable you to create a link that points to a specific part of a document. You can now add Background Bitmaps—used creatively in Web documents—to your own Notes documents. Horizontal Rules enable you to place graphical lines in your text to break up different parts of the document. You learn more about these features in Hour 18, "Working with Advanced Document Features."

- ☐ *Computed Text*   You can dynamically display what text is shown in a document by using a Computed Text hotspot. You learn more about this feature in Hour 18.

- ☐ *Calendar Printing*   This was perhaps the most requested feature after it was found missing in Notes 4.5; you can now print your calendar entries from within Notes by using the Calendar Style you prefer. You learn more about this feature in Hour 20, "Working with Notes Calendaring and Scheduling."

As you can see, Lotus has added many enhancements to Notes 4.6. This book shows you the most effective ways to learn and use these new features.

Task 1.2: Starting Notes

To start Notes, locate the Lotus Notes icon on your Windows, OS/2, Macintosh, or UNIX desktop. The placement of this icon depends on how your company installed Notes on your PC.

The person who installs Notes on your desktop can determine where the icon appears on your desktop. You might have a group or menu option called Lotus Notes that includes the Lotus Notes program. You might want to copy the icon to your Windows or OS/2 Startup folder so that Notes starts automatically each time you start Windows or OS/2.

Start Notes as you would any other program. Place your mouse pointer on the Notes icon and double-click. As Notes starts, it briefly presents a splash screen of the Lotus logo. You then see a screen similar to that shown in Figure 1.1, which shows a Notes workspace as it typically appears when you first install Notes. If your company has customized your Notes installation, you might see additional database icons on your workspace pages. You learn what to do with database icons shortly.

Figure 1.1.

Lotus has made few changes to the workspace for Notes 4.6. If you are upgrading from Notes 3, however, you will find quite a few new features.

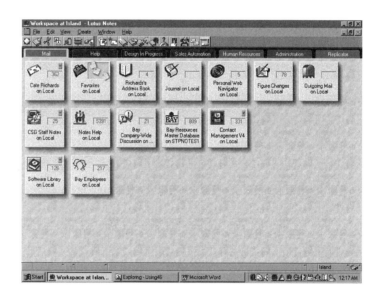

If you are new to Windows 95, the startup procedure for Notes might seem a little different than what you are used to. Simply choose Start, Programs. Find the menu option in which your Notes program is located (usually Lotus Applications). Click the Notes menu item. Notes then starts.

For other operating systems, follow your standard procedures for starting a program.

Task 1.3: Using the Menu Bar

Near the top of the Notes screen is the menu bar, which contains such words as File, Edit, View, Create, Actions, Window, and Help when you first start Notes. Each word represents a menu of operations. Table 1.1 briefly summarizes the operations available through each menu on the menu bar.

When you first start Notes, the menu bar does not display all menu commands available to you. Some commands are context sensitive—available only when you are performing particular functions.

Table 1.1. Menu operations.

Menu	Operations Accessed
File	Enables you to perform database operations, print documents, configure your environment, work remotely (not connected to a network), manipulate attachments, bring information from word processors and other programs into Notes, and save information from Notes to other programs.
Edit	Contains functions for moving, copying, and making other changes to documents; checking spelling; linking; working with unread marks; searching for text; and undoing the last command that you performed.
View	Enables you to determine what information you see onscreen.
Create	Enables you to create messages, documents, folders, views, agents, database designs, sections, tables, objects, hotspots, and page breaks. In Notes Release 3, this menu was called Compose.
Actions	Enables you to perform functions on a document, text, or database. You can move documents to folders; categorize documents; enter, change, or delete field values; edit, send, and forward documents; and perform such advanced actions as truncating, untruncating, and resaving documents.
Text	Enables you to alter the size, color, and font style of text within your message and to set tabs and margins.
Window	Provides a list of open Notes windows and enables you to switch from one window to another. You also can elect to tile, cascade, minimize, and maximize windows through this menu.
Help	Provides online help to all Lotus Notes functions and enables you to determine the version of Notes that you are using.
Table	Enables you to alter a table's size, color, borders, rows, and columns only when your cursor is located in a table.

Menu	Operations Accessed
Attachment	Provides actions you can perform on highlighted (selected) attachments, such as detaching selected documents. This menu command is available only when attachments are present in a document.
Section	Controls section attributes; for example, you can delete a section. This menu command is available only when collapsible sections are highlighted (selected) in a document.
Hotspot	Controls hotspot properties. You can delete the hotspot or change the way it appears in the document. This menu command is available only if a hotspot is selected in the document.

Other menu commands appear in the menu bar when you apply special functions in Notes. For example, if you insert a Lotus 1-2-3 worksheet into a document, a 1-2-3 Worksheet command appears in the menu to give you a quick way to manipulate the object's properties.

Task 1.4: Using Databases and Workspace Pages

You have already learned that Notes stores information in databases. Even if you use Notes only for sending and receiving electronic mail, you still need to learn how to manage databases, because your mailbox is a database. If you use Notes to its fullest, however, you and your coworkers will store and share many different kinds of information—status reports, customer records, sales prospects, various kinds of "paperwork," budgets, and so on. You might want to access dozens of different databases at different times. Organizing this information is the key to using Notes effectively.

Each database that you work with is represented by an icon located on a workspace page. When you first Notes, just below the SmartIcons you see what looks like a set of six file folder tabs, each representing a workspace page. You can think of workspace pages as categories of data. Just as you might use different drawers in a file cabinet to contain related files, workspace pages enable you to organize your databases into as many sections as you want (you start with six). You decide what to call each workspace page and which database icons you should place on each workspace page.

You can add, delete, and rename workspace tabs as you need them. You learn more about how to do this in the section "Customizing Your Workspace" in Hour 2, "Customizing Your Workspace."

Notes predefines a seventh tab, Replicator, that enables you to set up Notes to replicate database information between your remote PC and a Notes server, run agents, and send and receive mail when working remotely. You learn more about this tab in the section "Setting Up the Replicator" in Hour 24, "Working Remotely."

You can display any workspace page by clicking the tab associated with that workspace page. Each database appears as a box containing a name and a small icon. The icon is usually a picture that you can associate easily with the database's topic. A database of unsolved problems might have an icon that looks like a question mark, for example, or perhaps a frowning face. Sometimes each box displays other information about each database, depending on how you set up your preferences.

You decide what to call each workspace page tab. Many users label the first workspace page Mail and use it to contain the databases that they need to send and receive email, such as their mailbox and an address book that lists the users in their company. If you use Notes exclusively for mail, this workspace page might be the only one that you use. Together, the six workspace pages comprise your workspace.

Each Notes user can arrange his or her workspace pages in any convenient manner and can place any database on any workspace page. Notes does not require that everyone who uses a particular database puts that database on the same page. The organization of your workspaces is completely up to you.

Task 1.5: Using the SmartStatus Strip

The SmartStatus strip appears at the bottom of the screen. This strip of icons and messages displays information about network and hard disk activity, mail, database access levels, text attributes, and various status messages (see Figure 1.2). The strip is divided into segments that contain indicators. Table 1.2 describes the indicators in each segment.

Table 1.2. Understanding the status bar icons.

Status Bar Segment	Description
1	The first segment indicates disk or network activity. If a lightning bolt appears, Notes is accessing data across the network. If a modem appears, Notes is accessing the server via a remote dialup. The segment is blank when Notes isn't performing network access.
2	The second segment shows the current font that you are using. This segment is used only when you're editing a

Status Bar Segment	Description
	document or designing a new form and your cursor is located in a rich text field (see Hour 14, "Working with Text"). If you click this segment, Notes displays a list of available fonts and enables you to select a font.
3	The third segment—the font size segment—is, like the font segment, available only during editing. The font size segment displays the current text point size. Clicking this segment displays a list of the available point sizes. You can select a new point size by clicking one of the sizes in the list.
4	The fourth segment—the style segment—enables you to select a predefined style, such as bold red text. You will learn how to create styles in Hour 14.
5	The fifth segment displays status, error messages, and new mail messages. Check this section to see whether or not Notes is trying to communicate with you.
6	The sixth segment—the access level segment—indicates your permission level for the database that you now are accessing. You learn about the various access levels and how to interpret the icon in this segment in Hour 5. If you click this segment, Notes displays a message explaining the meaning of the symbol, as well as a list of all groups to which you belong and which of those groups are relevant to your access of this database.
7	The seventh segment—the location segment—indicates how your machine is set up to work. For example, if your computer is connected permanently to a network, the segment might display Office (Network). Hours 2, "Customizing Your Workspace," and 24, "Working Remotely," discuss other settings, such as Travel (Remote), Island (Disconnected), and Edit Current. To switch locations, click the segment, and a list of defined locations appears for you to select from.
8	The eighth segment displays an envelope when there is no new mail for you to read. If you have new mail, the segment displays a small blue Inbox with a yellow envelope in it. Clicking this segment opens a small pop-up menu from which you can open your email or select email options to create new messages.

Figure 1.2.

The status bar displays current activities performed by Notes and enables you to quickly access some of the most used features in Notes through pop-up menu selection lists.

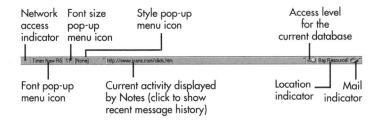

Task 1.6: Understanding Context-Sensitive Menus

You can access context-sensitive menus by clicking once with your right mouse button (right-clicking) anywhere in the Notes workspace. A context-sensitive menu of available commands appears next to your cursor, providing you easy access to the most commonly used functions in your current situation. The selections in this menu change as you perform different tasks in Notes. The context-sensitive menu in Figure 1.3 shows the commands available while you are entering text in a mail message.

Figure 1.3.

Context-sensitive menus help speed your work with Lotus Notes by placing some of the most common features that you need at the click of a mouse button.

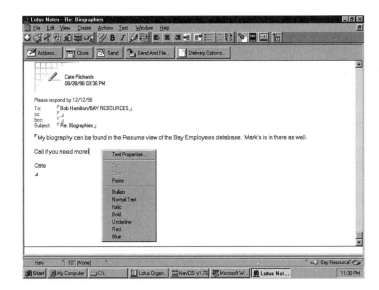

Task 1.7: Working with SmartIcons

Notes provides yet another way to perform common functions. Arranged along one edge of the screen (usually the top) is a row of icons, known as SmartIcons, that represent common functions (see Figure 1.4). SmartIcons represent the same operations that you can access with the pull-down menus, but they enable you to invoke these functions with a single click. For example, you can display the Notes ruler (explained in Hour 14) by clicking the SmartIcon that looks like a ruler instead of choosing View, Ruler.

Notes provides a SmartIcon for almost every operation, but the entire collection of icons would fill the screen. After deciding which operations you perform most often, you can tell Notes which SmartIcons you want to display.

Notes also displays context-sensitive SmartIcons—in other words, the icons displayed in the icon bar change according to where you are working at any given time. Context-sensitive icons display to the right on the SmartIcon bar; notice that these icons change as you perform different tasks in Notes. For example, when you open a database, the SmartIcons change to show icons used more often when looking for documents in a database—such as Expand and Collapse Category SmartIcons.

Figure 1.4.

SmartIcons provide shortcuts for performing menu commands.

Notes provides a default, *universal* set of SmartIcons to display. You can, however, add additional icons for Notes to display throughout your session in Notes that are not context sensitive. You also can choose whether Notes displays the context-sensitive icons or not by selecting File, Tools, SmartIcons, Context Icons. The default is to display context-sensitive SmartIcons.

If you want to hide the SmartIcons from your workspace, complete the following steps:

1. Choose File, Tools, SmartIcons.
2. Deselect the Show Icon Bar option in the SmartIcons dialog box.

Likewise, if you want to hide from the workspace only those SmartIcons that are context sensitive, deselect Context Icons. Finally, if you want to hide the icon descriptions that are displayed as "bubble help" when you point to an icon, you can deselect Descriptions. If you later change your mind and want to display any of these features, return to the SmartIcons dialog box and reselect these options.

You also can change which SmartIcon set Notes displays. To do so, open the SmartIcons dialog box and select from the drop-down list box the set that you want to use. You learn more about this dialog box later in this chapter.

Task 1.7.1: Changing the Position of SmartIcons

You can change the location of your SmartIcon palette. To do so, perform the following steps:

1. Choose File, Tools, SmartIcons. The SmartIcons dialog box appears (see Figure 1.5).

2. Click the down arrow in the Position list box.

3. Select the location in which you want to display the SmartIcons: Left, Right, Top, Bottom, or Floating.

4. If you do not want to customize your SmartIcons further, choose OK to save your settings and return to your workspace.

Figure 1.5.

Use the SmartIcons dialog box to add new icons to your SmartIcon bar, create custom SmartIcons, and change the position of the SmartIcons box.

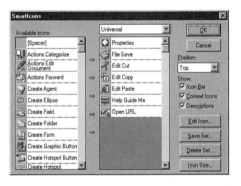

 If you are using Windows 95, you can reposition your Start menu by clicking anywhere within the bar and dragging it to a new position. This might make your workspace appear less cluttered at the bottom of your Notes windows.

By selecting Floating from the list of positions, you display the SmartIcons in a box (see Figure 1.6). You can drag the box to reposition it within the window. To resize the floating SmartIcons box, you can click any of the corners of the box and drag its borders until the box is the length or height that you want. Figure 1.7 shows the same set of SmartIcons floating after resizing.

Figure 1.6.

You can choose to float your SmartIcons on the workspace so that you can position them near the section of the page in which you are working.

Figure 1.7.

You can resize your floating SmartIcons box so that it is not in the way of the work that you are performing and is the shape that you want.

If you want to close the floating SmartIcons set, click the Close box in the window's upper-left corner. To redisplay the window, select File, Tools, SmartIcons, Show Icon Bar.

If you select Left or Right as the position for the SmartIcons, keep in mind that the height of your screen cannot display as many SmartIcons as the width of your screen does. If you find that one of these settings frequently results in truncating some of your SmartIcons from the set, you might want to select Top, Bottom, or Floating from the list or customize the SmartIcons set that you are using to display fewer icons.

Task 1.7.2: Customizing SmartIcon Sets

Although Lotus constructed a default set of icons named Universal that it considers useful, you are not locked into Lotus's choices. Within each set, you can add, remove, or rearrange icons, or even create new sets.

To customize the SmartIcon set, display the SmartIcons dialog box by choosing File, Tools, SmartIcons (see Figure 1.5). From the drop-down list at the top of the dialog box, select the SmartIcon set that you want to customize. The list box on the left displays all the available SmartIcons that you can put on a SmartIcon bar. Next to each icon, Notes displays the menu selections that you can make to perform the equivalent operation.

If you have not created any customized SmartIcon sets, the only set that your drop-down list of SmartIcon sets displays is universal. Although Notes enables you to edit this set, you might want to save the universal set under a different name by clicking the Save Set button, as described later in this section and then customizing the newly saved set of icons. This way, you can always restore the default set of SmartIcons to your workspace at any time.

The list box in the center of the dialog box shows the icons that now make up one of the available SmartIcon sets. (This section refers to this list box as the current set.) Select the set of icons that you want to customize.

To add a new icon to an existing set, find the icon in the list of available icons on the left side of the SmartIcons dialog box and drag it to the current set. Notes inserts the icon into the set. You can add the same icon to as many SmartIcon sets as you want. When you have added to the current list all the SmartIcons that you want, choose OK to save your changes and return to the workspace.

 At the top of the list of available icons is a special item called Spacer; it appears as a gray icon with no picture on it. If you insert this item in an icon set, Notes inserts a small gap between icons.

To remove an icon from the current set, drag the icon off to one side, out of the current set list box. (It doesn't matter where you drag the icon as long as it's out of the current set list box.) When you have removed all the SmartIcons that you want from the current list, choose OK to save your changes and return to the workspace.

Task 1.7.3: Resizing SmartIcons

Occasionally, you might want to change the size of the SmartIcons displayed. For example, you might want to increase the size of your SmartIcons when giving a presentation so that the audience can see which SmartIcons you are selecting. With the SmartIcons dialog box open, choose the Icon Size button. The Icon Size dialog box appears, as shown in Figure 1.8.

Choose Small (the default) if you want to display the SmartIcons in their usual size. Choose Large if you want to display large SmartIcons; of course, if you do so, you won't be able to display as many icons. Large icons, however, are ideal if you are using Notes to make a presentation or are working on a small screen.

Figure 1.8.

To increase the size of SmartIcons so that they are easier to see, choose Large in the Icon Size dialog box.

 You can create SmartIcons of your own that contain formulas to open databases, run agents, change font styles, and so forth. Though creating new SmartIcons is beyond the scope of this book, you can find instructions for doing so in your online Help database.

Workshop

Now that you have become acquainted with the Lotus Notes workspace, let's see what you remember! This workshop is provided to help review key terms that you have learned in this chapter, as well as review some of the most common questions asked when getting acquainted with Notes for the first time.

Key Terms

Review the following terms:

☐ *Menu Bar*   Located at the top of your Notes window, the menu bar displays the available menu commands that you can use during your Notes session. Each word represents a menu of operations available to you to perform specific operations in Notes.

☐ *Database*   A collection of documents that store related information. Notes displays databases on your workspace as square icons. You learn more about databases in Hour 5.

☐ *Workspace*   The window that Notes displays when you start Notes. It includes: the title bar, the menu bar, the SmartIcons bar, workspace (tabbed) pages that contain your database icons, the Replicator (a special workspace page where you manage database replication), and the status bar.

☐ *Workspace Page*   Tabbed folders used to organize subsets of database icons. Each page can hold 99 icons, and the page limit for the workspace is 32 pages plus the Replicator tab.

☐ *SmartStatus Strip*   Appears at the bottom of the Notes window as a gray bar divided into multiple sections. Each section of the SmartStatus strip displays information to you about the status of the activities or the Notes item you are working with at the time.

☐ *Context Sensitive*   When something is said to be context sensitive, it means that the item is available to you only when you are performing particular tasks. For example, the Context Sensitive menu that appears when you right-click your mouse button changes depending on the task you are performing. Context-sensitive features in Notes are provided to make it easier for you to find the appropriate menu command or SmartIcon given your particular situation.

☐ *SmartIcons*   Represent the same operations as menu commands but are provided as graphical buttons that you can push that perform operations with a single click—rather than as a series of clicks through menu commands.

Common Questions

Q I am working in Notes and can't find the SmartIcons to work with.

A Check to make sure you haven't changed the location of your SmartIcons, in which case they are just hiding from you. If you can't find them anywhere on your workspace, you probably just turned off the display of SmartIcons in an earlier session. Select File, Tools, SmartIcons, Show Icon Bar to redisplay the SmartIcon bar. If this does not work, you might have accidently deleted your UNIVERSE.SMI file. Check with your Notes Administrator for assistance in restoring this file.

Q I always use a particular set of menu commands to perform a function, and I want to cut down on the number of clicks it takes to perform that function.

A Check to see if there is a corresponding SmartIcon for the menu command sequence you are using. To do so, select File, Tools, SmartIcons to open the SmartIcons dialog box. Scroll through the SmartIcons in the left list box to see if there is a SmartIcon that performs the menu command sequence you use. If there is, click the SmartIcon once and drag it to the position in which you want it located on the right side of the SmartIcon dialog box. The SmartIcon will now be available to you throughout your session in Notes.

Preview of the Next Hour

Now that you have learned a little bit about what Notes is and have begun the process of learning your workspace, you will look further into customizing your workspace to meet your needs. The next hour looks at arranging your workspace so that you can find things more quickly.

Hour 2

Customizing Your Workspace

Goals for This Hour

Many Notes users spend most of their day working with the program. If your job requires a great deal of contact with other people, much of that interaction might involve exchanging messages through Notes. If you're going to work frequently with Notes, you will be pleased that you can customize most aspects of the program.

Your workspace page is the starting point for your Notes work each day. Although it is perhaps not as important to you as organizing the databases in which you work, organizing your workspace page can help you quickly locate those databases. If a well-organized desk is important to you, a well-organized workspace page will appeal to you as well.

You already know that your Notes workspace page is divided into workspace pages and that each database you access appears on one of the pages as a box with an icon. When you want to add a database to a workspace page or create your own database, the first step is to select the page on which you want the database to appear.

When you start using Notes, you probably will work with only a few databases: your mailbox, the Name & Address database, and perhaps one or two information databases that your department uses. Because the number of databases with which you work is small, you probably can put all your databases on a single workspace page.

As your familiarity with Notes increases and your use of Notes expands, you will work with more and more databases. Eventually, you might want to use more databases than can fit on a single workspace page (a single workspace page can hold 99 database icons). Long before that happens, however, your page probably will become so cluttered that you will want to organize it. The tasks in this chapter prepare you to do just that.

In this hour, you learn about arranging your workspace pages and icons, configuring Notes, and setting up your printer. You also learn a little bit about the special Notes file called DESKTOP.DSK. Specifically, in this hour, you will be

☐ Arranging your workspace pages

☐ Setting up your printer

☐ Changing your password

Task 2.1: Adding New Workspace Pages

Notes 4.6 enables you to add more workspace pages (tabs) to better organize your workspace. You can have up to 32 workspace pages in addition to the tab titled Replicator. Notes automatically adjusts the size of the tabs to accommodate the addition of extra tabs, and it adjusts the size of the words that you enter as tab titles. However, if you enter more text and tab combinations than Notes has room to display, the tabs on the right side of the workspace begin to disappear. If that happens, the only way you can move to those tabs is to highlight any tab and then press the right-arrow key to move to the tab to the right and view the contents of the hidden workspace pages.

To add a new workspace page, follow these steps:

1. Click the workspace page tab to the right of where you want to insert a new tab.

2. Choose Create, Workspace Page. If you haven't added a workspace page before, Notes asks whether you want to upgrade your desktop file.

3. Choose Yes to add the workspace page and upgrade your desktop file, or choose No to cancel adding the page.

You can right-click a page tab and select Create, Workspace Page from the context-sensitive menu as an alternative to steps 1 and 2.

When you add workspace pages to your workspace, you modify DESKTOP.DSK, the file that stores your personal preferences and setup information. After you modify this file in Notes 4.x, you cannot use the file with previous releases of Notes.

2

Task 2.2: Deleting Workspace Pages from Your Workspace

Just as you can add workspace pages to your workspace, you can also remove workspace pages. When you remove a workspace page, however, you also remove any database icons that you have positioned on the page. If you do not want to remove the icons from a workspace page, you must move them to another page before following these procedures.

To remove a workspace page from your workspace, follow these steps:

1. Click the workspace page's tab.
2. Choose Edit, Clear or press Delete.
3. Choose Yes to confirm the deletion or choose No to cancel it.

You can also remove a workspace page by clicking anywhere in the page you want to delete and then right-clicking and selecting Remove Workspace Page from the context-sensitive menu that appears.

Task 2.3: Naming Workspace Page Tabs

When your workspace starts to get cluttered, you might want to name the workspace pages so you can better organize your workspace and find things more easily. To name a workspace page, follow these steps:

1. Double-click the workspace page tab that you want to name. The Workspace Page properties box for the selected tab appears (see Figure 2.1).

Figure 2.1.

You can name your workspace pages by opening the Workspace Page properties box.

2. In the Workspace Page Name text box, type the tab's new name.

3. Select a color for the tab by choosing a color from the Tab Color list box.

4. Click the X in the upper-right corner of the properties box to close the properties box and put your changes into effect.

Task 2.4: Moving Databases on the Workspace

You can move database icons from one page to another at any time. Click the workspace page on which the database now resides, and then drag the database from that page to the tab belonging to the page where you want to place the database. As you drag, a box appears around the title of the workspace page tab on which the database icon will be placed. When the correct tab title is selected, release the mouse button. Notes moves the database to that page. You can move multiple databases by holding down the Shift key, clicking each of the database icons that you want to move, and then dragging the icons to the new page.

As you move icons from one workspace page to another, you might find that the icons on the pages become rather disorganized. You can tell Notes to "straighten up" a workspace page by selecting the page and then choosing View, Arrange Icons. Notes arranges all the database icons on the current page at the top of the page with no gaps.

You can also move the icons on your Notes workspace pages without using a mouse. To do so, follow these steps:

1. Select the icon that you want to move.

2. Press and hold down Shift+Ctrl.

3. Use the cursor arrow keys to reposition your icon.

4. Release Shift+Ctrl.

5. Press Enter when you have completed the move. The icons now appear on the newly designated workspace page.

Task 2.5: Working with Stacked Icons

Occasionally, you might want to keep more than one database icon for the same database on one workspace page. Perhaps you have access to the same database that is stored on more than one server on your network, or maybe you're working remotely and want to keep a replica of a database that is stored on your hard drive, as well as the icon pointing to the main database stored on your network. Regardless, after a while, your workspace page might become cluttered with all the copies of the database icons that are displayed.

To clean up the workspace page, you can set your workspace page to show all database replicas (identical copies) as stacked icons. Stacked icons take up less room on your workspace page and make it easier to work with all the databases at once. When you stack icons, the top-leftmost icon displayed on the workspace page appears at the top of the stack. Notes displays stacked icons with a stacked icon indicator in the icon's upper-right corner, as shown in Figure 2.2.

Figure 2.2.

You can stack replica copies of icons so that they take up less room on your workspace page.

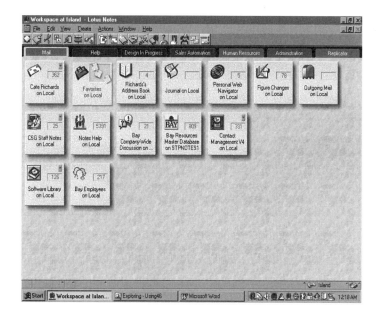

Task 2.5.1: Stacking Database Icons

If your icons do not appear to be stacked even though you are sure they are replicas, choose View, Stack Replica Icons. A check mark appears, indicating that the selection is active. Notes remembers this setting until you turn it off.

When you stack icons, Notes checks your location and displays either a *server replica* (if you are connected to the network in an office) or a *local replica* (if you are not connected to a network) at the top of the stack. As each icon reaches the top of the stack, it automatically displays in its title either the server name or "Local." Using these indicators, you can tell immediately which copy of the database you are using: a server copy (a network copy) or local copy (a copy stored on your hard drive). For example, in Figure 2.2, you see Cate Richards's database located on the Local hard drive.

Task 2.5.2: Using Stacked Icons

Typically, you store replica copies of databases on your hard drive when you are working away from a network (see Hour 21, "Working Remotely," for more information on creating replica copies of databases). You might also keep replica copies of a database on your hard drive if you are modifying a database's design but prefer not to make your changes directly in the production server copy.

Regardless of the reason for having multiple replicas of a database on your workspace page, you frequently might need to switch between the replica copies during your work session. Because the replica at the top of the stack is the database that Notes works on, you simply need to select a different replica to place on the top of the stack. To do so, follow these steps:

1. Click the stacked icon indicator (the down arrow) in the database icon's upper-right corner. The database icon menu drops down (see Figure 2.3).

Figure 2.3.

Select the database indicator to choose between replica databases when their icons are stacked.

2. Select the copy of the replica in which you want to work. For example, in Figure 2.3, the Local copy of the database is currently at the top of the stack (the check mark is displayed next to Local). To bring the network copy's icon to the top of the stack, select the name of the server in which the replica is stored. In this example, you would select BRSTPNOTES01/BAY RESOURCES.

 Hour 24 discusses the Replicate option in the Database Location menu. That hour also covers more about working with replica databases in general.

If you decide you do not want your replica icons stacked anymore, choose View, Stack Replica Icons to remove the check mark. Your icons are immediately removed from the stack and arranged on the workspace page.

Task 2.6: Deleting Database Icons from Your Workspace

From time to time, you may want to remove database icons from your workspace so that it isn't quite so cluttered. To do so, simply click the database icon once, and then press the Delete key (or select Edit, Clear). Notes will ask if you really want to remove the icon from your workspace page. Choose Yes to remove the icon, or choose No to tell Notes to leave the icon on the workspace page. If you want to remove multiple database icons from a single workspace page, press the Shift key and then highlight each of the database icons you want to remove before you press the Delete key. Notes will prompt you for each icon you highlighted before removing the database icon from your workspace page.

Removing the database icon and deleting the database are not the same thing. To delete a database, you select the database and choose File, Database, Delete. This command physically removes the database (if you have access permission to do so). When you delete a database, you are physically deleting the file from your hard drive or server—and you can't add it back once you delete it. When you remove a database icon, you only remove the icon from your workspace page. The file is still located on your hard drive or server, so you can add the database icon to a workspace page again.

Task 2.7: Compacting Your Workspace Page

When you add database icons, workspace pages, private views, and other features, they are stored in your DESKTOP.DSK file. If you later remove some of these features, Notes leaves some white space in the database where the definition used to be stored. Over time, this white space can accumulate, consuming valuable disk drive space. You can, however, remove the white space by compacting your DESKTOP.DSK file. Compacting recovers unused disk space by removing references to databases no longer on your workspace.

To compact your DESKTOP.DSK file, follow these steps:

1. Double-click any workspace tab. The Workspace properties box opens.
2. Click the Information tab. (The tab is marked with a bold lowercase i.) The Information page appears (see Figure 2.4).

Figure 2.4.

In the Workspace properties box's Information page, you can compact your DESKTOP.DSK file.

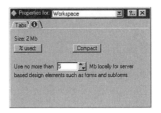

3. Click the % Used button.

4. If the percentage is over 85 percent, click the Compact button. (If the percentage is under 85 percent, you don't need to compact the file yet.)

You now have a cleaner DESKTOP.DSK file that takes up less space on your hard drive. You should periodically check the size of your DESKTOP.DSK file as a "housekeeping" measure, particularly if you are short on hard drive space.

Task 2.8: Setting Up Your Printer

You use your operating system software to tell your computer what kinds of printers are available. For example, in Windows 95, you use the Printers properties box. The only information that Notes needs is the printers that you want to use.

To set up your printer, use the following steps:

1. Choose File, Print to open the File Print dialog box shown in Figure 2.5.

2. Select the Printer button located in the upper-left portion of the dialog box. Notes then displays a list of available printers in the Print Setup dialog box (see Figure 2.6). If you have only a single printer available, Notes displays only that printer.

3. Select the printer you want to use, and then choose OK. After you select a printer, Notes routes all printouts to that printer until you change your selection.

Figure 2.5.

In the File Print dialog box, you can choose the Printer button to switch printers or make changes to your printer setup.

Figure 2.6.

The Print Setup dialog box lists the available printers. Select the printer you want to use or the printer for which you want to make setup changes.

2

The Print Setup dialog box also enables you to configure various aspects about how the printer works. To do so, you simply choose the Setup button. However, for most of your printing needs, you should not have to modify any of these options.

Perhaps the most common printer setup change is to switch between landscape and portrait printing. When you choose portrait printing, text is printed parallel to the short side of the paper (like a typical letter); when you choose landscape printing, text is printed parallel to the long side of the paper (like a typical certificate). You can make changes to the paper orientation through your operating system's printer setup, but you can make the same change by choosing File, Print, Printer, Setup. The Printer properties dialog box opens, as shown in Figure 2.7.

Figure 2.7.

You can switch between landscape and portrait printing in the Printer properties box (if your printer supports landscape printing).

The options available in this dialog box depend on the type of printer that you have selected, so you might see a slightly different Printer properties box for your printer. Figure 2.7 shows the Printer properties box for a Hewlett-Packard LaserJet 4P printer. In the Orientation combo box, select the paper orientation that you want to use, click OK, and then click OK again to save your settings. Typically, the page orientation settings remain effective until the next time you change them. However, some networks are set up and administered to always shift print settings back to their default.

If you have additional questions about the options that this dialog box displays for your printer, refer to your printer manual.

Task 2.9: Changing Your Password

Notes maintains several important pieces of information about you. Some of this information (such as your user ID number) isn't of personal concern to you but is vital to Notes. You can display some of the information by choosing File, Tools, User ID. Notes prompts you for your Notes password. Type your password and choose OK. When you choose this command, the User ID Information dialog box appears (see Figure 2.8).

Figure 2.8.

The User ID Information dialog box summarizes your personal ID information. You can choose the Set Password button to change your Notes password.

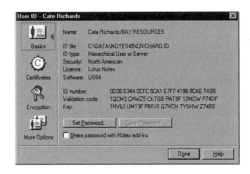

This dialog box provides the following information about your ID file:

- ☐ User name
- ☐ ID filename and location
- ☐ ID type
- ☐ Security (North American or International)
- ☐ License type
- ☐ ID number
- ☐ Software number
- ☐ Validation code
- ☐ Key

Opening this dialog box enables you to do the following:

- ☐ Change your user name
- ☐ Work with certificates
- ☐ Work with encryption keys
- ☐ Work with advanced options concerning your Notes ID

Don't change your user name, certificates, or other advanced options that you see in the User ID Information dialog box. Contact your Notes administrator for assistance. Modifying these settings might make it impossible for you to work with Notes. You should use this dialog box only to change your Notes password.

This book only covers changing your Notes password. If you need to perform any of the other activities in this dialog box, you should contact your Notes administrator, because modifying these features can cause a whole lot of trouble!

 If you change your user name, Notes removes all the certificates from your ID. That means you will have to acquire new certificates before you can use any shared databases (databases not on your local drive). Instead of doing it yourself, contact your Notes administrator if you need to change your user name! Your Notes administrator should make a backup copy of your Notes ID before changing your name (but just in case, you should back up your Notes ID as well). With this backup, you can access previously saved information even if you cannot do so with your new name and ID.

The User ID dialog box's most important option is probably Set Password, which enables you to change your password. Although security experts recommend that you change your password regularly, most people change their password only when they have a pressing need for a new one (for example, if a trusted friend who knows the old password turns out to be a snoop!).

To change your password, choose File, Tools, User ID. Enter your current Notes password when prompted. Then choose the Set Password button. The Enter Password dialog box appears, prompting you for your old password (see Figure 2.9). Enter your old password and then choose OK.

Figure 2.9.

To change your password, you must first enter your current Notes password in the Enter Password dialog box. You then type your new password when prompted.

Make sure you enter a password that others cannot easily guess but that you can easily remember. Unless your Notes administrator has a backup Notes ID with your original default password locked away for safe keeping, if you forget this password you also lose your access to Notes until a new Notes ID can be created for you. If you encrypted any data using your old Notes ID, you will never be allowed to access that information again!

The Set Password dialog box then prompts you to enter your new password (see Figure 2.10). Type in your new password and choose OK. As is always true when you enter a password, your new password doesn't appear on-screen as you type.

To ensure your security, avoid creating passwords that your acquaintances can easily guess. For example, don't use your child's or pet's name. Also, remember that passwords are case sensitive and you can decrease the chance of someone guessing your password by varying the case of the letters that comprise your password. For example, if you want to enter pluto3 as your password, type it as plutO3—capitalizing the O (or any other letter). Adding numbers to the password also makes it more difficult for others to guess your password.

The minimum number of characters required for a new password can vary, depending on the minimum character limit that your Notes administrator might have set when issuing your Notes ID. Lotus recommends a minimum character limit of eight, but your administrator can set the limit as low as zero. If Notes rejects your new password, try entering a password with more characters.

Figure 2.10.

You can enter a new password in the Set Password dialog box, but take note of the minimum number of characters that your Notes ID requires for a password.

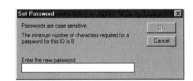

Finally, Notes prompts you for your new password again. This safety feature helps ensure that you typed the password correctly. Notes signals an error if you didn't type the same new password both times; otherwise, Notes accepts the new password, which you must use the next time that you start Notes or clear your logon. Choose Done to exit the User ID dialog box.

> The User ID dialog box includes a Clear Password button that you can click to remove your password. However, if you value your mailbox's security, do not use this option. Otherwise, after you clear your password, anyone who has access to your laptop or PC can access your Notes mailbox and even send mail under your name.

Workshop

Now that you have learned to arrange your workspace and configure your printer, you are ready to test your memory on a few key words or phrases that have been used this hour. This workshop will help you remember some of the key topics discussed by reviewing the key words and outlining the most commonly asked questions regarding workspace management and printer configuration.

Key Terms

☐ *Workspace*   The window Notes displays when you start Notes. It includes the title bar, the menu bar, the SmartIcons bar, tabbed workspace pages that contain your database icons, the Replicator (a special workspace page where you manage database replication, and the status bar.

☐ *Workspace pages*   Tabbed folders used to organize subsets of database icons. The workspace can contain up to 32 workspace pages (in addition to the Replicator page), and each page can hold 99 icons.

☐ *DESKTOP.DSK*   A file that contains information about your workspace, such as the database icons you have added to it.

☐ *Database*   A Notes database generally contains information in a single area of interest (such as a new product discussion, a set of industry news items, or all the processes, forms, and policies for a department such as customer service). A database can be used by an individual only, or it can be shared. If you've worked with other database software, you may think of the items within a database as "records." You can think of a document within a Notes database as a record, but a document is more sophisticated than a typical database record because it can contain rich text, pictures, objects, and many other types of information.

☐ *Database icon*   On the workspace page, a database icon is the square that identifies a database. Within each database, a database icon is the bitmap image that is embedded in the database to allow the users to quickly identify a database on the workspace.

☐ *Stacked icon*   Replica copies of a database from different locations (server A, server B, local, and so on) can be displayed as a stack in order to reduce clutter on a user's workspace.

☐ *Password*   Prevents other users from using your User ID to access shared Notes databases and identifies that you are allowed to use the Notes ID that the password is protecting. Once you set a password, Notes always prompts you to enter it when you access a Domino server for the first time after starting Notes. For security reasons, when you enter your password in the text box, the entry is not displayed on the screen.

Common Questions

Q You removed an icon from my workspace, and now I need to get it back. I try to open the database, but I can't seem to find it to add back. What is happening?

A There is a slight change that The Manager of the database set up so that the database would not show up in the Open Database dialog box, in which case you must know the exact path and filename of the database to be able to add it. You may need to contact your Notes administrator for assistance if the database is "hidden" from public view. However, if you used to have Manager-level access to the database, you may have accidentally deleted it by selecting File, Database, Delete instead of highlighting the database and pressing the Delete key. If you have a backup copy of the database, you can restore it. Otherwise, contact your Notes administrator to see if perhaps he or she made a backup of the database from the server.

Q You try to add a new workspace page to the workspace, and you are prompted that by doing so you will be upgrading your DESKTOP.DSK file and will not be able to undo this process. What should you do?

A Unless you plan to reinstall Notes 3.x on your workstation and want to use your current DESKTOP.DSK file (or unless you want to copy the current DESKTOP.DSK to another workstation running Notes 3.x), simply select Yes to tell Notes to go ahead and continue adding the workspace page.

Q You have added several workspace pages to your workspace, and now you can't see those to the far right side of your workspace—even though you know they are there. What do you do?

A Click any of the workspace tabs, and then use the right-arrow key on your keyboard to move from tab to tab until you find the one you are looking for.

Q You don't work on a remote computer, and therefore, you don't use the Replicator tab. How can you get rid of it?

A You can't. The Replicator tab will always appear at the right end of your workspace.

Preview of the Next Hour

Now that you have learned to arrange your workspace and set up your printer, it is time to learn about setting up your Notes Preferences. Your Notes Preferences control the environment in which Notes operates, and "tweaking" them can make working with Notes easier for you.

Hour 3

Specifying Your Notes Preferences

In Notes User Preferences dialog box, you can customize various aspects of Notes. Choosing File, Tools, User Preferences opens the User Preferences dialog box, which provides a single location for customizing all your global preference settings.

Goals for This Hour

The User Preferences dialog box consists of the following four sections:

- ☐ *Basics* is a panel that enables you to control startup options, the location of your Notes data directory, colors, and your User Dictionary.

- ☐ *International* consists of settings that enable you to customize the way Notes translates particular international symbols, casing, and collation. You also can select which international dictionary you want to use.

☐ *Mail* consists of settings that enable you to specify how you want Notes to treat your mail—for example, whether you want Notes always to save the mail that you send or to prompt you to confirm that you want to save mail each time you click the Send button. You also define the location of your mail database and which mail editor you are using and tell Notes how you want to check for new mail.

☐ *Ports* enables you to control the modem or network port that Notes uses to connect with the Notes server. Your system administrator can assist you with any changes that you might want to make in this pane, if you are unsure of the settings that you need to specify.

This hour teaches you how to customize Lotus Notes to work best with the tasks you want to perform in your work environment, by using the User Preferences dialog box. Specifically, you learn how to do the following:

☐ Customize the basic settings of Notes

☐ Customize the International settings

☐ Customize mail settings

Task 3.1: Using Basic Settings

The User Preferences dialog box always opens to the Basics settings as the default, as shown in Figure 3.1. Most of the settings that you make in this pane do not take effect until you restart Lotus Notes.

Figure 3.1.

The Basics settings pane enables you to change many of the default startup settings in Notes.

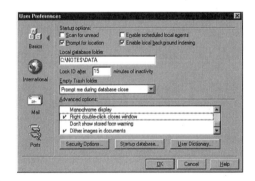

The pane's largest portion displays the Startup options, which consist of check boxes and text boxes that govern the actions that Notes takes each time you start Notes. The following sections describe the options.

Task 3.1.1: Scanning Unread Documents

If you want to cut the time you spend searching through a database to find documents you haven't yet read, you might want to use the Scan Unread feature in Lotus Notes. If you frequently want to scan for unread documents in one or many of your documents, you might want to tell Notes to simply prompt you whenever you start Notes to read your unread documents. If you choose the Scan for Unread option, Notes scans some or all of your databases for unread documents each time you start Notes. You can determine which databases Notes scans in the Scan Unread dialog box (for more information about scanning for unread documents, see Hour 6, "Understanding Documents").

Task 3.1.2: Prompting for Location

The Prompt for Location option causes Notes to display the Choose Location dialog box each time you start Notes. You might find this feature handy if you travel frequently with your laptop, because you can select any of the locations that you have defined in your Address Book. The locations that you define tell Notes whether it is on a network or is working remotely. They also enable you to tell Notes the phone numbers to call when you are working remotely and the time zone in which you are working. You also can change the date and time entries when prompted for your location. You learn more about this setting in Hour 24, "Working Remotely."

Task 3.1.3: Starting the Agent Manager

If you want to start the Agent Manager automatically when you start Notes, choose the Enable Scheduled Local Agents option in the User Preferences dialog box. With the Agent Manager, you can run agents (macros) in the background. This way, Notes automatically performs tasks that you set up, such as filing documents, finding particular topics, or sending mail at particular times.

Task 3.1.4: Indexing in the Background

Enable Local Background Indexing option enables you to create full-text indexes in the background so that you can continue working while Notes creates these indexes. A *full-text index* is a collection of files that indexes the database's text so that you can use queries to search for text anywhere in the database.

Task 3.1.5: Changing the Default Data Directory

By choosing the User Preferences dialog box's Local Database Folder option, you can specify where to keep Notes data files (databases, desktop settings, and so on). C:\NOTES\DATA is the default location, and you typically do not need to change this setting unless you have customized your file structure so that the location of Notes data changes. You can use this option to specify an alternative directory in which your local databases reside.

Notes 4.x uses C:\NOTES\DATA as the default data directory when the software is installed; this is a change from Notes 3, which used C:\NOTES as the data directory. Unless you change your data directory, this directory is where Notes looks for all your data files. If you choose File, Database, Open and do not see any databases listed, your data directory probably is not set correctly. Contact your Notes administrator for assistance.

Task 3.1.6: Setting the Automatic Logoff Point

The Lock ID After Minutes of Inactivity option enables you to specify how long Notes keeps your password active before logging you off. You specify the number of minutes since you last pressed a key or moved your mouse. After this duration, Notes logs off automatically, and you will have to reenter your Notes password the next time you access your database.

Don't choose a setting so short that Notes doesn't give you a chance to review a complex document, embedded chart, or spreadsheet. A setting between 15–30 minutes usually suffices to protect your Notes security while minimizing the number of times that you have to enter your password during a Notes session. Of course, you can log off anytime during the setting you select without shutting down Notes by pressing F5.

Task 3.1.7: Emptying the Trash Folder

Your mail database has a trash folder that contains all of the mail you have marked for deletion during a session. You can tell Notes how to empty the trash folder with three options:

- [ ] Choose Prompt Me During Database Close to have Notes ask whether or not you want to clear the mail in the trash folder each time you close your mail database. This is the default selection.

- [ ] Choose Always During Database Close to have Notes automatically clear the mail in the trash folder each time you close your mail database.

After you empty your trash folder, you cannot undo your deletion. You cannot get the mail back!

- [ ] Choose Manually to cancel automatic clearing of the trash folder. If you select this option, you must select Actions, Empty Trash to clear the mail in the trash folder.

Task 3.1.8: Selecting Advanced Options

You can select many advanced options that give you further control over many of Notes features when you start Notes. The following list summarizes these options.

☐ *Marking previewed documents as read*   Choose the Mark Documents Read when Opened in Preview Pane option if you want Notes to mark a document as being read when you preview it in the Preview pane (even if you haven't opened it). You learn more about the Preview pane in Hour 5, "Working with Databases."

☐ *Selecting monospaced font*   Notes normally uses proportional fonts, in which letters require varying amounts of screen space. In a proportional font, a capital M, for example, takes up much more space than a lowercase i.

> The Typewriter Fonts Only option tells Notes to display all information (including database titles, views, and documents) in a monospace font, in which all letters take up the same amount of space. You might find this option useful for checking the width of columns. If a column is wide enough in a monospace font to display its entire contents, the column probably will be wide enough when you switch back to a proportional (non-monospace) font.

☐ *Selecting large fonts for display*   The Large Fonts option tells Notes to display text in large letters. This option increases the font size displayed in the database icons (as well as the size of the database icons). It also increases the font in the views and forms as it is displayed on your workstation. The option does not change the size at which the font prints or the size at which other users' monitors display it—unless they also have selected the Large Fonts option. You might find this option handy if the regular characters are too small to read comfortably onscreen, if you need to view the screen from a distance, or if you are giving a presentation in which many people need to see the screen.

> Selecting the Large Fonts option might cut off text in your database titles. This truncating occurs because the text becomes too large to fit in the small areas. Also, the option specifies that Notes reorders the icons on your desktop so that they fit. If you deselect the option later, the icons still are stacked only four across rather than the standard six or more (depending on your monitor size and screen display).

3

☐ *Turning Internet URLs into hotspots*   By selecting the Make Internet URLs into Hotspots option, you tell Notes to convert Internet addresses into hotspots automatically if you are set up to have Notes interface with the Internet through Notes 4.x's web browser feature. A URL (Uniform Resource Locator) is the World Wide Web name for a document, file, or other resource. It describes the protocol required to access the resource, the host where it can be found, and a path to the resource on that host. If you are configured to access the web through Notes, click a URL hotspot to have Notes take you to the referenced web site.

☐ *Changing your workspace's texture*   You can choose to have Notes display the workspace with a three-dimensional, marbled look by selecting the Textured Workspace option. When you click a database icon with this selection, the icon appears to flatten against the workspace to indicate that it is selected.

> You must have 256-color-display capability to display a textured workspace.

☐ *Keeping the maximized workspace in back*   The Keep Workspace in Back when Maximized option enables you to keep the Notes workspace behind other open windows automatically when you maximize the Notes window. This way, each time you close a window, Notes returns to the most recently active window rather than the workspace.

☐ *Using monochrome settings*   When you select the Monochrome Display option, Notes displays everything in black and white (monochrome), even if you are using a color monitor and a Windows-based, OS/2, or UNIX operating system. Occasionally, you might find this option handy if you design databases and want to see how they look on a monochrome monitor.

☐ *Closing windows by right-double-clicking*   If you select the Right Double Click Closes Window option, you can close any open window by double-clicking your right mouse button while your cursor is anywhere within the window. If you were a Notes 3 user, you probably will want to select this option immediately!

☐ *Keeping all Notes windows within the main Notes window*   You can select the Keep All Windows Within the Main Notes Window (MDI) option to have Notes windows maximize only as large as the main workspace window. This option is the default selection. If you deselect this option, Notes windows opened within the main Notes window can be maximized to fill the entire screen—even if the main Notes window does not.

☐ *Enabling plug-ins*   A plug-in is a dynamic software module that extends the capabilities of the web browser when you are working with the Web Browser feature. There are many plug-ins available, such as those that run with Netscape, and that provide support for multimedia viewers, utilities, and applications within the context of a web browser. Notes supports plug-ins so that when you want to use a particular plug-in, you download it and install it on your hard drive. Then, when Notes encounters an HTML page with an object specified by the <EMBED> tag or with a URL whose data is supported by an installed plug-in, Notes loads the appropriate plug-in to display that object. To use these features, select the Enable Plug-ins option in Advanced Options.

> To ensure that Notes can find the plug-ins you have downloaded, install all of them in the same folder on your computer. If you have Netscape already installed on your computer, make sure all plug-ins are installed in the Netscape plug-ins folder.

3

☐ *Enabling Java applets*   You can tell Notes to enable Java applets so that you can view them with the Personal or Server Web Navigator. By default, this option is not selected. Even if you select this feature, you must also adjust the settings in your Location document's Java Applet Security section to use this feature. You learn more about working with the web navigators in Hour 22, "Understanding the Web Navigators."

☐ *Dithering images to match your display*   By selecting the Dither Images option, you tell Notes to use a particular pattern of pixels to convert a graphics image to something more appropriate for your particular display. You might select this option to fine-tune graphics images so that they appear sharper on your monitor.

☐ *Making Notes the default web browser*   You can tell Notes to be your default web browser by selecting this option. You will learn more about working with your web browser in Hour 19.

☐ *Securing your data*   When you choose the Security Options button, you can make selections in the Execution Control List (ECL). These selections can protect your data against the threats of mail bombs, viruses, Trojan horses, or unwanted application intrusions that you might encounter when surfing the Internet. ECLs provide a way for you to specify whether or not such executable files can execute— and what level of access to give the program.

ECLs are specific to your DESKTOP.DSK file on your PC, and you can control them to a very granular level, as shown in Figure 3.2. For example, you might stipulate that when a certain trusted colleague electronically signs a document, programs executed by that document can access documents and databases, as well as modify environment variables but cannot access the file system or external programs. This feature, introduced in Notes 4.5, can protect your data when you access documents from Notes locations.

Figure 3.2.

Execution Control Lists (ECLs) enable you to indicate what types of executable files can execute and what level of access to give the program.

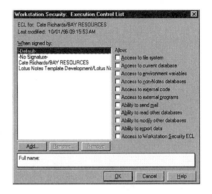

☐ *Choosing which database opens automatically when you launch Notes*   Select the Startup Database button to tell Notes which database, if any, you want to open automatically when you start Notes. The Startup Database dialog box, shown in Figure 3.3, lists the databases according to the workspace page in which they are located. You can select one database title and then choose OK to save your setting.

Figure 3.3.

You can select a particular database to open automatically when you first start Notes.

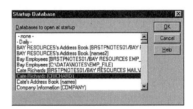

☐ *Changing the user dictionary*   Choosing the User Dictionary button causes Notes to display the User Spell Dictionary dialog box (see Figure 3.4). In this dialog box, you can add, update, and delete words that you have defined in your personal user dictionary. As you learn in Hour 6, you also can add words to your personal user dictionary while you are checking your documents' spelling. Typically, you open the User Spell Dictionary when you need to remove or correct the spelling of a word in this dictionary and use the spell checker interface to add new words and phrases.

To add new words to your dictionary, type the new word in the text box at the bottom of the dialog box and then choose Add. To delete a word, select it from the scrolling list box and then choose the Delete button. To edit an existing word, select the word from the scrolling list box, edit the text in the text box, and then choose Update. Choose OK to exit the dialog box and save your changes or Cancel to exit without saving your changes.

Figure 3.4.

In the User Spell Dictionary dialog box, you can make the Notes spell checker work more efficiently by defining words, names, and phrases that you commonly use.

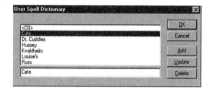

Do not press Esc to exit this (or any) Notes dialog box. If you do, you lose any setting changes that you have specified. Pressing Esc is the same as clicking the Cancel button.

Task 3.2: Using the International Settings

To display the options for International settings, click the International icon in the User Preferences dialog box. Notes displays the International settings panel shown in Figure 3.5. Through this panel, you can control characteristics that tend to vary from one country to another. These characteristics are described in the following sections.

The International settings do not change the currency denomination indicator nor the date format used in many countries outside of North America. You make these changes in your operating system.

For example, if you want to use British pounds Sterling, or the date format dd\mm\yy, you can open the Windows Control Panel and select the International icon. Change the Country setting to United Kingdom. The currency indicator and date format default then change to reflect the common format used in the United Kingdom.

Check your operating system's documentation for additional information on changing the international default settings.

Figure 3.5.

*You can change your
dictionary, import/export
character-translation sets,
and other settings that
typically change, based on
your international
location.*

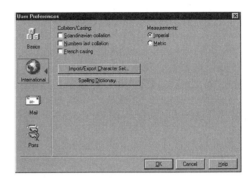

Task 3.2.1: Controlling Collation and Casing

In Lotus Notes, database designers can specify that a view lists items in a particular sort order—ascending or descending. Using the Collation/Casing options, you can tell Notes how to treat some of the characters when sorting. You can choose any or all of the options. If you choose Scandinavian Collation, Notes puts accented characters at the end of the alphabet (which is where Scandinavians put them). If you choose Numbers Last Collation, Notes assumes that numbers follow letters (therefore, part number 6X032 appears after ZY512). If you choose French casing, Notes discards accent marks when you change lowercase letters to uppercase.

When you import or export data from Notes, the program uses Country Language Services (CLS) files to translate accented letters and international currency symbols—such as the pound (£) and yen (¥) symbols. Notes also uses CLS files to determine the order in which to sort characters.

To re-sort the documents in an existing database with the selections made in this section, restart Notes and then press Ctrl+Shift+F9 after you open the database that you want to view.

The collation and casing options are off by default. If you choose these options, they won't take effect until the next time you start Notes.

Task 3.2.2: Changing the Unit of Measurement

The Measurements options enable you to specify Imperial units of measurement (inches, which is the default) or Metric units (centimeters). Your choice determines whether or not you must specify margins and tabs in inches or in centimeters. If you are displaying the ruler, this option changes the unit of measurement to inches or centimeters.

Task 3.2.3: Translating Files

When you are importing data into Notes from another application, the Import/Export Character Set button enables you to specify a file for translating foreign characters and symbols from a non-Notes file into Notes. When you press this button, the Choose Translation Table dialog box displays (see Figure 3.6).

You can either select an existing translation (CLS) file from the Choose New Import/Export Character Set Translation File list box, or type the path and filename of a CLS file that you want to use that is not stored in your data directory. Application designers typically use this option to populate a new database with information from another application. You can leave this setting unchanged unless you need a special translation file.

Figure 3.6.

The selection that you make in the Choose Translation Table dialog box determines how Notes translates characters when you import or export documents.

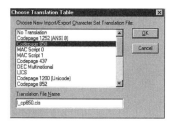

Task 3.2.4: Selecting a Dictionary

By using the Spelling Dictionary button, you can tell Notes which dictionary (such as French or British) to use rather than the American dictionary.

The dictionary files are not the same as your user dictionary, in which you add terms when you select Define while using the spelling checker. These files are located in your Notes program directories. The default file is English.

Task 3.2.5: Setting the Starting Day of the Week

You can specify the day of the week on which your week starts by selecting Week Starts On and then selecting the day of the week from the list. This setting is important if you use the Calendaring and Scheduling features, because Notes uses this setting when laying out the calendar pages. The default setting for this option is Sunday.

Task 3.3: Using Mail Settings

You can control how Notes accesses and processes your mailbox. Simply choose File, Tools, User Preferences and then click the Mail icon on the left side of the dialog box. Notes then displays the Mail setup options in the User Preferences dialog box.

> The first setting you see when you click the Mail icon in the User Prefer-
> ences dialog box is Mail Type. This setting enables you to identify which
> email package you plan to use when working in Lotus Notes. For most of
> you, the default will be Lotus Notes unless your system administrator
> instructs you otherwise. This book only covers working with the Lotus
> Notes email system. If you have another email option such as cc:Mail
> selected, contact your system administrator for instructions on working with
> that application.

Task 3.3.1: Saving Sent Mail

With the Save Sent Mail option, you can tell Notes how you want to treat mail when you
select the Send button (or choose Actions, Send Document). If you want to keep a copy of
each memo that you send, select the Always Keep a Copy option. If you do not want to save
a copy when you send a memo, select Don't Keep a Copy. If you want Notes to prompt you
to save every time you send a message, select Always Prompt.

> If you select Don't Keep a Copy, Notes doesn't prompt you to save a
> document when you select the Send button to send the message. Instead,
> Notes simply sends the document and closes it. If you later want to
> reference the document, you cannot do so unless the recipient sends it
> back to you. Selecting one of the other two options is safer if you think
> you might need to review any of the messages that you send.
>
> If instead of clicking the Send button, you right-double-click or press Esc to
> exit and send the document, the check box highlights your default
> selection for saving sent mail. You can deselect the option for that
> instance, however, before you click Yes to send the mail message.

Task 3.3.2: Selecting Your Local Address Books

If you travel often, you might want to carry more than one Address Book in which you can
select users' names from the list of available recipients. For example, in addition to your
Personal Address Book, you also might want to take your company's Public Address Book.

Your Personal Address Book's file, NAMES.NSF, must be located in your Notes data
directory. To configure Notes to access any additional Address Book, you must type or select
the Address Book's filename in the Local Address Books text box. You can click the Browse
button to select the filename, or you can type the filename directly in the text box. Use
commas to separate each filename.

The address books that you enter in this text box must be located in your Notes data directory (see the discussion on your data directory earlier in this Hour). Notes saves this text box's setting to your NOTES.INI, which is a special settings file that tells Notes where to find particular information and how to treat it.

> The maximum character length for this text box is 255 characters—the limit set by Notes in the NOTES.INI file.

When you select the Action bar's Address button while composing an email message, you can switch from one address book to another if you have defined both address books in the Local Address Books text box.

> When you send mail or use the Notes type-ahead feature to address mail, Notes looks in the first database that you listed in the Local Address Books text box, checks the next database, and so on. You should keep your Personal Address Book (NAMES.NSF) as your first entry and then list all subsequent databases in the order in which you want Notes to search them.

Task 3.3.3: Checking for New Mail

As you learn in detail in Hour 8, "Using Mail Basics," Notes notifies you when new mail arrives. By changing the number of minutes specified in the Check for New Mail Every Minutes setting, you can control how often Notes checks the server to see whether or not new mail has arrived. If you need to find out quickly when new mail arrives, enter a small number (perhaps 3 or 4). If you receive mail rarely, or if you do not need to be notified immediately, entering a larger number (15 or 20) saves your computer the work of checking frequently. If you clear the associated check box, Notes doesn't automatically inform you when new mail has arrived; you've got to check for yourself periodically.

You also can tell Notes how you want it to notify you of new mail—audibly, visually, or both. If you choose Audible notification, Notes plays a short tune whenever you receive new email. If you choose Visible notification, Notes displays a small dialog box to notify you that new mail has arrived. To clear this dialog box from your screen, choose OK.

Task 3.3.4: Signing and Encrypting Sent Mail

If you select the Sign Sent Mail check box, Notes checks the Sign box when you mail a document. Hour 4, "Understanding Access Control Lists and Security," describes this check box in more detail, which serves much the same purpose as a signature on a paper message.

When you select the Encrypt Sent Mail option, Notes automatically checks the Encrypt box when you close a mail document. See Hour 4 for more information about encrypting messages.

Task 3.3.5: Encrypting Saved Mail

If you check the Encrypt Saved Mail option, Notes encrypts mail stored in your mailbox on the server and in your hard drive if you work remotely and have a copy of your mail database there. Although you usually can assume that your mailbox is private and secure, a few people, such as your system administrators, can access your mailbox without your permission. You can use this option if you are particularly concerned about keeping the messages in your mailbox secure.

Task 3.3.6: Choosing a Document Memo Editor

You can select whether you want to use Microsoft Word, Lotus WordPro, or None as your mail document editor. If you select MS Word or Lotus WordPro, you will be able to use their respective word processing packages as the tool to type and edit text while creating documents in your mail database. If you select None, you will use the standard Lotus Notes word processing capabilities to create your mail documents. You will learn more about this feature in Hour 9, "Creating Outgoing Mail."

Task 3.4: Using Ports Settings

The Ports panel in the User Preferences dialog box provides options and buttons that enable you or your system administrator to configure how your computer communicates with your server and what kind of network or modem your computer has. After your computer is set up, you normally do not have to adjust any of these options if you are working on the network. If you need to change your ports setup but lack experience in doing so, consult your system administrator.

If you are working remotely, you might use the Ports preferences quite frequently. Because setting up your ports is beyond the scope of this book, contact your Notes Administrator for assistance setting up or changing your port settings.

Workshop

Now that you have learned to configure your workstation to work to your advantage, see what you have learned. This workshop will highlight the keywords and questions you may have when customizing Notes to work for you.

Key Terms

Review the following list of terms:

- [ ] *Agent Manager* Enables agents (macros) to run in the background. Notes can automatically perform tasks that you set up, such as filing documents, finding particular topics, or sending mail at particular times.

- [ ] *NOTES.INI* A special file typically stored in your Windows or Notes directory that controls many of the aspects of your Notes environment. When you customize Lotus Notes to work best for you, Notes updates the NOTES.INI file so that those changes are remembered for each working session. As customization selections are stored in the NOTES.INI file—which is stored locally on your workstation hard drive—these selections are specific to your particular workstation. If you use two different PCs to access Notes from different locations, you must make the customization selections twice (or copy the NOTES.INI file from one location to another).

- [ ] *Data directory* The directory specified for Lotus Notes to store all of your data files— your DESKTOP.DSK file, Notes databases that you store on your hard drive, your Personal Address Book, and your Notes ID to name a few.

- [ ] *Unread documents* Documents that you have either not read at all or have not read since they were modified by someone other than yourself. Notes typically displays unread documents in a color (usually red) that is different from documents that have been read, along with a star in the left-hand margin next to the document's name. The designer of the database can modify how a document is displayed, however, if it has not been read by you.

- [ ] *Dither images* An option that enables you to tell Notes to use a particular pattern of pixels to convert a graphics image to something more appropriate for your particular display. This option does not modify the graphic image permanently but tells Notes to display it in a format best supported by your particular display monitor.

- [ ] *URL* *(Uniform Resource Locator)* The standard Internet protocol that enables web clients to request specific pages from web servers. When you type in a URL— for example, **http://www.lotus.com**—the web client (your browser) sends the request to the HTTP server. Each web page has its own URL.

Common Questions

Q How can I log off Notes without waiting for the timeout feature?

A Log off manually by pressing F5.

Q Why is logging off Notes a good idea when not using the application or when leaving the workstation?

A If the workstation is unattended, anyone can access all files (for good or bad) as though he were the user. Updating, copying, editing, and deleting are all possible if the user has those permissions.

Q What is an ECL and why is it important?

A An Execution Control List (ECL) is a security feature. The ECL protects your data against the threat of mail bombs, viruses, Trojan horses, and unwanted application intrusions that you might encounter when surfing the Internet and are specific to your DESKTOP.DSK file on your PC. ECLs can specify whether such executable files can execute.

Q I am used to double-clicking the right mouse button in Notes 3.x to close a document or exit a database. Now I have been upgraded to Notes 4.6 and can't perform that feature, which is a real time-saver. How do I re-enable this feature?

A Select File, Tools, User Preferences and select the Right Double Click Closes Window option in the Advanced Options list box. You must restart Notes before this option will be available to you.

Q I want to carry a copy of my company's Public Address Book on my laptop when I am working remotely so that I can select user's names when addressing mail. I figured out how to make the replica copy of the Public Address Book onto my hard drive (see Hour 24), but when I try to use the Address button in my email database to access the Public Address Book, it doesn't list it as available.

A Remember, you need to tell Notes if there is more than one address book that you want to use in your working sessions. Refer to Task 3.3.2: "Selecting Your Local Address Books" in this Hour's lesson to guide you through making these selections.

Preview of the Next Hour

Now that you have Notes set up to work as you prefer, it is time to prepare for actually working with Notes databases. Before you can do that, however, you need to review a few brief lessons on Notes security. The next Hour's lesson walks you through an understanding of Lotus Notes security and working with your Notes ID and password.

Hour 4

Understanding Access Control Lists and Security

Goals for This Hour

Before you can work in a Notes database—whether it is your Mail database or another one in which you are interested—the Database Manager must grant you access to the database. If you have tried to open a Notes database on a server, you already know that you need your Notes password before you can go any further. If you do not have access to the database or do not know your password, you can't open the database. In fact, you can't even add a database to your workspace if you do not have access to it. Notes security provides many ways to protect the information with which you are working.

In this hour, you discover how Notes secures the databases and the Notes environment in which you are working. You learn about the following:

- ☐ Understanding Notes security
- ☐ Working with access control lists

☐ Changing your Notes password

☐ Making a backup copy of your Notes ID

☐ Requesting and receiving an updated certificate

Task 4.1: Understanding Notes Security

Whenever people store and distribute data, there is always the danger that prying eyes will intercept or even alter that data. Some data might be subject to simple nosy snooping—perhaps an employee that wants to examine personal records of other employees. Other data might be critical to a project's success, making it attractive to corporate spies. Whatever the reason, much of the information passed around inside companies is secret from somebody.

Notes provides several features to protect your information in various ways, and you learn about these features in this hour.

Task 4.1.1: Learning the Four Levels of Security

Notes offers significant control when it comes to securing your data. There are several security options available to you, ranging from protecting a Notes server from unwanted eyes to verifying the author of a single field of information to prevent forgery. The following list introduces you to the four levels of Notes security:

☐ *Server-Level Security*   Before you can access a database on a server, you must have access to the server. The server administrator controls server access through the use of certificates attached to your ID file and server access lists. This is the first and most general layer of security.

☐ *Database-Level Security*   Database security for any database on a server is handled by the database access control list (ACL). The ACL lists users and servers and assigns them rights to that particular database. Access levels range from Manager—who has total access to the database—to No Access. The Database Manager creates and controls the ACL and can use a combination of individual names and group names to simplify the management of who can access the database.

An additional database-level security feature is local encryption, which encrypts local databases (those stored on your hard drive) so that only specified users can access them.

☐ *Document-Level Security*   Document security consists of the document's read access list, which refines the ACL for that document; this means that if someone has Reader access or better in the ACL but is not listed in any read access list, he or she cannot read the document. If they are not readers in the ACL, they cannot read the document even if they are listed in the document's read access list.

☐ *Field-Level Security*   Certain fields on a form can be encrypted by using encryption keys, so only users with the correct key can read those fields. The database designer specifies that fields are encryptable, and when an encryption key is associated with the document, all encryptable fields are encrypted with the key.

> Encryption means encoding data so that only those who have the encryption key can read it. Essentially, when you encrypt information, you scramble it in a way that makes it unreadable to anyone that does not have the code (often referred to as the key) to un-encrypt it. Users who have the proper key then perform a related task when they open the document that converts the scrambled message back to its original form.

Task 4.2: Working Your Notes ID

The key to protecting your information in Notes is your Notes ID file. All security features in Notes work through the information contained in your ID file. Through your ID file, Notes grants you access to the information you're supposed to see and keeps you out of documents and databases that are off limits to you.

Your Notes ID file contains the following information:

☐ Your name

☐ Your Lotus Notes license, which gives you permission to use Lotus Notes

☐ Your private and public encryption keys, which Notes uses to encrypt and decrypt messages

☐ Your password

☐ Encryption keys and certificates

You can usually find your ID file in the Notes Data directory—look for a file with an .ID extension. For example, the ID file for Cate Richards probably would look something like this: crichard.id. Some users keep their ID file on a floppy disk as extra security because it can be locked up at night, they can take the file with them when they travel, or they can place it in their home directories on their LAN, so it can be accessed from any workstation on the LAN.

Task 4.2.1: Working with Your Password

If your ID file is your gateway to Notes, your password is your key to your ID file. Notes will not enable you to use the information stored in your ID file until you have entered your correct password. This means that you can not access most of the information in Notes without knowing your password. By requiring you to enter your password, Notes can ensure that only you can use your ID file and the information it contains.

It is crucial that no one but you knows your password. With your password and access to your ID file, someone else can access your mailbox, read and compose documents in databases to which you have access, send messages with your name, and decrypt messages you receive.

The first thing you need to keep in mind regarding your Notes password is that it is case sensitive—in other words, it matters whether you type your password in uppercase, lowercase, or a combination. For example, if your password is changeme, and you type it as CHANGEME or ChangeMe (or any other case combination), you will be prompted that your password is incorrect because you entered it in the wrong case.

When your system administrator installs Lotus Notes on your PC, he or she creates an ID file that contains your initial password. You should immediately change this to a new password. Follow this procedure to change your ID password:

1. Choose File, Tools, User ID. Notes displays the Enter Password dialog box (see Figure 4.1). Notes asks you to type in your current password before you can access any of your user options.

Figure 4.1.

Type your password exactly as it was given to you. Remember, passwords are case sensitive!

2. After you've typed your password, click OK to display the User ID dialog box (see Figure 4.2).

Figure 4.2.

Click the Set Password button to change your password.

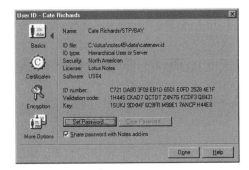

3. Click the Set Password button to change your Notes password.

4. Notes prompts you for your current password to ensure that it is really you trying to change your password.

5. Notes displays the Set Password dialog box, which reminds you that Notes pass-words are case sensitive; this means that if you capitalize any letters in your new password, you must capitalize those same letters each time you use your password in the future. Enter your new password and choose OK.

6. Notes displays another Set Password dialog box. Enter your new password again, and choose OK. By making you repeat your password, Notes ensures you didn't mistype your password the first time. If the two attempts to enter your new password don't match, Notes makes you repeat steps 3 through 5.

> As you type your password, you might notice that a random number of Xs appears for every letter or number you type. This prevents someone looking over your shoulder from telling how many characters are in your password simply by counting the Xs.

Try not to forget your password. If you do, ask your system administrator to create a new ID file for you with a new password or forward a backup copy of your ID to you, if your system administrator made one. Forgetting your password can cause some difficulty because there is unique encryption information that is stored within each ID file that cannot be re-created. You will lose access to information encrypted by your user ID if you have to change IDs. See Task 4.2.2, "Backing Up Your ID File," for information on protecting a copy of your ID file.

Task 4.2.2: Backing Up Your ID File

When Notes was installed on your computer, the person who installed it created a Notes ID file for you. As previously mentioned, this file contains information about you, such as your name and other technical information that Notes requires. This ID file is your key to Notes. Without it, you cannot perform most of the functions for which you use Notes; most important, you cannot access your mailbox.

Your ID file, in your Notes Data directory, has an ID extension. The first part of the filename is part of your real name. Robert Richards, for example, can find a file called RRICHARDS.ID in his Notes data directory.

Because you must have this file to access Notes, your best strategy for protecting it is to copy this file to a disk. You can copy this file as you would copy any file to a disk:

1. Open Windows Explorer on your PC by selecting Start, Programs, Windows Explorer from your Windows task bar. (Note: if you are not using Windows 95, follow your operating system instructions for opening your system's file manager.

2. In the left directory tree of Windows Explorer, locate the Notes subdirectory. It is typically either in the root (c:\) or in the lotus (c:\lotus) subdirectory. Click the Notes subdirectory to open it.

3. Locate the DATA subdirectory within the Notes directory and click to open it.

4. In the NOTES\DATA directory, locate and click your Notes ID file. You will recognize it by its .ID file extension.

5. Make sure there is a floppy disk in the drive and then select File, Send To, 3½ Floppy (A). Windows copies your Notes ID to your floppy disk. Make sure you store your floppy disk in a safe place.

Task 4.3: Working with Access Control Lists

When working with a database, you might discover that Notes does not enable you to perform all possible operations. As mentioned before, each database has a manager who is responsible for that database, and one of the manager's responsibilities is to set an access control list (ACL) that maintains data security and integrity.

The ACL defines three important things related to database access:

☐ Who has access to a given database (the list can contain user names, server names, and group lists)

☐ What users can do to the database

☐ Which users belong to certain roles (the roles define which users have access to specific forms and views)

Only the Database Manager (or any user with manager access) can manipulate the ACL. Within the list, the manager arranges all users into one of the seven access levels shown in Table 4.1. Users at each level can perform only certain tasks. The list can include group names so that the manager can assign the same access privileges to an entire department or workgroup with just one entry.

 Whenever you read instructions in this book for performing operations, keep in mind that Notes might not enable you to proceed if the Database Manager hasn't placed you at the required access level for certain operations.

Table 4.1. Notes access levels.

Category	Tasks Enabled
No access	Cannot access the database
Depositor	Can create new documents but cannot edit or read existing documents, even those that he created
Reader	Can read documents but cannot edit documents
Author	Can create, read, and modify her own documents; can read documents created by other users; can delete documents created by herself
Editor	Can compose, edit, read, and possibly delete documents (which is a suboption that can be toggled off or on for each user), including those created by other users
Designer	Has the same access rights as the editor level and can also create, edit, or delete design elements such as forms and views
Manager	Has complete access to all facets of the database, including the ability to delete it from the hard disk and change the ACL

Your assigned access level can (and probably will) vary from one database to another, because the manager for each database decides your level of access. Consider the following examples:

☐ For a database containing sales reports, you have author access. This access level enables you to create new sales reports and change them later. In addition, you can read sales reports entered by other users, but you cannot edit other people's sales reports.

☐ For a database handling suggestions, comments, and complaints, you have depositor access, so you can add new suggestions to the database, but you cannot read or edit them after they have been saved. When you have such access, the database is much like an anonymous comments box hanging on the wall.

☐ For a database containing technical support material, you have editor access. This level enables you to add new documents, edit documents that you have created, and edit documents that others have created.

☐ For a strategic plans database, you might be assigned no access unless you are an executive. At this level, you basically cannot do anything with the database.

There are many options available to the Database Manager when assigning access to a database. This hour's lesson only presents a few of the most used options. If you are interested in learning more about ACL settings, check out the online Notes Help database.

To find out what access level you have been granted to a specific database, select the database icon and look at the third block from the right on your status bar. This block displays an icon representing your access level. You can click that area of the status bar for a textual description of your access level.

Workshop

Now that you have reviewed how Notes secures the information with which you are working, review some of the key concepts of this hour's lesson. This workshop provides you with some of the keywords discussed in this hour and highlights some of the more common questions asked about Notes security.

Key Terms

Review the following list of terms:

- [ ] *Access control list (ACL)*   The access control list of a database provides the Database Manager with the ability to control what users and servers can access a database, and what tasks those users can perform.

- [ ] *Encryption*   Encoding data so that only those that have the encryption key can read it. When you encrypt data, you scramble it in a way that makes it unreadable to anyone that does not have a code to decrypt it.

- [ ] *Certificates*   A certificate is an electronic "stamp" attached to your User ID by a Notes certifier that is controlled by your Notes Administrator. Certificates enable access to specific servers. When you were registered as a Notes user, your User ID should have included the certificate(s) required to access the servers you need for your job.

- [ ] *Database Manager*   A person responsible for maintaining access and the design of a Notes database. You can find out who the manager(s) of a particular database are by selecting File, Database, Access Control. You can easily send mail to the manager of a database by selecting Create, Mail, Other, Special\Memo to Database Manager.

☐ *Notes ID*   A User ID is a file that uniquely identifies a Notes user. Every Notes user or server has a User ID, which determines your access privileges to Domino servers. When you try to open a database on a server, the server looks at your User ID to see if you have any certifiers in common with the server. If you do, access is allowed; if you do not, access is denied.

Common Questions

When working with Lotus Notes, you might experience a few situations in which Notes does not enable you to perform a function that you think you can. This is often due to the security features built into Notes or incorporated into the design of a database. This section highlights a few of the typical security-related questions you might have regarding Notes:

Q You typed in your Notes password, and you know you spelled it correctly, but you keep getting prompted that your password is incorrect.

A Check to make sure you are typing your password in the correct case. One of the most common problems is that the Caps Lock key on your keyboard has been pressed, and you are typing your password in reverse case. If that does not correct your problem, then verify that the Notes ID you are using is yours by checking the name in the Password Prompt box. If your name does not appear in the prompt box, then someone might have used your PC and switched to their ID, and then forgotten to switch back. If this happens, select File, Tools, Switch ID, and then select your ID file from the file list box. Finally, think back — did you change your password and forget? If so, then switch to a backup copy of your ID, or contact your Notes Administrator for assistance.

Q I am trying to open a new database from my Notes server, but a message tells me that Access is Denied.

A The Database Manager of that particular database has not included you in the access control list of the database. Contact the Database Manager for assistance.

Q I keep getting a message from Notes that my ID is about to expire.

A You are getting close to the expiration time specified by your Notes Administrator when the Notes ID was first created. Follow the instructions in this hour's lesson to request and update your Notes certificate.

Preview of the Next Hour

Now that you have gained an understanding of the various ways in which Notes keeps your information safe, it is time to start working with databases in Notes. The next hour's lesson walks you through opening a database, reading the information in the database, and understanding many of the properties of the database that can help you in your daily work.

Hour **5**

Working with Databases

Everything in Notes is stored in a Database. Even your Notes mail is a database. To work effectively in Notes is to understand Notes databases and the components of those databases.

Goals for This Hour

This hour, you will really start to get into Notes—from adding the database to your desktop to examining the different views and folders and creating your own Portfolios. Here is what you can expect to learn in this hour:

- ☐ Adding databases to your desktop
- ☐ Understanding views and folders
- ☐ Understanding database properties
- ☐ Deleting a database from your desktop
- ☐ Creating and managing Portfolios

Task 5.1: Accessing Notes Databases

Before you can access the data contained in a Notes database, your workspace must include a database icon that represents the database. You can add an icon to your workspace for any database to which you have been granted access rights. (You learned more about access rights in Hour 4, "Understanding Access Control Lists and Security.")

Adding a new database icon to your workspace is quite simple. Just choose File, Database, Open, or press Ctrl+0.

Notes then displays an Open Database dialog box similar to that shown in Figure 5.1. The dialog box presents a list of the Notes servers available from your machine and a list of all Notes databases on the selected server.

Figure 5.1.

The Open Database dialog box lists the available Notes servers and databases.

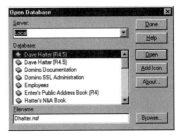

From the Server list box, you can select the server on which the database of interest resides. After you select a server, the Database list box displays the title of each database on the server. If your selected server is not a local server (for instance, if you are working remotely), you can click select File, Mobile, Call Server to dial the server and see which databases are available. You also can choose File, Database, Open or press Ctrl+0, because if you then type in the name of a server for which you have a dialup connection and press Enter, you will be prompted to call the server.

The list of databases that you see might not include every database on the server because the database designer or database manager might have chosen to hide certain databases from the Open Database dialog box or because some databases reside in other Notes Named Networks. In addition, you do not necessarily have access rights to every database in the list. If you do not see a database listed but know its actual filename, you can type it into the Filename text box and open the database if you have sufficient access rights. You also can check the Database Catalog, which should contain the majority of databases resident on that server to see if the database is listed. The filename for the Database Catalog on the server is CATALOG.NSF. If you cannot find a database that you think exists, see your administrator.

When you select a database from the list, the database's actual filename displays in the Filename text box below the Database list box. If you want to add a database icon to your workspace and open the database, choose the Open button, which places the icon on your workspace and opens the database. If you want only to add the database icon to your workspace, choose the Add Icon button. (If you want to add several icons, you should use the Add Icon button because opening each database is unnecessary.)

When you are trying to determine the use of a particular database, the About button can help you. When you choose this button, the database's About document (if one exists) displays. This document should provide information on the database's intended use.

As in all Windows applications, choosing the Help button displays context-sensitive help. When you're in the Open Database dialog box, choosing this button displays information about the dialog box. If you cannot find a database by its title, click the Browse button to display the standard File dialog box, in which you can search for a database by its filename (see Figure 5.2).

Figure 5.2.

In the Choose a Notes Database or Template File dialog box, you can browse the Notes server.

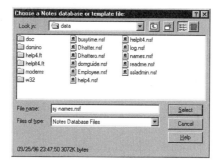

5

After creating an icon for the database that you want to access, you are ready to begin working with the database. To open a database, double-click its icon on the workspace. The Notes database user interface provides panes that consist of a series of smaller windows. These windows work together to simplify navigation through views and folders.

Figure 5.3 shows information in a Notes database; your databases might appear different if the developer has created a custom Navigator with a different look and feel. Instead of presenting one large view window, Notes splits the screen into three distinct window panes separated by gray lines. Each of these panes has a distinct and useful function:

- [ ] The pane in the top-left corner is the Navigator, a hierarchical structure of graphics objects that represent parts of the database.

- [ ] To the right of the Navigator pane is the View pane, which displays data from documents in the currently selected folder or view. (The following sections discuss folders and views in detail.)

☐ Below the Navigator pane and the View pane is the Preview pane in which you can view the contents of a document without actually opening it, saving you significant time and effort. The Preview pane cannot be displayed when you first open a Notes database. To display this pane, choose View, Document Preview. Alternatively, you can move your mouse to the separator bar just above the status bar at the bottom of your Notes screen, where your mouse pointer changes shape. Clicking and dragging up reveals the Preview pane. Perhaps the quickest way to display this pane is to double-click the separator bar to open the Preview pane. Double-clicking again closes it.

You can resize each of these panes to suit your taste. You can even hide the Navigator and Preview panes if you don't find them useful or want to use the screen real estate in other ways.

Figure 5.3.

The Preview pane splits the screen into three panes when you view a Notes database. You can determine how the Preview pane appears by choosing View, Arrange Preview.

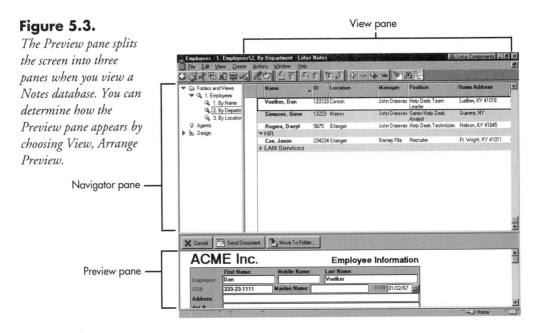

Task 5.2: Understanding the Navigator Pane Symbols

The standard Navigator pane (also referred to as the Folders Navigator pane), contains symbols and text that guide you as you work in the opened database. The symbols in Table 5.1 are present in most Folder Navigators. Database designers can incorporate additional symbols and graphics in custom navigators they build to make it even easier for you to find your way around. For example, if you open the Help database installed with Notes, you find different Navigator panes.

Table 5.1. Common symbols found in most database navigators.

Symbol	Represents	Description
📁	Folders	Folders store related documents or groupings of documents. Folders can contain documents and other folders. You can drag documents from the View pane to the right of the Navigator pane and drop them in folders to store related topics.
🔍	Views	Views are represented by a small magnifying glass. Unlike folders, their contents are determined by a selection formula and sorted according to criteria defined by you or the database designer. You learn more about views in the next section.
💡	Agents	Agents are represented by a small light bulb. These user-created programs automate common user processes, such as archiving mail.
📐	Design	A small triangular ruler represents the design menu in the Navigator. Selecting a design menu displays a list of design elements in the view to the right (see Figure 5.4). This feature might not display if you don't have the capability to modify the database's design.
▼	Twisties	Small, solid triangles appear next to items in views, panes, or documents that can be expanded. Click a twistie pointing right to expand the section. Click the twistie pointing down to collapse the section.

5

If you click the symbols next to the identifying text, the views to the right of the pane display the corresponding information.

Figure 5.4.

By selecting the design menu, you can view a list of designs in the view to the right. The design menu doesn't appear if you lack access permissions to modify the database's design.

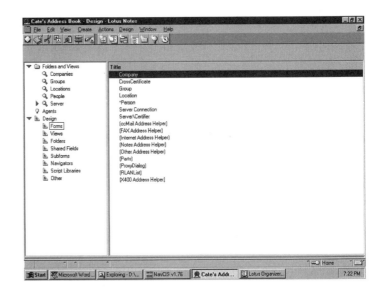

Task 5.3: Accessing Folders and Views in the Navigator Pane

Because the Navigator pane uses graphical icons and presents your choices in a hierarchical structure that you can expand or collapse, it is easy to use. The folder at the top of the tree represents folders and views. You click this icon to expand a diagram of the folders and views available in the database. A folder icon represents each folder or subfolder, and a magnifying glass represents each view. The currently selected icon turns blue; all other icons remain yellow. Figure 5.5 shows the Navigator pane.

Figure 5.5.

The Navigator pane provides a graphical interface for navigating through your folders and views.

Task 5.4: Previewing Documents in the Preview Pane

In the Preview pane, you can select a document in a view or folder, and save time by viewing the contents of a document without actually opening it. By using this tool, you can scan through a database very quickly.

The Preview pane is flexible. Not only can you resize it, you can place it in a variety of onscreen locations. To change the Preview pane's placement, choose View, Arrange Preview. Then click the button corresponding to the placement you want.

If you don't find the Preview pane to be useful, you can disable it. The View, Document Preview menu option works as a toggle switch to enable and disable the Preview pane. If a check mark is visible next to this menu option, the Preview pane is enabled.

You can use several methods to select a document in a view or folder. The mouse and scroll bars enable you to navigate through the documents; then, click the document in which you are interested. You also can use the cursor keys to move the selection bar to the document that you want.

If the first column of a view or folder is sorted, you can type in the first few characters of the item that you want to find. The Quick Search dialog box appears, containing the characters you have typed, and when you press Enter or click OK, Notes moves to the first document that matches the characters you entered. For example, if you use a view that displays all your customers' names sorted alphabetically by last name and are looking for Philip Krezewicz, typing Krez should be enough to move you directly to the correct document.

After selecting the document of interest, you can open (for reading or editing), print, or delete the document. These topics are covered in Hour 6, "Understanding Documents."

Task 5.5: Using Views

Each view has a selection formula (created by the database designer) that tells the view which documents to display. For instance, a view in a sales tracking database might select only orders for which the total sale price is greater than $50,000.

Usually, each row in a view represents a document. However, documents can span multiple rows so that more information can be displayed. Each column in the view can either display data from a field in the document or use a formula to compute a value to display.

Task 5.5.1: Using Columns in Views

As you can see in the View pane shown in Figure 5.6, several columns display data from this view in the database. The View pane's leftmost column is a special feature in Notes views and folders—the marker column. This column displays a variety of system information and is separated from the view's other columns by a thin gray line that extends the length of the view. If you delete a document, for example, you see a small, blue trash can icon in this column. If you have not opened a document, this column displays a star.

Figure 5.6.

The Marker column displays unread marks (red stars) for documents that have not been read and trash cans for documents marked for deletion.

Unread mark →

Delete icon →

Marker column —

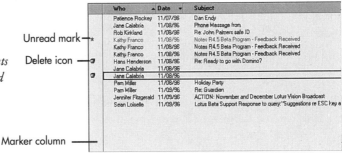

The database designer is responsible for choosing the icons that display in the columns of views and folders, as well as the colors that indicate different aspects of a view or folder, such as unread documents. You cannot change the icons that appear in the view marker column, although the developer might choose not to display them at all.

Unless the database designer explicitly disables the feature, Notes views and folders enable you to resize columns dynamically. To resize columns in any view or folder, simply click the line separating any two columns, drag it sideways until the column reaches the width that you want, and release the mouse button.

Task 5.5.2: Using Categories

The database designer determines which data elements from the underlying documents the view should display and how to organize those elements. For most databases, the designer creates many views so that users can easily navigate through the database, using whatever information they find most useful. For example, in a customer database, you might have the following three views:

☐ *Contacts by Company*, which displays all the customer documents in the database, sorted and categorized by company name and contact name.

☐ *Contacts by State*, which displays all the customer documents in the database, sorted and categorized by state and then by company name.

☐ *Complaints by Customer*, which displays all the complaint documents in the database, sorted by customer.

By selecting different views, you can examine different "snapshots" of the data; in fact, a view need not display all the documents in the database. A view named Calls This Week might display only a subset of customers to whom you spoke this week, whereas a view named Calls Next Week might display all your calls scheduled for next week.

In the view shown in Figure 5.7, the phone numbers within Bay Resources are organized by location: Detroit, Miami, Orlando Bay Services, Orlando, and St. Petersburg. The Location categories are not documents, and you cannot open them as you can open documents. Sometimes categories can be expanded or collapsed. If a small triangle appears to the left of the category, click the triangle to expand or collapse the category.

Figure 5.7.

In this example, Orlando is expanded and the other Bay Resources Locations are collapsed.

Expanded category ——

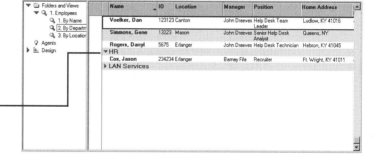

 In most views, the database designer uses boldface to distinguish category titles from document titles. However, only the designer can select this font option in the view's design.

To avoid information overload, you can temporarily limit the amount of information that the view displays. To do so, you *collapse* a category. When you double-click the category's name, all the documents in that category disappear. Alternatively, you can select the category and press the minus (–) key; select the category and choose View, Expand/Collapse, Collapse Selected Level; or click the View Collapse SmartIcon. Notes doesn't delete the documents themselves from the database, but instead stops displaying them while the category is collapsed.

You also can expand and collapse views by using SmartIcons, as shown in Table 5.2.

Table 5.2. SmartIcons that help you collapse and expand view categories.

Icon	Contents	Action
⊞	Single plus sign	Expands one category level
⊟	Single minus sign	Collapses one category level
⊞	Multiple plus signs	Expands all categories
⊟	Multiple minus signs	Collapses all categories

> Categories are not documents; they act only as headings so that the user can group documents together logically. If you double-click any of the categories in a view, you expand or collapse that category. Categorization is a feature that the database designer builds into views and folders.

If you are interested only in phone numbers in the St. Petersburg area, for example, you can collapse the Detroit, Miami, and Orlando categories so that the view displays only the numbers for St. Petersburg. Later, you can expand the other categories—that is, redisplay the phone numbers in other locations—by double-clicking the other category names. Alternatively, you can expand the other categories by selecting them and pressing the plus (+) key; selecting them and choosing View, Expand/Collapse, Expand Selected Level; or clicking the View Expand SmartIcon.

If you are working with a database that has dozens of categories and are interested in only one, collapse all categories by choosing View, Collapse All; by pressing the Shift and minus (–) keys (you have to use the minus key on the numeric keypad); or by clicking the View Collapse All SmartIcon. Then double-click (or use any of the previously mentioned methods) the category that you want to expand.

Similarly, you can expand all categories by choosing View, Expand All; by pressing the Shift and plus (+); or by clicking the View Expand All SmartIcon.

The capability to quickly expand and collapse categories in views and folders makes working with data much easier.

Task 5.6: Closing a Database

To close a Notes database, close any open documents by using one of the following methods:

1. Press Esc.

2. Press Ctrl+W.

3. Click the view or folder window's Control-menu box and then choose Close (the Control-menu box is the small application icon in the window's upper-left corner).

4. If you have used Notes 3.x before, you might have used a double-right click to close a document. You can still do this in Notes 4.6 but only if you switch on the option from File, Tools, User Preferences and check the Right double-click closes window option in the Advanced options section.

Don't worry about forgetting to save changes that you have made to open documents, because Notes prompts you to save them.

Task 5.7: Deleting Database Icons and Databases

When you no longer are interested in a particular database, you can delete it from your workspace without deleting the database file from the server or hard drive that stores the file. To do so, follow these steps:

1. Select the workspace page on which the database resides, if it is not currently showing.

2. Click the database that you want to remove. (Don't double-click, or you'll open the database.)

3. If you want to delete more than one database from the same workspace page, hold down the Shift key and click the other database icons that you want to delete.

4. Press Del; choose Edit, Clear; or click the Edit Clear SmartIcon.

5. Notes prompts you to confirm that you want to delete these icons from your workspace (see Figure 5.8). If you are sure, choose Yes to delete the selected icons from your workspace; if you have changed your mind, choose No.

Figure 5.8.

Notes prompts you to confirm that you want to delete the selected database icons.

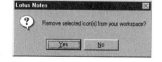

5

Deleting database icons does not actually delete the database file but instead only removes the icon from your workspace. Other users who access the database still see the database icon on their workspaces and can still access the database. In fact, later you can restore the same database icon to your workspace.

> When you delete database icons from your workspace, you leave gaps where the icons used to be. You can fill in the gaps easily by dragging other database icons into these empty positions. Alternatively, you can choose View, Arrange Icons to have Notes rearrange the icons on the workspace and fill in all the gaps.

If you have the appropriate access rights for a given database, you can permanently delete the database file.

> The following instructions explain how to delete a database and all its information permanently from the hard disk in which the file resides. If you perform this procedure on a database, you will lose all data that the database contains!

To delete a database permanently, perform the following steps:

1. Click the database icon of the database that you want to delete. This selects the database.
2. Choose File, Database, Delete. The dialog box shown in Figure 5.9 informs you that you are about to delete the database permanently and asks whether you are sure that you want to do so.
3. Choose Yes to delete the database permanently from the server or hard drive, or choose No to cancel the deletion.

Figure 5.9.

Notes displays this dialog box to warn you that you are about to delete the selected database permanently.

You have manager access to all Notes databases stored on your workstation (other than any that have been stored with local ACL enforcement). These include important system databases such as your mail database, your Notes log database, and your Private Name & Address Book database. In addition, you have manager access to your mail database on the Notes server. You should not delete any of these databases without first seeking your Notes administrator's advice. There is no good reason to remove these icons, as you will find yourself using these databases (particularly your mail database) quite often.

Task 5.8: Creating and Managing Portfolios

One thing to consider in Notes is how to keep logically connected databases together. One option is to create a new workspace page and move related databases there, but you might consider that wasteful if you're only trying to organize two or three databases that make up a particular application. This is where a Portfolio comes in handy.

New in version 4.6, a Portfolio looks like an ordinary Notes database, but in reality it is a container in which you can collect related databases.

Figure 5.10 shows the Portfolio icon that is added by default to your workspace on installation. This Portfolio, called Favorites, contains your mail file, Personal Address Book, Journal, and Personal Web Navigator. You can add to this Portfolio or create new Portfolios according to your own requirements. For example, you might create a Portfolio containing your client tracking database, product catalog, and order entry database. Together, these databases make up your Sales application.

Figure 5.10.

The Favorites Portfolio created on installation.

Portfolios are also good for providing company information for employees. Many companies publish employment policies, safety regulations, organization charts, and company bulletins via Notes. Because Portfolios can be stored on the server as well as locally, new employees can add a single Portfolio to their workspace and have access to all the databases they need without having to hunt down each one individually.

Portfolios can be deleted and replicated just like any other Notes database, but remember that these actions affect the Portfolio's NSF file and not the database collection held within. So when you delete a Portfolio, you're just deleting the Portfolio itself and not the databases referenced in that Portfolio. Replicating a Portfolio replicates the Portfolio NSF file, not all the databases referenced within.

Task 5.8.1: Navigating Inside a Portfolio

To access a Portfolio, double-click its icon on the workspace. Figure 5.11 shows the open Favorites Portfolio. The following sections are indicated in the figure:

☐ On the top-left side you see the Portfolio Title. This displays the name of the Portfolio. Clicking it enables you to edit some of the Portfolio settings.

☐ Below the Portfolio title, the Portfolio Navigator displays a "tile" representing each database that has been added to the Portfolio.

☐ On the right is a standard View pane that reflects the contents of the database you have chosen from the Portfolio Navigator.

Figure 5.11.

The contents of the Favorites Portfolio.

Portfolio Title

Portfolio Navigator

View pane

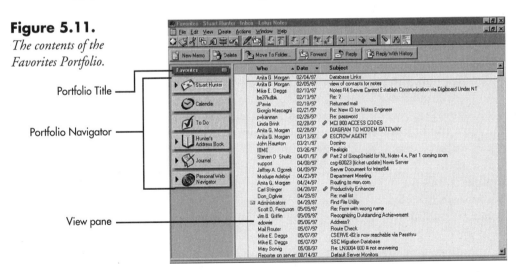

Each database contained in the Navigator pane displays the tile for the database and a twistie. Clicking the twistie expands that database, displaying the folders, views, and design elements that make up the database, as shown in Figure 5.12. Once expanded, the database behaves much like you would expect. Clicking the folders and views changes the contents of the View pane on the right, and any Action bars associated with these views appear in place beneath the SmartIcon Palette. Clicking the database twistie again collapses the database back to a tile.

Figure 5.12.

The Portfolio Navigator with the mail file expanded.

 When added to a Portfolio, your mail file is treated as a special case. The Calendar and To Do sections are displayed as individual tiles below the main Mail tile. You can't delete these sections, and you can't add other sections from the mail file or from any other database.

Unlike databases stored on the workspace itself, you can't display the unread document count or server name of the selected database. Right-clicking a database in a Portfolio limits you to replicating the database or selecting another replica copy from your workspace to work with. Therefore, instead of right-clicking, you must work through the menus to perform common database actions.

5

 You might be disconcerted to find that if you add a database to a Portfolio and then delete the original icon from the workspace, the next time you start Notes, the icon magically reappears. You can't have a database in a Portfolio that isn't also present on your workspace. The best that you can do is create a new workspace page and move the unwanted icons to it.

When dealing with databases, you get used to the idea that when you open a database, the view you see is the one that was active when you last closed the database. This is not how databases work within Portfolios. Regardless of the database and view you were accessing, when you exit the Portfolio and then re-enter it, the view you see in the right pane will be the *last* view you accessed in the *first* database in the Portfolio list. In the case of Favorites, this normally is your mail file.

Task 5.8.2: Creating a Portfolio

The Notes administrators or developers in your company might have created general-purpose Portfolios for you to use, but it's easy to create your own by following these steps:

1. Select File, Database, New to display the New Database dialog box, as shown in Figure 5.13. You first choose the location for the new Portfolio, either locally (which is the default) or on a Notes server if you have the rights to do so.

Figure 5.13.

Creating a new Portfolio by using the PRTFLO46.NTF template.

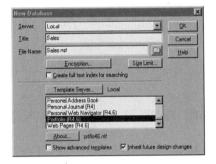

2. Give the new Portfolio a title and a filename. The most important part is to ensure that the Portfolio's design is based on the Portfolio template (PRTFLO46.NTF). Otherwise, you're creating an ordinary database, not a Portfolio.

3. Click OK. The new empty Portfolio opens onto your screen.

Task 5.8.3: Editing a Portfolio

After you have created an empty Portfolio, you need to add databases to it, and you will probably want to customize the way they are displayed. The simplest way to add databases to a Portfolio is to drag and drop them from the workspace to the Portfolio icon, where they appear in the order you dropped them. Unlike when you drag a database icon from one workspace page to another, the database icon won't disappear when you drag it onto the Portfolio icon; it remains in place. Although you can continue to add databases to your Portfolio, the Portfolio Navigator is limited to displaying a maximum of 20 databases.

To further customize the way the databases appear, left- or right-click the Portfolio Title and select Edit Portfolio, as shown in Figure 5.14.

Figure 5.14.

Selecting the Edit Portfolio command enables you to customize the way the databases appear.

Figure 5.15 shows the Edit Portfolio view of the Portfolio database. In the View pane on the right, you can see a list of all the databases that are contained in the Portfolio.

Figure 5.15.

The Edit Portfolio view.

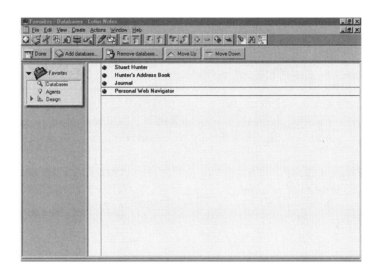

When you double-click one of the databases listed in the view, you are taken to the Database Information form for that database. Here, the only thing you can change is the displayed name of the database, as shown in Figure 5.16. Doing this doesn't change the title in the actual database, just the name as it is displayed in the Portfolio.

Figure 5.16.

Changing the displayed name for a database in a Portfolio.

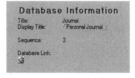

At the top of the view, the buttons on the Action bar enable you to perform various actions that affect the contents and order of the Portfolio database. Table 5.3 lists these buttons.

5

Table 5.3. Buttons on the Portfolio action bar.

Button	Action
Done	Takes you back to the Portfolio, saving any changes you have made.
Add database...	Brings up a dialog from which you can select databases from your workspace to add to the Portfolio (see Figure 5.17).
Remove database...	Removes the selected database from the Portfolio.
Move Up	Changes the order of the databases by moving the selected database up the list.
Move Down	Changes the order of the databases by moving the selected database down the list.

Clicking the Add database or Remove database buttons on the Portfolio Action bar brings up a new dialog box. Figure 5.17 shows the dialog box for adding a database to the Portfolio.

Figure 5.17.

Adding a database to the Portfolio.

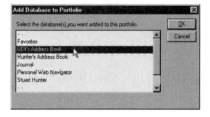

When you have finished customizing the Portfolio, click the Done button on the Action bar to return to the Portfolio Navigator.

Workshop

With this hour completed, you should feel comfortable with adding and removing databases from your Desktop. You can identify the different parts of the database display and manipulate them to look the way you want. You understand the difference between a Folder and a View, and you know how to expand and collapse views to get just the information you want. You also learned how to create and manage Portfolios and now have an understanding of some of the properties that affect how a database works.

Key Terms

Review the following list of terms:

☐ *Database*   A collection of Notes documents with something in common is held in a Notes database. The database is represented on your workspace page by an icon.

☐ *Template*   A building block for databases. Rather than creating a new database from scratch, you can base it on a template where much of the design has already been defined. Templates have .NTF file extensions.

☐ *Database Catalog*   A file on the Notes server, with the filename CATALOG.NSF, where most if not all of the databases on the server are listed.

☐ *View*   A representation of the documents held within a database. A formula controls what documents appear in the view. A database can consist of many views showing different documents, sorted in different ways with different information in the columns.

☐ *Folder*   Like a view, except there is no formula dictating the contents of the folder. You determine that by dragging documents from views into folders.

☐ *Navigator*   That part of the database on the left side where you click to switch between views and folders. Your developers might create Navigators that look nothing like the standard Navigator with graphics and hotspots to navigate around the database.

☐ *Portfolio*   A collection of databases accessible from a single place on your workspace page. They are created with a special template, and you can then drag databases onto them.

Common Questions

Q Is a Notes database the same as other databases I have heard of such as Oracle and Access?

A Yes and No. There are similarities. Oracle and Access are examples of "Relational" databases useful for storing structured data such as accounting and sales information. Notes is known as a "Hierarchical" database and is more adept at handling semi-structured or unstructured information such as discussions and reports that might contain other files (spreadsheets, graphics, sound files, and so on). In addition, the Notes database also contains all the forms and views that you use to create and view the data, whereas typically those items would be held outside of a relational database that just contains the data.

Q If I accidentally delete a database as opposed to just removing the icon from my desktop, can I "undelete" it?

A Sorry, that is why you have to be very careful. If you accidentally delete a database, your only hope is to find a backup copy of the database somewhere. Quite often, though, you do not have the rights to delete a database from the server.

5

Preview of the Next Hour

Now that you know how to access the databases, in the next hour you will learn how to access the documents that you can see in the views and folders. You will learn how to create new documents, edit existing documents, and delete those that you no longer need.

Hour 6

Understanding Documents

Goals for This Hour

Now that you know how to access a database and how its various parts work, it is time to learn how to add information to one. You add information into a database by filling out forms that database designer creates. These forms are then saved as documents in the database. This hour teaches you how to do the following:

☐ Locate, open, and read a document

☐ Use fields within documents, such as keyword field, rich text field, and others

☐ Save documents

☐ Close documents

Task 6.1: Locating, Opening, and Reading Documents

To open an existing document, select it in a view or folder and double-click it. If you have reader access to the database, your screen displays the document in read mode, so you currently cannot edit it. You can easily tell that a document is in read mode by noting the absence of brackets around any fields.

In read mode, you can see all the data in the document and can elect to print it, but you cannot edit it. To edit the document, press Ctrl+E. (You can click the Actions Edit Document SmartIcon if you have the appropriate access level.) When the document is in edit mode (in which case you'll notice the small gray brackets around the editable fields), you can change any of the data elements to which you have access. Figure 6.1 shows a document in edit mode. Alternatively, you can double-click a document to put it in edit mode.

Figure 6.1.

When you place a document in edit mode, small gray brackets enclose the fields that you can edit.

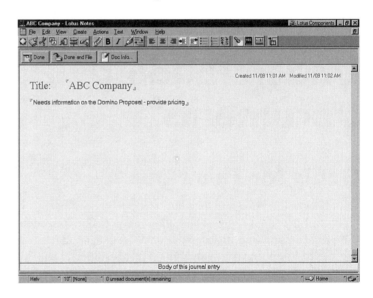

To compose a new document, open the Create menu, which lists all the forms available in the database, as shown in Figure 6.2.

Figure 6.2.

The Create menu lists all available forms.

In Figure 6.2, the menu lists the forms available in the Employee database. This database happens to have only one form: Employee. To create a new employee, choose Create, Employee. Notes displays a new document such as the one shown in Figure 6.3. You can now enter data in the document.

Figure 6.3.

When you choose Create, Employee, Notes creates a new Employee document.

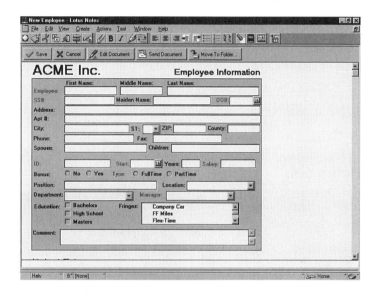

Remember that the Access Control List for each database controls your ability to create, read, and access documents. The database manager sets the ACL.

Task 6.2: Using Fields in Documents

6

Most documents contain several fields that are analogous to the blanks on a paper form.

The database designer determines the number, data type, and placement of fields within a form.

On Notes forms, editable field boundaries are identified by small, gray, square brackets. Usually, each field has a label that explains the type of data the user should enter into the field.

If the database designer has included field help (a useful feature to help guide users when entering data), you can find additional information on how to use the field and what kind of data you are expected to enter. To find this information, choose View, Show, Field Help.

You can move the cursor from field to field by using the directional arrows, the Tab key, or by clicking the field in which you want to place the cursor.

Notes supports a variety of data types for fields. You might encounter a mixture of different data types when working with fields inside a Notes form. Figure 6.4 shows a sample form named Employee Information. This form contains many of the different supported data types.

Figure 6.4.

The Employee Informa-tion form includes many types of data fields.

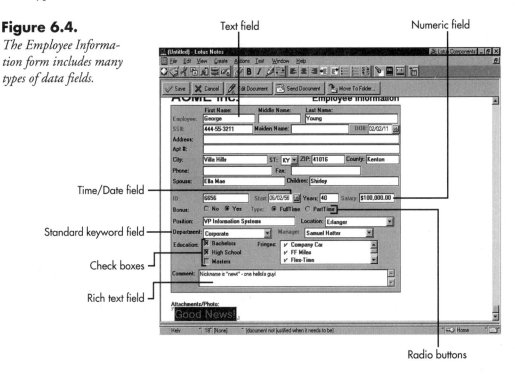

The following sections describe the field types.

Task 6.2.1: Using Text Fields

You can use the text data type to store alphanumeric data (essentially any character) that isn't used mathematically. In the Employee Information form in Figure 6.3, examples of text fields include Employee, SS#, Address, City, ST, ZIP, and Phone.

Task 6.2.3: Using Rich Text Fields

The rich text field (RTF) data type also stores alphanumeric data that isn't used mathematically. However, you can format data in a rich text field. You can change such font features as style, size, and color or format text, insert objects from other applications, insert file attachments, and display graphics. In Figure 6.4, Comment is a rich text field.

> You cannot use the tab field to move from a rich text field to the next field on a form. In a rich text field, pressing the Tab key moves your cursor to the next tab position within that field.

Task 6.2.4: Using Keyword Fields

The keyword data type stores text but enables you to choose a value from a list of predefined choices. For example, a list of possible household salary ranges can be defined as <$10,000, $10,001–$20,000, $20,001–$40,000, $40,001–$60,000, or >$60,000.

There are three ways to display the list of keywords: standard keywords, check boxes, or radio buttons, as described in the following list.

> Check boxes are square; radio buttons are round. You can select as many check boxes as you want, but you can select only one radio button in a group of radio buttons.

☐ *Standard keywords*   In Figure 6.4, the Position and Department fields are standard keyword fields. You can choose only one of the positions defined in the list. When you position your cursor on such a field, repeatedly pressing the Spacebar cycles through the keyword list, or you can display a keyword by typing the first letter. If you want to see all possible keyword selections in a dialog box, place the cursor in the field and press Enter; or click the Entry Helper button (the small gray down-arrow button next to the field) if it is visible to change the field to one of the values listed in the dialog box; then select an item and press Enter (or choose OK).

6

> Most keyword fields present a fixed set of values from which you are to select one value. The database designer can, however, enable you to enter something other than one of the predefined selections or can enable you to select multiple items from the list. When a keyword field enables new values, the Keywords dialog box contains an input box into which you can enter new text.

☐ *Check boxes*   In a check box field, each box represents one entry in the predefined list. By default, check boxes are not mutually exclusive, so you can select all that apply. For example, the Education field in Figure 6.4 lists three degrees. An X appears next to each one that applies, whereas the absence of an X indicates the choice does not apply.

☐ *Radio buttons*   Each button in a radio button field represents one item in the list, and you must choose one of several mutually exclusive items. In the Type field in Figure 6.4, for example, you can specify the type of employee by clicking the corresponding radio button once (a block dot appears in a selected radio button). You can select only one radio button per field.

Task 6.2.5: Using Time/Date Fields

A time/date type field enables you to enter a time or date. If the value that you enter is an invalid time or date value, Notes prompts you to enter a valid one. As was shown in Figure 6.4, the Start field contains the date that the employee started work.

Task 6.2.6: Using Numeric Fields

The numeric data type expects a numeric value—numbers only, no text, punctuation marks, or other characters—such as the number of employees in a company or the number of calls made to a customer. If you enter a nonnumeric value in a numeric field, Notes prompts you to enter a valid value. The form in Figure 6.4 contains two numeric fields: Salary and Years. (The field containing a phone number was not designed as a numeric field because no calculations will be performed on this field.)

Task 6.2.7: Using Names Fields

Names fields can be of three data types: authors, readers, and names. Authors and readers fields control the security of each document. If a person's name is listed in a readers field, she can only read a document, but if she is listed in an authors field, she can edit the document, as well. The names field type does not directly affect security but does indicate to Notes that the values held within are only names. Depending on the design of the database, names fields might or might not display on your form.

Task 6.3: Saving and Closing Documents

Now that you know how to compose and edit documents, you need to know how to save or cancel your changes. When you finish reading or editing a document, you have three options:

☐ Save it

☐ Save and close it

☐ Close it without saving

To save any Notes document, press Ctrl+S or click the File Save SmartIcon. Neither action closes the document.

To close a Notes document and return to the folder or view, perform any one of the following actions:

☐ Press Esc

☐ Press Ctrl+W

☐ Right double-click, if it is enabled in the user preferences

Performing any of these actions causes Notes to check whether you have made any changes to a document. If you have made changes, Notes prompts you with the dialog box shown in Figure 6.5.

Figure 6.5.

Notes prompts you to confirm that you want to save your changes to a document.

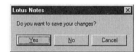

If you want to save your changes, choose Yes. To close the document without saving changes, choose No. To avoid closing the document (and not save the document), choose Cancel.

Workshop

Now that you know how to work with documents, review what you have learned. This workshop is designed to help answer anticipated questions that might arise and to review important new terms that you have learned.

Key Terms

Review the following list of terms:

☐ *Document*   The basic "storage unit" in a Notes database. Each document holds one or more items that store a variety of types of data: text, numbers, dates, images, sound, and so on.

☐ *Text field*   Often referred to as alphanumeric, this field contains any character— letters, punctuation, spaces, and numbers that are not used in calculations. Information in text fields can be displayed in views.

☐ *Numeric field*   This field is used to store numbers that you use in mathematical formulas. If a value is entered into a numeric field that is not a number, Notes prompts you with an error message.

6

☐ *Keyword fields* This field includes radio buttons, dialog lists, and check boxes that provide a predetermined list of choices.

☐ *Rich text field* Like a text field, this field enables the input of text, but the text can use fonts, colors, and formatting. Rich text fields also can contain attachments, graphics, embedded objects, and just about anything else in electronic format. Information in rich text fields cannot be displayed in views.

☐ *Time/date field* This field is used for input of values that represent a date or time.

Common Questions

Q How do I create a new document?

A From the menu bar, select Create + document name.

Q How do I know whether or not my document is in edit mode?

A When a document is in edit mode, all editable fields have small, gray brackets in the top left and bottom right corners. If the field can be encrypted, you will see red brackets rather than gray ones.

Q When I press Ctrl+E or double-click a document, it does not go into edit mode.

A If a document does not seem to go into edit mode, it might be due to one of two things. You do not have permission to edit the document—in other words, security is set so you do not have editor access to that document. Or, there might be an absence of editable fields on that particular document.

Preview of the Next Hour

Now that you have learned how to work with documents, you are ready to print something that you or a co-worker has entered into a database. In the next hour, you will learn how to print documents and views in Notes.

Hour 7

Printing Documents and Views

Goals for This Hour

Even though Notes is an online system—in other words, it is built primarily to view information online—there are many times you may want to print information from a database.

One of the most valuable things you can print from Notes is a view. Often views are categorized and display information that you want that's pulled from many documents, much the way you print out reports from other types of databases. For instance, you may want to print a phone list view that displays all of your clients with their phone numbers and addresses. Or you might want to print a calendar view with your schedule to take home and put on the refrigerator.

There are also many times when you must print a document, such as when a change in a production process is approved and that approval must be printed and then given to assembly people who are not on Notes. Or perhaps you are a Sales Executive and you want to print an automated client letter to fax to your client. All of these examples lead to one thing: learning to print from Notes.

Notes provides tremendous flexibility when printing documents and views. You have several options for specifying what to print:

☐ Print a single document

☐ Print selected documents

☐ Print the entire view

There are two basic, slightly different ways to print a single document:

☐ Print a selected document from a view or folder

☐ Print an open document

In this hour, you will learn how to accomplish those tasks.

Task 7.1: Printing a Document from a View or Folder

Printing a document from a view or folder is simple. Follow these steps:

1. Select a document either by clicking it or by clicking in the view marker column (and thus placing a check mark in the column).

2. Choose File, Print, or press Ctrl+P, or click the File Print SmartIcon to display the File Print dialog box shown in Figure 7.1

3. Make any custom printing settings from the File Print dialog box (discussed below) and click OK.

Figure 7.1.

The File Print dialog box with a single document selected for printing.

In the File Print dialog box, you can control many aspects of printing, including the following:

☐ The Printer button enables you to select a printer other than the one currently selected (the name of the currently selected printer appears next to the printer icon) or to change the setup for a printer. (The section "Specifying a Printer" explains how to specify other printers.)

☐ In the Print Range panel, you can set a range of pages within the selected document to print. This range applies only to printing individual documents.

☐ Select the Draft Quality check box to specify lower-resolution printing, which speeds the printing process. You might also need to select this option if the selected printer does not contain much memory.

☐ With the Copies setting, you can indicate whether you want to print multiple copies of the document.

☐ Select the Graphics Scaled to 100% check box to print graphics at their original size. You cannot select a different percentage than what the size is.

☐ The View Options section presents the most important options in this dialog box.

In the View Options section, you can specify that Notes print only selected documents or print the entire view. When printing documents, you can also choose the Form Override button to select a form to print in addition to the form that the document was saved with.

The Form Override feature of Notes can be quite useful. For instance, if you use a database that includes a form specifically designed to speed data entry but that is very unattractive when printed, you can design a separate form for printing. When you decide to print the document, use Form Override to select the form designed for printing to ensure that you print your document using the more attractive format.

When printing multiple documents, you can select one of these three options in the Document Separation field:

☐ *Page Break Between Documents* enables you to eject a page and start printing the next document on a new page.

☐ *Extra Line* doesn't eject a new page, but it literally inserts one blank line after each document to make the printout somewhat easier to read.

☐ *No Separation* doesn't separate documents, but instead begins printing the next document in the queue immediately following the previous document.

The Document Separation settings do not apply when you are printing only a single document.

Finally, you can select the Reset Page Numbers check box, which works with the Page Break setting, to reset the page number to 1 for the first page of each document.

After you select the proper settings, choose OK to send the document to the printer.

7

> Before you print, you might want to see where your pages will break and
> how words will wrap for a given document. To see what the printed
> document will look like, open the document and choose View, Show,
> Page Breaks. Notes displays a heavy black line wherever the printout will
> have a page break.

Task 7.2: Printing the Open Document

Printing a document that's currently open in Read or Edit mode is similar to printing a single document from a view or folder. You can choose File, Print or click the File Print SmartIcon to display a slightly altered File Print dialog box (see Figure 7.2).

Figure 7.2.

*The File Print dialog box
for a single document.*

This dialog box offers fewer choices than the version that opens when you begin in a view or folder, but it is essentially the same. However, because you are printing a single open document instead of a view, there is no View Options section, you cannot select Form Override, and you cannot insert page breaks. Choose OK to send the document to the printer.

Task 7.3: Printing Multiple Documents from a View

Printing selected documents is quite similar to the first option for printing a single document. You open a view or a folder, and then select multiple documents by clicking in the view marker column next to each document that you want to print. (A small check mark in the view marker column indicates that you have selected a document to be printed, as shown in Figure 7.3.)

After selecting all the documents you want to print, choose File, Print or click the File Print SmartIcon. The File Print dialog box opens, offering the same options as if you were printing a single document. However, the View Options and Document Separation selections now take on new importance.

Figure 7.3.

When you select multiple documents in a view, check marks appear next to each of their titles.

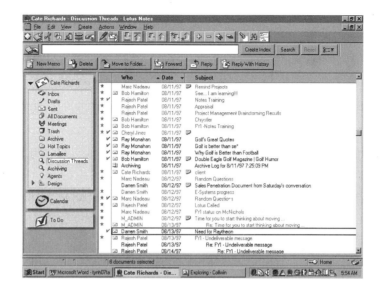

Make sure that the Print Selected Documents option button is selected, and select Page Break as the Document Separation setting. You can also choose Form Override to print each selected document with a form other than the one with which the document was last saved. You may want to do this, for example, if the form associated with the document is not attractive when printed and another form has been designed for printing.

After specifying all of your printing settings, choose OK to send the print job to the printer.

Task 7.4: Printing a View

As you learned at the beginning of this hour, you might want to print an actual view instead of printing the documents displayed within the view. Notes makes that quite easy to do. You simply open the view that you want to print and choose File, Print. (Alternatively, you can press Ctrl+P or click the File Print SmartIcon.) The familiar File Print dialog box opens (refer to Figure 7.1). In the View Options section, choose the Print View option button. Set the other print options, such as Copies, to meet your needs, and then choose OK to send the view to the printer.

A special type of view that you may want to print is one of the four calendar views. There are four types of calendar views: two days, one week, two weeks, and one month. When printed, these views look just as they appear on the screen. You print one of these views just as you would a standard Notes view. When printing a calendar view, however, you'll find one new option called Print Selected Days in the File Print dialog box. If you select this option, you can specify a date range to print outside the conventional week or month time frame.

7

If you select the Print Selected Days option in the File Print dialog box, Notes will not print in a calendar format. Instead, it prints all items for the date range in a list format categorized by date. If you want a calendar look on the printout, you must print one of the four calendar views without using the date range option.

Task 7.5: Printing a List of Documents in a Folder

Printing documents from folders is much like printing documents from views. To print a list of documents from a folder, just select the documents that you want to print, and then choose File, Print or click the File Print SmartIcon.

Task 7.6: Specifying a Printer

When Windows was installed on your workstation, a default printer driver should have been installed and selected for the printer that you use most frequently. When you print from Notes, the program sends your output to the default printer unless you specify a different printer. Often, it is helpful to have access to a printer other than your default printer. For example, having access to a printer with 8.5×14-inch paper is particularly helpful if you are printing wide views that scroll off the screen. Having access to multiple printers, then, might enable you to take advantage of some options that your default printer does not support, such as an envelope feeder.

Each time you print something from Notes, a Print dialog box appears. What type of Print dialog box appears depends on the type of item you are attempting to print. Each of these dialog boxes displays a Printer button above the currently selected printer (indicated by a printer icon).

To change printer drivers, choose the Printer button or click the File Print Setup SmartIcon. Notes displays a dialog box that lists all the printer drivers installed on your workstation (see Figure 7.4).

Click to select a printer driver from the list, and then choose Setup to display a property sheet for the selected driver. Figure 7.5 displays the dialog box for the HP LaserJet 4M driver.

Figure 7.4.

The Print Setup dialog box displays a list of installed printers.

Figure 7.5.

The dialog box for an HP LaserJet 4M printer.

Task 7.7: Using Headers and Footers

With Notes, you can set global headers and footers for all documents in a database. Headers and footers print on every page of a document and can enable you to identify printed documents. The headers at the top of this book's pages are a good example of this concept. In the header, you often see such information as the chapter's title and the page number.

To set a header or footer, choose the Print tab of the Database properties box. Notes displays the Print page, as shown in Figure 7.6. From this page, select the Header option button to create a header. Then, in the text box below the button, enter the text that you want your header to display. While you are entering info in this field, a green check button is displayed. When you finish entering your text, click the green check button to accept the changes, or click the red cancel button to reject the changes. You can choose the Footer option button to enter text you want printed in the footer; the Footer button works exactly the same way as the Header button.

Immediately beneath the text box are several buttons for the header or footer. Table 7.1 shows each button and describes how the buttons make it easy for you to automatically add certain information to the header or footer.

7

Figure 7.6.

In the Database proper-
ties box's Print page, you
can set headers and
footers.

Table 7.1. Buttons for creating headers and footers.

Button	Function
	Inserts a page number, which the text box displays as &P
	Inserts the current date, which the text displays as &D
	Inserts the current time, which the text box displays as &T
	Inserts a tab, which the text box displays as I
	Inserts the code &W, which tells Notes to print the window's title

Using these buttons in a header formula, for example, you can print the current date and time, insert a tab, print the text "Test Header," insert another tab, and then print the current page number. In the text box, such a formula would look like this:

&D&T|Test Header|&P

When printed, the header would look something like the following:

10/21/96@10:10PM → Test Header → Page 1

From the Print page, you can also adjust font settings—such as typeface, size, and style—for the header or footer. To change the typeface for the header or footer, simply select a new font from the Font list box. To change the size of the font, select a font size from the Size list box. To change the font style, select the style from the Style list box.

The font settings for the header and footer are mutually exclusive, so you can use different font settings for the header and footer.

Workshop

Now that you have learned about printing documents and views in Notes, let's see what you remember. This workshop is designed to help answer anticipated questions that may arise while you are printing and to review important new terms that you have learned.

Key Terms

☐ *Calendar view*   A special type of view that displays dated information in a calendar format.

☐ *Printing a document*   Prints a document(s) in the format of the form in which they are displayed when open, instead of as the list of documents that are displayed in the view.

☐ *Printing a view*   Prints all document information as it is displayed in a given view, instead of printing document(s) as they are displayed when opened. A view that is printed looks more like a report in other databases.

☐ *Headers and footers*   Specified information that is printed at the top (header) and bottom (footer) of every printed page. These are set in the Database properties box. You cannot see headers or footers displayed online; they are added to the document only when it's printed.

Common Questions

Q When I try to print a view I get a document instead. Why?

A Most likely, a document is already selected in the view when you open it, and therefore, the print options default to printing the document. To print the view, select the Print View option in the File Print dialog box instead.

Q Can I have a different type of header or footer on a specific document without changing the database settings?

A Yes, select the Document properties box (choose File, Document, Properties) to display the Print dialog box for the document. Set up the header and footer information for that document on the Print tab of the dialog box.

Preview of the Next Hour

Now that you have learned the basics of working with databases and printing documents in databases, it is time to turn your attention to a special database provided to you in Notes: your Mail database. The next hour's lesson gets you started working with Notes Mail.

7

Hour **8**

Using Mail Basics

Goals for This Hour

Electronic mail (email) is one of the most important and useful tools to come out of the "information age," making communication with coworkers quick and easy, regardless of geographical and time barriers.

The Notes email system is a friendly, robust client/server system modeled after Lotus's bestselling, standalone email package, cc:Mail. NotesMail makes it very easy to communicate with other Notes users (and with other mail systems, such as Microsoft Mail or Internet mail, if you have the proper hardware and software), and is very flexible. You're not limited to sending messages to other users; you can also send file attachments and embed objects, such as spreadsheets or graphics, in an email message.

After completing this hour, you will be able to do the following:

- [ ] *Understand the advantages of using email*   Email can help you work more productively. You will learn some of the tips and techniques for taking advantage of using email.

- [ ] *Work with your mailbox*   Mail is a Notes database and provides forms and tools for organizing your work and your time. You will learn the parts of your Mail database and how to use them.

☐ *Create and send mail*   Many options are available in creating mail that affect your
mail message's delivery and appearance.

☐ *Forward, print, and delete messages*   By forwarding messages, you can share them
with users who were not included in the original distribution. You can also print
messages when you need to or delete them if you no longer need them. This hour's
lesson shows you how.

Task 8.1: Understanding the Mail Navigator Pane

The Mail navigator contains several default folders and views that you can access by clicking
their icons or names. You can expand each folder or view by clicking its icon. Notes then
presents a list of other views and folders in the database. Each view is represented by a yellow
magnifying glass icon, and each folder is represented by a file folder icon. Figure 8.1 shows
the Navigator pane.

Figure 8.1.

*The Mail navigator pane
displays available views,
folders, custom views,
and the Design views.
Click the triangle that
indicates collapsible
sections to expand them.*

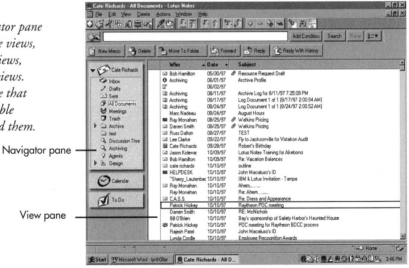

To display your Preview Pane, select View, Show, Preview Pane. You will
then be able to read a Notes document from the view by simply highlighting it instead of opening the actual document.

These are the default folders and views in the Mail database:

- [ ] *Inbox*   This contains all incoming mail. Mail documents will stay in the Inbox until you delete or move them. The Inbox is the default view and will be active when you open a database for the first time. From then on, whatever view you had open when you last closed the Mail database will be the view you are returned to when you open the database again.

- [ ] *Drafts*   This contains all mail messages you save as drafts (works in progress). Notes does not mail messages saved as drafts until you direct it to mail them, which means you can start a mail message anytime and finish it at a later time. Personal Stationery you create is also saved in this view. You will learn more about creating Personal Stationery in Hour 12, "Working with Advanced Mail Features."

- [ ] *Sent*   All mail messages you send are displayed in this view unless you move or delete them. By default, Notes keeps a copy of all messages. To change this setting, refer to Hour 3, "Specifying Your Notes Preferences."

- [ ] *All Documents*   This displays all mail messages that are in your Mail database; it comprises a combination of messages that are sent, filed in folders, and available in all other views.

- [ ] *Meetings*   This displays a list of meetings you have created or to which you have accepted an invitation. They can be sorted by date, time, and subject.

- [ ] *Trash*   This contains documents marked for deletion that have not yet been deleted. Select this view to see all documents marked for deletion. If you see documents in your Trash view that you don't want to delete, simply drag them into another folder.

- [ ] *Discussion Threads*   This displays mail messages grouped with their replies so that you can follow an entire conversation (found under Folders and Views).

- [ ] *Archiving*   This lists the documents you have archived from this database. Archiving saves space in your Mail database.

- [ ] *Agents*   They automate tasks, such as managing documents, manipulating fields, and importing information from other applications.

- [ ] *Design*   As a Lotus Notes user, you can design Notes databases, views, and forms. Design is beyond the scope of this book. You can access the Design menu only if you have a Notes license that enables you to do so. Consult your Notes administrator if you have questions over which type of license you have.

Notes also provides two additional view selections in the Mail navigator to assist you in finding your Calendar and To-Do information. These two selections are separated from the mail views and appear as buttons. These two additional views are:

☐ *Calendar*   Your personal appointments and calendar are displayed in this view. You can view the calendar by month, week, or two-week period—just to name a few. For more on calendars, see Hour 20, "Working with Notes Calendaring and Scheduling."

☐ *To Do*   This displays documents created with the Task form. You will learn about To-Do lists in Hour 20 as well.

You can determine how documents are displayed within some of these folders and views. For example, you can sort the documents in your Inbox by sender (Who) or by date. Not all views and folders give you sort capabilities, but you can easily find those that do by looking for a triangle located next to the column header. If you see a triangle pointing up, that means that the column can be sorted and is displayed in ascending order. Click once in the column header, and the sort order will change to descending. If you do not see a triangle, no sort options are available (see Figure 8.2).

Figure 8.2.

The column headers indicate sorting capabilities.

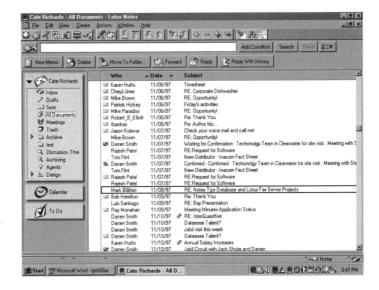

The first column in all views is a special column called the marker column. It's separated from the other columns in the view by a thin, vertical gray line that extends throughout the length of the view. This column displays a variety of system information. For example, if you delete a mail message by selecting the message and pressing your Delete key, Notes places a small, blue trash can icon in this column. Read marks (red stars) appear in this column until your mail message has been read. You can select mail messages you want to print or view by clicking once in this column; Notes places a check mark next to each mail message you mark (see Figure 8.3). Other icons that you may see in the Mail database are explained in Table 8.1.

Table 8.1. Common NotesMail icons.

Icon	Description	Location
Yellow envelope	Sent mail of normal or low importance	View or folder column
Red envelope	Sent mail of high importance	View or folder column
Paper and pencil	Draft (unsent mail message)	View or folder column
Paper clip	Attachment icon	View or folder column
Torn sheet of paper	Truncated document	View or folder column
Trash can	Deleted message	View marker column
Star	Unread mail	View marker column
Check mark	Selected document	View marker column
One piece of paper over another	Stationery	View or folder column
Exclamation point	Important document	View or folder column
Hands shaking	Invitation	View or folder column
Man waving	Appointment	View or folder column
Document with lightning	Event	View or folder column
Finger with string	Reminder	View or folder column
Calendar with date	Anniversary	View or folder column
Document with check mark	To-Do	View or folder column

Some views have categories. Categories are not documents; they act only as headings so that the documents can be logically grouped together. If you click any of the categories in a view, you can expand and collapse the categories. The Drafts view enables you to categorize documents by providing you with a list of categories (see Figure 8.4) with twisties next to the category titles.

Figure 8.3.

*The marker column with
unread marks and check
marks. Placing check
marks next to documents
allows you to perform
some menu functions
(such as view, print,
delete, and move to
folder) on groups of
documents at one time.*

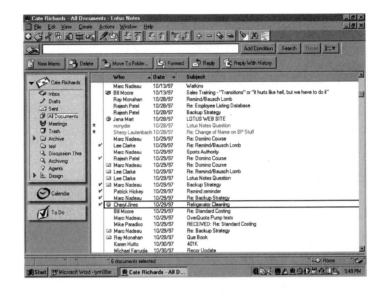

Figure 8.4.

*To expand and collapse
categories quickly in the
Drafts view, use the +
and − SmartIcons.*

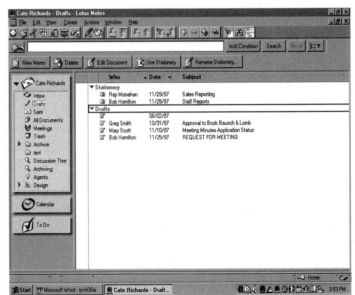

Task 8.2: Using the Inbox View

A great deal of the time you spend in the Mail database will be in the Inbox view. The first
column to the right of the marker column is titled *Who* and displays the sender's name. In
the column heading, you see a triangle, indicating that the column can be sorted in ascending

order. The default view sorts your mail by the date it was sent, according to the entry in the *Date* column, which can also be sorted. The last column is the *Subject* column, which displays the contents of the subject line of each mail message. Because Notes does not require you to supply information in the subject line when you create mail, this column may sometimes be blank. Email etiquette, however, suggests that supplying information in the subject line is not useful only to the recipient, it also helps ensure that your mail will be read by the recipient.

If you are using server-based mail, your mail may not appear in a view as quickly as it arrives in your mailbox on the server. Notes can notify you of new mail with a beep or a message on your screen. If you don't see new mail in your Inbox view, refresh your view by pressing the F9 key or by clicking the Refresh icon located in the header of the first view column.

Task 8.3: Receiving Mail Notification

Generally speaking, most people want to know when they have new mail as soon as possible. By default, when new mail arrives in your mailbox, Notes plays a short tune to indicate that you have new mail. You can also set a user preference that will display a small dialog box to give you a visual notification of new mail. (For more information on user preferences, see Hour 2, "Customizing Your Workspace.") In addition, if you look at the status bar, there is a small icon in the lower-right corner that will provide visual cues to indicate the arrival of new mail. A small dim envelope is displayed when you have no unread mail messages in your mailbox. If an Inbox with a piece of paper is displayed, you have unread (possibly new) mail messages in your mail box.

If you want to quickly access your new mail, click the Inbox icon in the lower-right corner of the status bar and choose Scan Unread Mail from the list.

You can control how often Notes checks for mail as well as whether Notes should notify you audibly or visually when new mail arrives. If you disable the notification features of Notes, you will need to check your mailbox from time to time to see if you have new mail. In Hour 2, you learn how to edit the default settings for mail notification and scanning.

To take advantage of the mail notification features, you must leave Notes running constantly on your workstation, even if you are using other applications. You can minimize Notes if you need to run other applications, but ending your Notes session prevents you from getting mail notifications. (It does not prevent you from receiving mail, however.) If Notes is minimized and you receive new mail, the Notes icon displays an envelope in addition to its usual graphic.

Task 8.4: Reading Incoming Mail

In order to access the data in a mail message, you must at least select the document in a view or folder. Selecting mail messages is just like selecting documents in a regular Notes database. Simply choose the view or folder that is most useful in your search and navigate to the message you want. For instance, if you wanted to reply to a message your boss sent you today, the Inbox folder or the All Documents view would probably be the most helpful. Once you find and select the message from the boss (by placing the selection bar on that document), you can read the mail message and create a reply.

Alternatively, you can click the All Documents view in the navigator (or choose View, All Documents) and then choose View, Show, Unread Only (see Figure 8.5). Once you have selected a particular document to read, you can enable the preview pane to scan the contents of the document without actually opening the document, or you can double-click the document to open it in Read mode.

Figure 8.5.

View, Show, Unread displays only unread mail in the Inbox view. To return to the Inbox view that shows all documents, deselect Show, Unread Only.

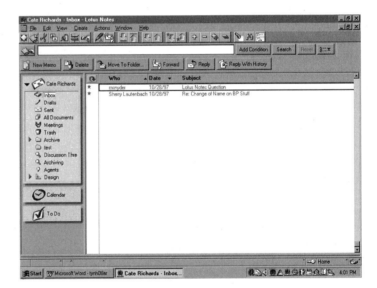

Task 8.5: Printing Mail Messages

Even though you work with your mail electronically 99 percent of the time, occasionally you may want to print a copy of a mail message you have sent or received. Printing a mail message is exactly the same as printing any Notes document. The following steps serve as a quick reminder for printing documents:

1. Select the message you want to print. (Remember, if you are in a view or a folder, you do not have to open the message to print it.) If you want to print the mail message that you are reading, proceed to the next step.

2. Choose File, Print, or click the File Print SmartIcon. The File Print dialog box appears. (See Hour 5, "Working with Databases," for more detailed information about this dialog box.)

3. Select the appropriate settings for this document in the File Print dialog box.

4. Choose OK to print your document.

Remember that users can disable printing capability fosr messages they send to you.

Task 8.6: Closing Messages

When you finish reading a mail message, you can close the message and return to the folder or view you were in by taking any of the following actions:

☐ Press Esc.

☐ Press Ctrl+F4.

☐ Click the view or folder window's Control-menu box and then choose Close. (The Control-menu box is the small application icon in the upper-left corner of the view or folder window.)

You will see two Control-menu boxes: one for Notes (in the upper-left corner) and one for the view or folder window (just below the program's Control-menu box). Make sure that you click the view or folder window's Control-menu box. If you inadvertently click the Notes Control-menu box, you are prompted to exit Notes. Be sure you click the correct one.

Task 8.7: Handling Your Mail with the Status Bar and SmartIcons

As you are probably well aware by now, Notes provides many ways to accomplish the same task, particularly in the area of email. One of the most useful features that Notes provides is the mail section in the far-right corner of the status bar.

When a dim Envelope icon is displayed, you have no new mail. When new mail is transferred to your mailbox, an Inbox with a piece of paper in it appears. You can click this icon to display the menu shown in Figure 8.6.

Figure 8.6.

The Mailbox feature can be accessed from the status bar.

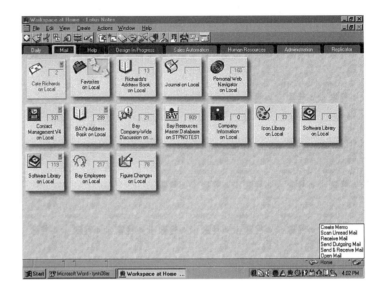

Choose one of the following options from this menu:

☐ *Create Memo*   You can select the Create Memo option to open your mailbox and create a new blank mail memo, just as if you had chosen Create, Memo in your mailbox.

☐ *Scan Unread Mail*   Selecting the second option opens your mailbox and opens the first unread mail message in your mailbox. You can then navigate among the unread documents until you have read all of them. If no unread mail messages are found, the status bar displays this message: "There are no unread documents in your mail file."

When you use this method to read an unread document, you actually open the document, which means that Notes no longer considers the mail message unread.

☐ *Receive Mail*   You can select this option to initiate a server connection and begin replicating your local mailbox with the server copy of your mailbox. Any new mail that is queued at the server mailbox is then transferred to your local mailbox (but outgoing mail is not sent). For more on replication, see Hour 24, "Working Remotely."

☐ *Send Outgoing Mail*   Selecting Send Outgoing Mail, the fourth option, initiates a server connection and routes pending mail from your workstation to the server's mailbox (but incoming mail is not received). This option is for remote users.

☐ *Send & Receive Mail*   The fifth option performs the actions of both the Receive Mail and Send Outgoing Mail options. This is also for remote users.

☐ *Open Mail*   The final option, Open Mail, opens your mailbox and displays the last view or folder that you used.

In addition to the status bar, Notes provides a context-sensitive set of NotesMail SmartIcons that are available when you open your mailbox. Using these SmartIcons can make your NotesMail sessions easier and more productive. Table 8.2 shows the default NotesMail SmartIcons and describes their functions.

Table 8.2. The Default NotesMail SmartIcons.

Icon	Name	Description
	Actions Edit Document	Opens the selected document in Edit mode
	Actions Forward	Forwards the selected document
	Navigate Next Main	Goes to the next Main document in the current view or folder
	Navigate Previous Main	Goes to the previous Main document in the current view or folder
	Navigate Next	Goes to the next document in the current view or folder
	Navigate Previous	Goes to the previous document in the current view or folder
	Navigate Next Unread	Goes to the next unread document in the current view or folder
	Navigate Previous Unread	Goes to the previous unread document in the current view or folder
	View Expand	Expands the current category
	View Collapse	Collapses the current category
	View Expand All	Expands the entire view (All Categories)
	View Collapse All	Collapses the entire view (All Categories)

continues

Table 8.2. continued

Icon	Name	Description
	Edit Find	Launches the Search dialog box
	View Show/Hide Search Bar	Toggles the full text search bar off and on
	View Show/Hide Preview Pane	Toggles the document preview pane off and on

Task 8.8: Deleting Messages

As mail messages accumulate in your mailbox, the time will come when you decide that you no longer need certain messages. Unneeded mail messages clutter your mailbox, making it harder to find the important messages, and occupy precious disk space, decreasing the performance of your mailbox. If you keep every mail message you receive, you will begin to consume a large amount of disk space, and your administrator will probably tell you to clean out mail you no longer need.

Consider the following techniques for conserving disk space:

☐ After you read an incoming message, delete it unless it contains information you really need to keep.

☐ If you frequently need to keep messages for a long time—for example, if you work in a legal department, you might need to keep a message or a return-receipt message as proof that you responded to a problem—you can print the message and delete the electronic copy. You can also move the message to an archive mailbox.

☐ Regularly scan your mailbox (at minimum once a month) for unneeded messages. When you identify these messages, delete them.

☐ Often, you may receive mail messages that have file attachments. If you don't really need the attachments, but you want to save the mail messages, delete only the attachments. Deleting unneeded attachments can conserve significant space because the attachments are stored within your mailbox as well. See Hour 18, "Working with Advanced Document Features," for more on attachments.

8

Because of the way Notes allocates storage space for databases, your Mail database can eat up inordinate amounts of disk space if you do not delete mail messages frequently. This is particularly important for remote users, as disk space on most notebook computers is usually at a premium. The moral of this story is to delete your unneeded mail frequently: It makes it easier to find mail you need to keep, it saves disk space, and it increases the performance of your Mail system.

You delete mail messages in the same way you delete documents: Simply open your mailbox and choose the view or folder you find most useful for viewing mail. Select the message or messages you want to delete, and then press the Delete key on your keyboard or click the Edit Clear SmartIcon. This marks that message for deletion. Notes does not delete the message immediately, however; it moves the message into the Trash folder. This is an extremely useful feature, because if you decide that you really don't want to delete any of the marked documents, you can rescue them from the trash simply by opening the trash folder and moving the documents back out.

If you are certain that you want to delete the documents in the Trash folder, click the Empty Trash button on the action bar, or press the F9 key, or close the database. When you perform any of these actions, Notes displays a dialog box warning you that you are going to delete the documents permanently and asking you to confirm the operation.

You also can delete a message while you are reading it by pressing Delete. Notes flags the message for deletion (displaying the trash can icon in the view marker column) and immediately takes you to the next message in your mailbox. This procedure works only when you're reading a message, however; pressing the Delete key when you are composing a message has a very different effect: It deletes the text your are typing, but not the document.

Task 8.9: Exiting Your Mailbox

To exit your mailbox, you can use any of the following methods you learned earlier for closing a database:

- [ ] Press Esc.
- [ ] Press Ctrl+F4.
- [ ] Double-click the Control-menu box for your mailbox view.

As in any database, if you have flagged messages for deletion, Notes displays a prompt that asks you if you want to delete the flagged documents permanently. If you click Yes, the messages you have flagged are deleted permanently from your mailbox. If you click No, the messages remain in your mailbox, and the deletion flag is removed.

Workshop

Now that you have learned how easy it is to work with your NotesMail database, let's review a few key terms and questions that may occur while you are working with mail. This workshop provides you with a quick overview of the key points of this hour's lessons.

Key Terms

Review the following list of terms:

☐ *Mail navigator*   The default navigator pane located on the left side of your NotesMail database when it is open. This navigator provides you with a quick and easy way to find the documents you have stored in your mail database.

☐ *Inbox*   The view that automatically displays messages that you receive. Messages stay in the Inbox until you either delete them or move them to a folder.

☐ *Sent view*   Shows all messages that you save when you send them. You can change whether Notes automatically saves the messages you send by modifying the User Preferences for mail (see Hour 3, "Specifying Your Notes Preferences").

☐ *Drafts view*   Shows all messages that you have created but have not sent. This view also displays any custom stationery you have created (see Hour 12, "Working with Advanced Mail Features" for more information on creating stationery).

Common Questions

Q   I created a document and saved it without sending it, but now I can't find it. What happened to it?

A   Chances are, you are looking for it in the wrong view. Switch to the Drafts view, and you should be able to find it.

Q   I received some email from someone else in my company, but I can't seem to find it in my Inbox view. Where did it go?

A   You either deleted it, or you moved it to another folder. Check the folders in your database or open the All Documents view to see if your document is there. If you have enabled archiving in your mail database, the document may have been moved to your Archive mail database, so you should check there as well.

Q   I just deleted a document, but I have decided I need it again. Is there anything I can do?

A As long as you have not exited the database (or refreshed the database by pressing F9) and answered Yes when prompted to permanently remove the document(s) from the database, you can still undelete it. To undelete the document, simply highlight it and press the Delete key again. Notes will remove the deletion marker (the small trash can icon) from the document, and you can continue to work. If you already answered Yes when prompted to permanently delete the document, the only way to recover it is to contact your Notes administrator to see if a backup copy of the database was made that can be accessed to restore the document. The chance of a backup copy being made is not usually a good one, so be careful when deleting documents!

Preview of the Next Hour

Now that you have learned the basics about your NotesMail database, it is time to learn how to create and send mail. The next hour will teach you the basics of creating and addressing email.

Hour 9

Creating Outgoing Mail

Goals for This Hour

Being able to read your email is only half the story. You also need to be able to create and send email. In this hour you will learn how simple it is to create email for friends and colleagues in your own organization and around the world.

Creating email requires you to be familiar with several functions. Here is what you can expect to learn:

- ☐ Composing an email message
- ☐ Addressing an email message to individuals and groups
- ☐ Understanding moods, delivery options, and return receipts

Task 9.1: Creating a Mail Message

The Notes email system is very flexible and supports several types of mail messages that you can send and receive. To send a mail message, choose Create to see a list of all of the forms available in your Mail database. Figure 9.1 shows the default forms available in the standard Mail database.

Each of the default forms in the Mail database was designed to provide a certain type of functionality. You will now examine the most common and useful forms in detail.

Figure 9.1.

The Create menu in the Mail database displays all available forms in the database Inbox view. This menu is context sensitive and will change from database to database.

The Memo form is the standard form. You use it most of the time when you send mail messages to other users. To create a new memo, choose Create, Memo. A new memo, like that shown in Figure 9.2, is displayed on your screen. Notice that the format of the standard Notes mail message, called a memo, is similar to an interoffice memo or standard business letter.

Figure 9.2.

You can access the Mail Memo form through the menu or by clicking the New Memo button on the Action bar.

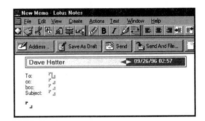

At the top of the Memo form, you see the envelope section, where you can begin to address the mail. Notes computes the username of the user ID currently in use at the workstation (your username if you are sending mail), the date, and the time, and places this information into this section.

The first four lines provide the addressing information and a snapshot of the contents of the message. These are the parts of the envelope:

☐ The To field displays the name or names of the primary recipients of the message. If you are reading a message you received, obviously your name appears in this field; if other names also appear in the To field, those individuals also received the mail.

☐ The cc field displays the names of secondary recipients to whom the mail was sent. (cc is an abbreviation for carbon copy, a holdover from the days when carbon paper was used to make copies. Some things just never die!)

☐ The bcc field displays the name or names of other recipients to whom the mail was sent. If you send a mail message with names specified in the bcc field, the recipients named in the To and cc fields will not know that the person or persons specified in the bcc field also received the mail. (bcc is an abbreviation for blind carbon copy.) If two people are listed in the bcc field, each sees only his own name and does not know that the other person was sent a copy.

☐ The From line (the colored bar at the very top of the envelope area) indicates the name of the sender of the mail message. The name in this field is automatically generated by Notes based on the user ID currently in use when a mail message is composed. In addition, the date and time the mail message was sent are normally displayed in this bar.

☐ The Subject line indicates what the mail message is about. When you send a message to another user, you should include a subject as a matter of common courtesy (and good etiquette) so that the user can have an idea of what the message pertains to without opening the message. While you are not required to enter a subject for your mail message, I recommend that you do so not only so the recipients have some idea of what the message is about, but also because many other mail systems will not accept mail that contains no subject.

Next is the text of the message, commonly referred to as the body. The body of a NotesMail message can be virtually any length and can contain embedded objects, such as pictures, sounds, and charts. It can also contain file attachments. You will learn about these other features in Hour 12, "Working with Advanced Mail Features."

The body field in a NotesMail message is a special type of field known as a *rich text format* (RTF) field, in which can store any type of data from formatted text to graphics and sound. You can learn more about the powerful features of RTF fields in Hour 5, "Working with Databases."

Task 9.2: Addressing the Mail

The first editable field, To, is the field you use to list the primary recipients of this message. If you know the exact username of the recipient, you can type it in. For example, if you want to send mail to John Smith, enter **John Smith** in the To field.

Each Notes user must have an account and a Notes ID file that contains that user's Notes username and password (along with other information). Notes maintains a directory of each user's username for security purposes and to identify users to the mail system. The Public Address Book serves as the repository for all user information and plays a critical role in the Notes email system. Hour 13, "Using the Personal Address Book," briefly describes the Public Address Book.

The Memo form uses a Notes feature called *Type-Ahead*. If this feature is turned on, when you type the first few characters of a user's name in any of the address fields (To, cc, or bcc), Notes looks up the name in the Public and Personal Address Books as you type. If Notes finds a match, it completes the name for you; if Notes does not find a match, the status bar displays a message stating that the name was not found in the Address Book.

You can control which, if any, address book Notes will use for Type-Ahead addressing. To do so, you use a setting in the Location document of the Personal Address Book. See Hour 13 for details.

Of course, Notes doesn't always find the name you're really looking for. If you are sending a message to Bob Dolby and the address book contains more than one Bob, Notes completes the address line with the first Bob it finds in alphabetical order (by last name). For example, if you were to type **Bob D** in the address line, Notes might complete the address line with Bob Dobbs instead of Bob Dolby. If this happens, simply continue to type the person's name as if the address line were still blank. As you do, Notes continues to zero in on the name you're typing.

If you want to send the message to several people, you can enter several recipients' names separated by commas. If you make a mistake and enter the wrong person in the To field, you can delete the name by pressing the Backspace key, by selecting the entire name and pressing the Delete key, or by typing the new name to replace the old. Figure 9.3 displays an example of multiple recipients on a memo.

You can also send email to several people by using groups. Your administrator may have set up several groups to be used as *mailing lists* in the Public Address Book. For example, you might be able to send email to everyone in the Marketing department by entering the group name Marketing in the To, cc, or bcc fields. Look at the Groups view in the Public Address Book to see what groups are available. Note that many of these groups may be intended for use in determining who can access a particular database instead of for use as a mailing list. Ask your administrator if you are not sure. You can also set up personal groups in your Personal Address Book. See Hour 13 for details on creating personal groups.

Figure 9.3.

An example of multiple recipients on a memo.

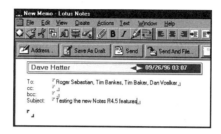

9

Once you have added the names of all of the primary recipients, you can press the Tab key to move to the cc field (or you can simply click the cc field). If you want to send a copy of this message to other users, you can enter those names in this field. For example, if you want to send email to Roger Sebastian, but you want Rick Flagg and Chris Clark to receive copies for reference, you must put Roger Sebastian in the To field and Rick and Chris in the cc field, as shown in Figure 9.4.

Figure 9.4.

Sending a copy of a message to several users.

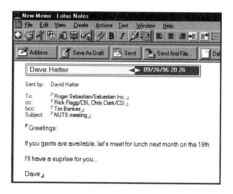

When you reply to a mail message that contains names in the cc field, consider using the Reply to All feature of Notes (as described in the section "Replying to a Message" in Hour 10). This sends your response to everyone who received the original message.

All three of the named users will receive the mail, just as if you had included them all in the To field. However, by putting Roger in the To field and Rick and Chris in the cc field, you indicate to Roger that although the mail is primarily intended for him, you also sent the information to other users. By copying Rick and Chris, you let them know what you sent to Roger.

In some instances, you might not want the primary recipients to know that you have sent a copy of the mail to another party. In such cases, you can use the bcc field to send a copy of the message to other users without notifying the recipients named in the To and cc fields that a copy was sent to someone else. Figure 9.5 shows a message that is sent to Roger Sebastian, carbon copied to Rick Flagg and Chris Clark, and blind carbon copied to Tim Bankes. Only the sender and Tim Bankes will see the contents of the bcc field and know that Tim received this message. This new memo has recipients specified in the To, cc, and bcc fields. The bcc field will never display more than one name except in the sender's copy of the memo. If two people are included in the bcc field, each will see only his or her own name.

Figure 9.5.

Use the To, cc, and bcc fields.

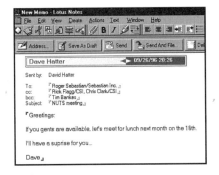

You've learned that you can type names directly into the various addressing fields or let the Type-Ahead feature fill in the Memo form for you. In addition, you can choose recipients' names from an Address Book. Click the Address button on the Action bar to display the Mail Address dialog box, from which you can choose recipients directly from the Personal Address Book (see Figure 9.6).

Figure 9.6.

You can click and drag names from the left pane of the Mail Address dialog box to the right pane. When you drag a name to the right pane, drop the name onto the To, cc, or bcc field.

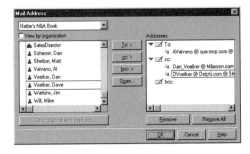

Task 9.3: Specifying the Subject

Once you have all of the addresses entered, you can tab to the Subject field. In this field, you enter a brief description of the contents of the message. This description is displayed in all of the mail views and folders (see Figure 9.7). Because the subject is the first thing the user will see regarding your message, it should be as explicit and concise as possible. Although you can enter up to 256 characters in the Subject field, many views and folders will truncate the text in the display. (Not to worry, your subject will not be affected; this description is for display purposes only.)

Figure 9.7.

You cannot format text in the subject line, and you should keep your subject lines short but informative. This will help others to determine the purpose and impor-tance of your message.

Task 9.4: Creating the Body of the Message

After you have entered the address and a brief subject, you are ready to enter your actual message, which is known as the body. Although this field appears to be small, because it is a rich text field, you can enter just about as much text or graphics as you want, and you can attach files or embed objects from other applications, such as a 1-2-3 spreadsheet or a Word document. The red markers around the field indicate that it can be encrypted for extra security. Figure 9.8 shows a completed mail memo ready to send, with several different types of data objects in the body. It contains an MS Word document as an attachment, an embedded wave file, an embedded bitmap file, and a doclink.

When you add attachments to your mail, you should supply the recipients with information regarding the attachment. Although the attachment will display a file name, that isn't always a sufficient description of the file or your purpose for sending it. You'll learn more about attaching files and embedding objects in Hour 18, "Working with Advanced Document Features." You'll learn about using the spell checker in Hour 16, "Working with Basic Document Features."

Figure 9.8.

A mail memo with several different types of data objects in the body.

Task 9.5: Mailing Options

There are several delivery options that affect how and when your mail is delivered. To examine or change these options, click the Delivery Options button on the Action bar at the top of the form. Notes then displays the Delivery Options dialog box (see Figure 9.9).

Figure 9.9.

The Delivery Options dialog box.

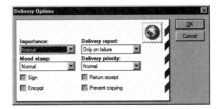

For a good percentage of your mail, it won't be necessary to access the Delivery Options dialog box. If you are sending mail to someone on the same Notes server who is using server-based mail, that mail will be delivered immediately.

The following sections discuss in detail how to use the settings in the Delivery Options dialog box.

Task 9.5.1: Choosing a Mood

You can use the Mood Stamp drop-down list to select a mood for your mail. A mood stamp helps set the tone of your mail message by assigning an accompanying icon that represents your mood. The mood stamp is displayed next to the subject line in the recipients' Mail database and in the mail memo when it is opened. Figure 9.10 shows the Good Job mood stamp in a memo.

Figure 9.10.

The Good Job mood stamp is a nice way to acknowledge accomplishments.

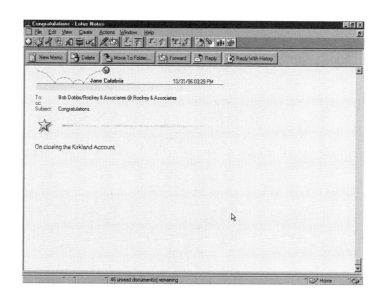

Think carefully about the delivery options you choose, but don't think for too long. Some people can get trapped by the many choices available for mood stamps and spend more time selecting a mood than they did creating the mail memo. The default mood is Normal, which assigns no icon. The other choices are outlined here:

- ☐ *Confidential*   This indicates that the recipients should not share this information with others.
- ☐ *Flame*   This indicates that you are angry about something. (It does not mean that the mail message is important.)
- ☐ *FYI*   This means that the mail message is for your information only, and no action or reply is required.
- ☐ *Personal*   This indicates that the mail is of a personal nature and should not be shared with others.
- ☐ *Private*   This is similar to Confidential; the information contained in the mail is for the distribution list only.
- ☐ *Thank You*   This indicates that you are showing your appreciation for something.
- ☐ *Good Job*   This lets the recipients know that they are being commended for a job well done.

☐ *Joke*   This tells the recipients that the message has a light, jovial tone.

☐ *Question*   This lets the recipients know that the message is a question that requires an answer.

☐ *Reminder*   This indicates to the recipients that they should not forget to do something.

Task 9.5.2: Setting the Delivery Priority

The Delivery Priority field is a drop-down list from which you can choose one of the following settings: Low, Normal, or High. Each of these options has an effect on the speed and cost with which the mail is routed by the server. Just as you would expect, High priority mail is routed the quickest, regardless of the cost. Low priority mail is the slowest, but it is the most economical. Normal is the default setting and is sufficient for most mail messages.

If you communicate only with other Notes users via a LAN connection (a persistent connection to the network) or if you have only one server, this setting has little effect on the speed or cost of routing. If you communicate with other Notes users across leased-line or dial-up connections, this setting becomes more important, as it can have a significant effect on delivery time and cost.

For instance, High priority mail is routed immediately, regardless of the routing cost. Low priority mail is sent only between midnight and 6:00 a.m., which is more cost effective because connect charges are considerably lower during the off-peak hours. Normal priority mail is routed according to various settings the Notes administrator determines. If you are cost-conscious and the promptness of the mail is not very important, use the Low setting. Conversely, if the mail is very important and must be delivered as soon as possible, use the High setting.

Task 9.5.3: Generating a Delivery Status Report

In most cases, if your mail message cannot be delivered to your intended recipients, the Notes server sends you a message indicating that it had a problem delivering the mail message, along with a suggested corrective action to take. If you have sent a message and do not receive a Failure report message, you can assume that your mail message has been delivered. For very important messages, you may want to have the Notes server send you a Delivery report to let you know that your mail was delivered successfully to the recipient's mailbox.

The Delivery Report drop-down list has four possible settings: Only on Failure, Confirm Delivery, Trace Entire Path, and None. The default setting is Only on Failure, which causes Notes to send a delivery report if a routing error occurs. You can change the setting by typing the first letter of the setting you want (O, C, T, or N) in the box, or by clicking the down arrow and selecting from the list.

If you change the Delivery Report field to Confirm Delivery, the Notes server notifies you when your mail is delivered (or it notifies you of a delivery failure). A Delivery report from the server appears in your mailbox like any other NotesMail message.

> A Delivery report does not indicate that the mail message recipient actually read the message. It tells you only that the mail message was successfully delivered to the recipient's mailbox.

The Trace Entire Path setting tells Notes to return a confirmation message from each hop along the routing path between the sender and the recipient. If you are having trouble sending and receiving mail, this can be a valuable troubleshooting tool because you can see where the mail died on the routing path. If you communicate only with users on the same server, Trace Entire Path probably is not very useful. Your Notes administrator may ask you to use this if you are having difficulty with your mail; otherwise, you'll not need it.

If you change the Delivery Report field to None, you will not receive a notification, even if the delivery fails. Though it's not often used, this setting may be useful if you are sending an unimportant message to many people (known as spamming on the Internet) and you don't care if Notes cannot deliver the message to someone. For instance, if you were going to send an FYI-type mail to an entire department, you might use this option.

Task 9.5.4: Requesting a Return Receipt

Request a return receipt if you want to receive a message from the server when a recipient opens your mail message. This can be very useful when you need to be sure that a user has received and read (or at least opened) your mail (see Figure 9.11). To enable this feature, simply select the Return Receipt check box in the Delivery Options dialog box. An X appears, indicating that it is enabled. To disable this feature, click the check box a second time to remove the X.

Task 9.5.5: Encrypting the Message for Security

The Encrypt check box enables you to encrypt your mail message with your private key. This provides additional security because any user who receives this message must possess a copy of your public key in order to read it.

If you want to encrypt a message, just select the option.

Figure 9.11.
This return receipt indicates that a mail message was read. Use this for your most important messages.

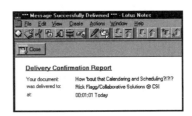

Task 9.5.6: Adding an Electronic Signature

With the Sign check box, you can attach an electronic signature to your mail. An electronic signature is derived from your unique key stored in your Notes ID. It is virtually impossible to duplicate an electronic signature, which guarantees that any mail or document that is signed by your Notes ID actually came from you (or at least from your Notes ID).

Electronic signatures and encryption are extremely secure methods for protecting mail messages (or any document for that matter), but they are dependent upon the physical security of your Notes ID. Anyone who can access your Notes ID and knows your password can impersonate you! The moral of this story is to keep your ID secure and your password to yourself, and change your password frequently.

All Notes encryption keys are based on the 64-bit RSA standard, which creates almost unbreakable encryption codes and requires a public key and a private key. If you encrypt a mail message or a document and then lose your Notes ID file—or even forget your password—chances are good that your information will be irretrievably lost! You should use encryption only when security is paramount.

Task 9.5.7: Preventing Copying

Place a check in the Prevent Copying check box of the Delivery Options dialog box to enable this feature. When you enable Prevent Copying, recipients of the mail message cannot copy the message to the Clipboard, print it, or forward it to other users. This helps ensure that confidential information is not leaked to others through the NotesMail system.

Task 9.6: Using Microsoft Word or Lotus WordPro as Your NotesMail Editor

Some users do not find the basic word processing features available in Notes powerful enough to generate complex documents. Other users prefer to use the skills they have acquired in a particular word processing application instead of learning how to use yet another editor. For these reasons, in the past, many users created documents in Word or WordPro and then attached the documents as file attachments into Notes mail memos. Now, however, Notes enables you to compose your Notes mail with Word or WordPro directly so you don't have to attach a file. This allows you to create much more sophisticated message contents than you can create with the standard Notes mail editor.

You can use Word or WordPro only as your **mail** editor. You cannot use them as the editor in any other Notes databases. In addition, you can use only Microsoft Word 95, 97, or later and Lotus WordPro 97 or later.

To change from the standard Notes editor to Word or WordPro, select File, Tools, User Preferences. Then select the Mail icon. Figure 9.12 shows the Document Memo editor field, where you can change the default entry of Notes to either Microsoft Word or Lotus WordPro.

Figure 9.12.

Selecting Microsoft Word as your Notes mail editor.

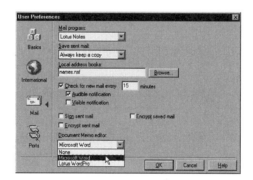

After you select your Notes mail editor, you will have a new option in the Create, Mail menu. In addition to creating a Memo which uses the standard Notes mail editor, you can choose either a Word memo or a WordPro memo depending on your selection (see Figure 9.13).

It might take a few seconds longer than usual to load your chosen editor and open the mail editing window, but your word processor will appear on-screen, displaying a blank screen with an addressing window open on top of it. You can choose to address the mail memo now or to cancel the window and address the memo later. Then you can compose your mail message using all the tools of your chosen editor, utilizing the same menus and toolbars that you are used to.

Figure 9.13.

*Creating a new memo
using WordPro.*

A new button also appears on the Action bar: the Envelope button (see Figure 9.14). In a standard Notes mail memo, you can address the mail memo directly in the memo itself. You do not have this option with either of the two other editors, so this button brings up an addressing dialog box where you can enter the names of the recipients of the memo. (This is the same addressing dialog box that was open when the memo first appeared.)

Figure 9.14.

*The Envelope button
gives you access to the
dialog box in which you
address mail to the
recipients.*

Figure 9.15 shows a mail message being edited in Lotus WordPro with the addressing dialog box open; Figure 9.16 shows the same mail message being edited in Microsoft Word. Notice the specific differences in the menu and toolbars. Although the File menu still displays standard Notes options, the other menu items reflect those of the editor you have chosen.

Figure 9.15.

*Addressing a mail
message with WordPro as
your Notes mail editor.*

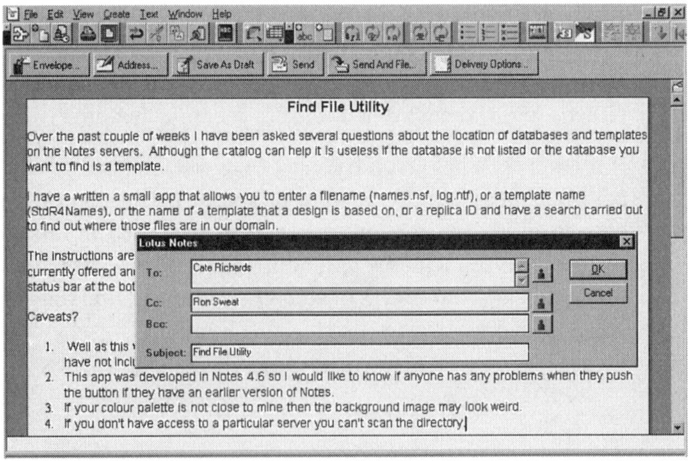

Figure 9.16.

Editing a memo with Microsoft Word.

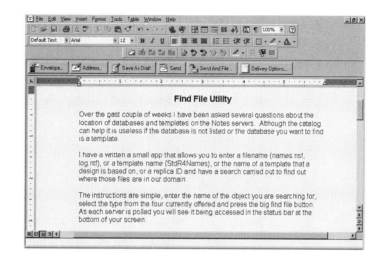

9

If you choose the Help menu (see Figure 9.17), you will see that it now allows you to choose between help for Notes and help for your chosen editor.

Figure 9.17.

The Help menu offers help for Notes or for your chosen editor.

When you finish entering and formatting your email message using the tools available to your selected editor, you can send the memo in the normal way.

When the recipient opens the memo to read it, if he has the editor you used to create the memo in the first place (Word or WordPro), that editor will automatically open and display the memo. If the recipient does not have the editor used to create the memo, it will be displayed in the standard Notes mail editor, in which case, some formatting may be lost.

Workshop

Having completed this hour, you should now be comfortable with creating and sending email messages. You have learned how to address messages to individuals, as well as groups.

Here are some of the words you should be familiar with and some common questions you might have.

Key Terms

Review the following list of terms:

- ☐ *Memo* You may think of a memo as a brief communication, and often it is. But in Notes, the memo is the basis of email. It is the document where you create an email message, it can be as brief or as lengthy as you like, and you can include graphics and file attachments as well.

- ☐ *Groups* If you regularly send email to the same group of people, you might get tired of having to type the names in individually every time. Using groups that you have set up yourself in your Personal Address Book or that have been set up for you in the Public Address Book, you can send mail to all of those individuals by entering a single group name.

- ☐ *Return Receipt* A means of asking Notes to inform you when your email has been read by the recipient(s). Note that if you are mailing outside of your own domain (such as to the Internet), there is no guarantee that the recipient's email system acknowledges return receipts.

Common Questions

Q Can I send email to everyone in my company at once?

A If your administrator has set up a group, perhaps called "Everyone," you may be able to. It is best to see what the company policy is for sending mail to such groups, though, because the CEO may not be happy at receiving an email from you trying to sell your car. Such groups are usually set up for company-wide communications, such as financial results, HR policies, and so on. Certainly, if this is your job function, approach your Notes administrator about setting up such groups if they don't exist.

Q How private are my email communications?

A Most companies have a policy stating that they can inspect a user's mail file at any time for any reason. Your Notes administrator has access to your mail file on the Notes server but will normally access it only at your request to help sort out a mail problem or when directed to by management. If you are sending email out via the Internet, you have very little guarantee of privacy as it is a public network and your mail must pass through the mail servers of several other companies to get to its destination.

Preview of the Next Hour

You now know how to send and receive email messages. In the next Hour, you will learn how to send email to people within and outside of your company.

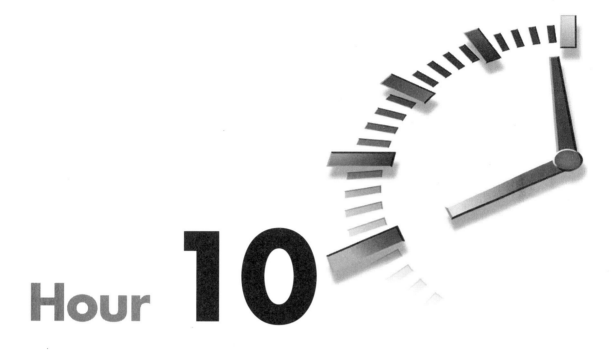

Hour **10**

Sending Outgoing Mail

Goals for This Hour

The last few hours have spent time on using mail and the separate mailing options. Now, all that's left for you to do is send mail. This hour will teach you the following:

- ☐ The different ways to send and/or save your email messages
- ☐ Sending email to other Notes users outside your company
- ☐ Sending email to the Internet
- ☐ Forwarding a message

Task 10.1: Sending Your Message

After you have selected the settings you want, you are ready to save and/or send your mail message. Press Esc to close the message, and Notes displays the Close Window dialog box shown in Figure 10.1. You can choose to send the message in any of the following ways:

☐ The Send and Save a Copy option button tells Notes to send the mail and place a copy of the mail message in your mailbox, where it is stored in the Sent folder. This is the default option for this dialog box and is recommended for any mail that you might need to refer to in the future.

☐ The Send Only option button tells Notes to send the message, but not place a copy of the mail message in your mailbox. If you are sending mail that you don't need to keep (maybe a joke, for instance), you can use this option to save space in your mailbox.

☐ The Save Only option button tells Notes not to send the message but to save a draft of the mail messages in your mailbox. All mail messages that you elect to save without sending will be considered drafts and can be seen in the Drafts view until you send them. This can be very handy if you don't have time to finish a mail message and want to work on it later.

☐ The Discard Changes option button tells Notes to ignore the changes in the mail message. If you are composing a new mail message, this option causes the new message to be neither sent nor saved. If you are editing a message, all edits are discarded, and the saved mail remains unchanged.

Figure 10.1.

The Close Window dialog box for mail messages can be accessed by pressing the Esc key or Ctrl+W.

When you have chosen the option you want, click OK to take the action you have selected. Choose Cancel to ignore the action you have selected and return to the mail message. Pressing Esc while this dialog box is displayed is the equivalent of selecting Cancel.

You can also use the Send or the Send and File buttons on the Action bar to send the mail. To send the mail and store a copy in your Sent folder, click the Send button. To save a copy to a different folder, click the Send and File button, which will send the mail and launch the Move to Folder dialog box so you can choose the folder in which to store the copy.

Task 10.2: Sending Mail to Other Notes Users Outside Your Company

If your Notes server has the ability to communicate with a Notes server at another company, you can send email messages to people on the other server. You may need to check with your Notes administrator to confirm that you can do this. You can also check your Public Address Book. You may find that in addition to the employees listed, there are listings for people that your company contacts frequently via another Notes server or the Internet. These might be vendors, customers, information sources, or servers in other locations. If someone is listed in the Public Address Book, you should be able to send mail to him or her, no matter where that person is located.

Your Notes administrator may have added address books from other companies to your server. If so, you will be able to access multiple Public Address Books when you perform address lookups. These multiple Public Address Books are called *cascading* address books.

Even if users from another company do not appear in your Public Address Book or in a cascaded address book, you should still be able to email them as long as your Notes server is connected to theirs. If you are sending mail to someone not listed in the address book, you simply need to address the email properly. The address must include the person's domain (which is almost always the company name; your contact at the other company should provide this information) preceded by an at sign (@). For example, to send a message to Dan Voelker at ABC Company, you would address the message as follows:

```
To: Dan Voelker/ABC Company@ABC Company
```

This notation tells Notes that Dan Voelker is not in your domain (your company's Public Address Book) but is outside your organization, and that this message should be forwarded to the ABC Company server upon the next connection. Once the mail message is delivered to the mailbox on the ABC Company server, that company's server routes it to Dan Voelker's mailbox.

If you communicate frequently with people in other companies, you can make it much easier on yourself by adding their addresses to your Personal Address Book. To do so, you must add a Business Card document for each person with whom you want to communicate, just as you would for people in your own company who are not in your domain. The primary difference for adding people outside your company is that you must place the person's full email address in the Email address field. For more information, see Hour 13, "Using the Personal Address Book."

10

If you have received mail from someone outside your company who is not in either of your address books, you can easily add that person to your Personal Address Book for future use. Simply select the mail message that you received, and then choose Actions, Mail Tools, Add Sender to Address Book. This creates a new Business Card document and automatically copies the sender's information into it.

Task 10.3: Sending Mail to the Internet

Not all Notes servers are configured to send and receive mail to the Internet, so you should confirm with your Notes administrator that you have this ability. To route Internet email, your Notes administrator will have set up a special domain name (such as SMTP) that you will use to indicate that you want the mail to go out to the Internet. If you can send and receive Internet mail, the process is the same as sending any Notes email message, and the key is how you address your mail.

A typical Internet address has the form *name@domain.com*, where *name* is the name of the person you're sending to, *domain* is the name of that person's domain (an Internet domain is different from a Notes domain), and *.com* is the type of domain (in this case, a commercial entity). Other domain types include .edu for educational organizations, .org for nonprofit organizations, and .gov for government organizations.

For example, suppose you have a friend, Rose Wezel, who works at XYZPDQ Manufacturing, which has an Internet account. You want to send a message to your friend, so you create a new mail message and address it like this:

```
Rose Wezel@XYZPDQ.com@SMTP
```

When the mail router sees this message, it knows from the @SMTP suffix that this message is intended for the Internet, so it sends the message to the correct server for conversion and transmission to the Internet. Even if you forget to enter the @SMTP in the example, the mail *might* still be routed correctly, as your administrator can choose to have any mail to an unknown domain passed to the Internet by default.

 If you frequently communicate with Internet users, you can add these people to your Personal Address Book in the same way you add Notes users, to make it easier for you to address mail messages.

Task 10.4: Forwarding a Mail Message

You might often receive mail messages you want to send to other users who were not included in the original distribution list. To do so, select any mail message and choose Actions, Forward, or click the Forward button on the Action bar, or click the Forward SmartIcon. You see a new Memo form that looks much like a regular memo, except that the body of the memo contains the whole mail message you were reading or had selected (see Figure 10.2).

Figure 10.2.

A message forwarded to Ron Reeves.

10

You address a forwarded message using the steps you learned earlier in this chapter for addressing any message. You can edit the body of the memo if you need to add to or change the original message or include additional information with the old message. When you finish, send the message as you would any other. You are not restricted to forwarding only mail messages. You can forward any document that you can access simply by selecting it in a view or opening it on-screen, and then choosing Actions, Forward or clicking the Forward SmartIcon.

You can see from the figure that the original mail has been copied into the body of the new mail message and that other text has been added. Forwarding mail messages makes it easy to distribute information to other users.

Remember that unless you enable Prevent Copying in the Delivery Options for your mail messages, any recipient can easily forward your mail messages to any number of other users without your knowledge. This includes Internet users if the appropriate Message Transfer Agents (MTAs) are in place. A major security breach could result, so keep this in mind when mailing confidential information.

Workshop

Having completed this hour, you should be able to ensure security with return receipts, encryption, and delivery reports.

Here are some of the words you should be familiar with and some common questions you might have.

Key Terms

Review the following term:

☐ *Domain* Normally, everyone who is listed in the same Public Address Book is in the same domain. The Public Address Book is like the company phone book, giving you details on how to contact anyone in your company. Sending email to people in your own domain is easy because these people are "known" to Notes. Sending email outside of your domain, such as to the Internet or to a supplier, is more difficult because your administrator has set up some routing information so that Notes knows how to deliver the email. Whenever you use an @ sign in a mail address, you are sending email outside of your domain.

Common Questions

Q Can I send email with figures, file attachments, and formatting such as bold and italics to other email users?

A If you are sending email to another user in your own domain or another Notes domain that's directly connected to your own, yes. However, if you are sending mail to another domain, such as to the Internet or a cc:Mail user, you cannot be sure. Many email systems do not support text formatting or inline graphics. Your graphics and file attachments may be lost, or they may be listed as separate files at the bottom of the recipient's email message.

Q How long does it take for a message I send to get to an Internet recipient?

A This can vary greatly. Your administrator may queue Internet mail until, say, 50 messages are received, and then send the batch out to the Internet. It will also depend on how many other computers there are between your Notes server and the recipient's mail server and whether you have sent a large file attachment. Although it can be as quick as a few minutes, don't be surprised if it takes 2 hours or, in rare cases, up to 24 hours. After a day, if the recipient has not received the email and you have had no delivery failure report, you should probably re-send it or have your administrator troubleshoot the problem.

Preview of the Next Hour

This hour completes a three-hour run of learning about using email with Lotus Notes. The next hour focuses on file attachments.

10

Hour 11

Working with File Attachments

Goals for This Hour

"Once upon a time" when two people in a company wanted to share an electronic file, one of them had to copy the file to a floppy disk and send the disk via the mail or take it to the other person's office. Some of the more fortunate could copy the file to a public directory on a network instead so that another person could access it. Now, most email packages provide the capability of attaching files to the email messages. This process of attaching files to an email and sending it is exactly the same as copying the files to a disk and sending them via housemail—only much faster and more efficient. While this hour's lesson focuses on using file attachments in your mail database, it is important to note that file attachments can be created in any database document that has a rich text field (see Hour 6, "Understanding Documents," for more information on rich text fields). This hour's lesson teaches you everything you need to know about working proficiently with attachments. You will learn how to do the following:

- ☐ Attach a file(s)
- ☐ Detach file attachment(s)
- ☐ View a file attachment
- ☐ Launch a file attachment
- ☐ Delete file attachment(s)

Task 11.1: Attaching Files

You can attach a file (or files) to any mail document—or any document that has a rich text field in it. The first step is to create a new message. When the new mail message is on the screen, work with it as you would any mail message until you are ready to attach the file.

You can attach any file, regardless of its format, to a Notes mail message (or any other document containing a rich text field). For instance, if you have an office in Germany to which you must send the latest sales figures, you can attach the 1-2-3 spreadsheet to a mail message and send it. Likewise, you can attach the Access database with the latest inventory data and mail it to a colleague in a different office.

> Although you can attach files at any time while composing the message, it might help to attach the file first. By attaching the files first, you eliminate the possibility of accidentally forgetting to attach the files when you send the mail.

To attach one or more files, follow these steps:

1. Place the cursor in the body portion of the memo and then choose File, Attach or click the File Attach SmartIcon. The Create Attachment(s) dialog box appears (see Figure 11.1).

   You must be in the Body field to attach a file. File attachments can be attached only in rich text fields, and Body is the only rich text field in the mail message.

2. You can use the "look in" drop-down box to select the folder where the file(s) you want to attach resides. The list box below will display all the files in the selected folder. By default, the Create Attachment(s) dialog box points to the last folder you accessed with this dialog box. If this is the first time you're using it, it should point at the Notes directory C:\NOTES.

Figure 11.1.

The Create Attachment(s) dialog box is simple to use; just select the file(s) to attach.

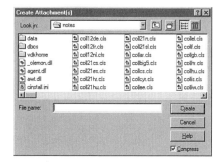

3. Select all the files you want to attach by clicking the files in the list box. If you want to select multiple consecutively-listed files, hold down the Shift key while clicking on the first and then the last file you want to select. If you want to select multiple files that are not consecutively listed, hold down the Ctrl key while clicking each file you want to select. Selected files are highlighted with a blue bar and will be displayed in the filename text box.

4. Click Create. Notes inserts an icon in your document that represents each of the attached files. Notes uses the file extension of each file you attach to scan the Windows registry to try to identify the source application (the application that created the file) so that an icon representing the application that created the file can be displayed.

For example, if you insert an MS Word document, the MS Word icon is displayed in the mail message to represent the file attachment. If Notes cannot identify the file attachment (its capability to identify file attachments is based on your operating system), an icon that looks like a blank, gray piece of paper with the right edge folded over is inserted. Figure 11.2 shows a sample memo with several different file attachments.

When you have attached the files, address the mail as you normally would, enter the subject, and add any text to the message body that might help the recipient understand the attachment. After the file is attached, you still have complete editing capability in the Body field.

You can insert text above, below, beside, or between the attachments and move the attachments as if they were text. After you finish the message and attach the files, send the message as you would any other.

11

Figure 11.2.

A mail message displays the icons of known file types when they are attached.

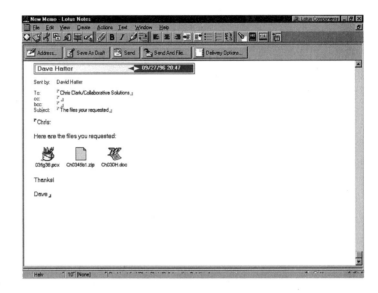

Task 11.2: Detaching Attachments

When you open your mailbox, you should be able to immediately identify mail messages that have attached files. This is because all the standard views and folders display a paper clip somewhere in the View pane to indicate that a file has been attached, as Figure 11.3 shows.

Figure 11.3.

The All Documents view displays messages with attachments with a paper-clip icon.

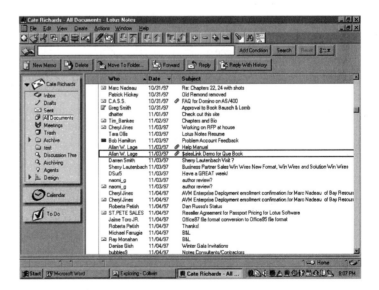

The position of the paper clip might vary from view to view and folder to folder, but it is displayed in all the standard views and folders that ship with Notes 4.6. Be aware that if custom views and folders have been specified for the database, the paper-clip icon might not be displayed. This is at the discretion of the designer.

To detach one or more of the attached files (extract the file from the mail message and store it in a file on your disk), follow these steps:

1. Open the mail message that has attachments. You see the corresponding icons in the body.

2. When you select any or all of the attachments, a new menu option, Attachment, appears between the Actions and Window options (see Figure 11.4).

   From this menu, choose Detach (a bit of a misnomer because it does not detach the attachment from the message but saves the file separately). Notes displays the standard file dialog box asking where you want to copy the file and what the filename should be.

   The original filename of the attachment is the default value for the new filename, but you can give the file a new name. Pick any directory you want. Notes detaches the file from the message onto your hard disk.

Figure 11.4.

The Attachment menu on the main menu bar mimics the features that are available when you double-click the attachment.

Or, you can double-click any of the attachments to display the Attachment properties box and view, launch, or detach the attachment (see Figure 11.5).

Figure 11.5.

The Attachment properties box enables you to use a number of options for an attachment.

Attached files stay in a mail message even after you detach, launch, or view them (*launching* and *viewing* are described shortly). You can extract the attachment as many times as you want.

You can detach the file to your hard disk, for example, and then detach it again to a disk (specify A: or B: as the directory). If you forward the message to someone else, the attached file goes with it.

> File attachments are often quite large and can quickly consume precious disk space. If you find yourself running low on space, you can open mail messages and delete their attachments while retaining the mail message itself. See "Deleting Attachments" later in this hour for details.

Task 11.3: Viewing Attachments

Sometimes you get file attachments that you want to look at before you detach them onto your workstation's disk. To view only the contents of an attachment, you can select the attachment and open the Attachment property sheet by double-clicking the icon.

Click View to open the Universal Viewer and examine the file contents. Or, you can select an attachment and choose Attachments, View.

The Universal Viewer enables you to examine the most popular file formats, such as Microsoft Word, Microsoft Excel, Microsoft Access, Lotus 1-2-3, Lotus Word Pro, and many others. However, you might receive files that the Universal Viewer cannot understand. If this occurs, an error message appears when you try to open the attachment. If you get an error message, you will need to find the application that originally created the file to view it.

Task 11.4: Launching Attachments

Not only can you extract the files to disk or view and print the contents with the Universal Viewer, you also can launch (start) the application that created the file and begin editing the file immediately. For the Launch function to work correctly, however, the following must be true:

☐ Unless the attached file is an executable file, such as a Lotus ScreenCam movie, you must have access to a copy of the application that created the file attachment, either from the hard disk on your workstation or from a drive on a network server. In other words, you can launch 1-2-3 by double-clicking a file with a WK4 extension only if you have 1-2-3 available from your computer.

☐ The application that originally created the file must have been successfully installed and configured in the Windows Registry for your system.

Launching a file is not foolproof because end users can name a file anything they want. For example, even though a file might look like a 1-2-3 spreadsheet (has the extension WK4), it might actually be an ASCII text file, which means that the file will not launch correctly in Lotus 1-2-3. If you cannot launch a file, consult your operating system manuals and your Notes administrator for more information.

> A malicious user might send you a virus or other harmful program as a file attachment that infects your computer when launched. If you receive mail that has an executable file from a suspicious source or you are suspicious of an attached file, do not launch it! Scan the file with an antivirus program or consult your administrator to learn about the Execution Control List feature of Notes. See Hour 3, "Specifying Your Notes Preferences," for more information about Execution Control Lists (ECLs).

To launch an attachment in its associated program, select the file and open the property box by double-clicking the attachment's icon. You can then click the Launch button to open the file with the application that originally created it.

When you elect to launch, Notes starts the application that created the file and opens the file in that application. For example, if the file was created in 1-2-3, Notes starts 1-2-3 and loads the attachment into 1-2-3 for editing. If the file is an executable program, Notes executes the program.

> Notes does not automatically update the file that is attached in Notes when you edit it in the application in which it was created. If you modify a file that has been launched, you need to save it to your hard disk and then reattach it in Notes, following the instructions to attach a file given earlier in this hour.

Task 11.5: Deleting Attachments

Normally, attached files remain in a message until the message is deleted. This can quickly consume an inordinate amount of disk space. You can, however, keep the mail message but delete the attachments to save disk space.

Some reasons for deleting attachments include the following:

☐ The mail message has important information, but you don't need the file attachments.

☐ You detached the files or launched the files with the host application and saved the file to disk. Either of these choices creates a copy of the attached files on disk, meaning that you now have redundant copies of the files on your workstation that consume disk space. By deleting the attachment from the mail, you free up this space.

☐ Files were erroneously attached to the mail message. You don't want to send the files, but you do want to send the mail message. If you delete the message, it deletes the attachments, but you must retype the mail message.

To delete an attached file or files, execute the following steps:

1. Open the document in edit mode. If you are viewing the document or have the document open in read mode, press Ctrl+E to switch to edit mode.

2. With the document open in edit mode, select the files you want to delete.

3. Press the Delete key or choose Edit, Clear. You also can click the Edit Clear SmartIcon.

4. Notes prompts you with a dialog box indicating that the delete operation cannot be undone. If you are sure you want to delete the attachment, choose Yes; otherwise, choose No to cancel the delete operation.

Workshop

Working with attachments can save you a lot of time when you need to send or receive files from other users. This workshop will highlight some of the key terms highlighted in this chapter. It will also provide answers to some of the more common questions users ask when working with attachments.

Key Terms

☐ *Attach a file*   Create an electronic file attachment to a Notes document for storage or mail routing.

☐ *Launch a file*   Automatically opens a file attachment's associated application, and then opens the attached file for you to work with. You will need to save and reattach a file if you want to share your edits with other users.

☐ *View a file*   Automatically launch the Universal Viewer in Notes to read the contents of an attached file. You will be able to read, copy, and print a file in the viewer, but you will not be able to edit it.

☐ *Detach a file*   Copy a file attachment from a Notes document to your local drive.

☐ *Delete a file*   Physically remove a file from the Notes document.

Common Questions

Q I launched a file to edit it, but none of my coworkers can see the changes I made in the file. What's wrong?

A Chances are, you made changes in the file but did not save the file and then reattach it to your document in Notes. If you saved the file you were editing in the application you edited it in, locate the file and follow the directions for attaching files in this hour's lesson. If you did not save the file in the application in which you launched it, you must edit again and then save and attach the file as instructed in this hour's lesson.

Q Why do I get the message `Cannot execute the specified command` when I select the File Attach SmartIcon to attach something?

A You do not have your cursor in a rich text field. Select OK to clear the error message and then locate a rich text field (like the body of your memo) in which to place the cursor. Now you should be able to attach your file.

Q I detached a file but did not pay attention to which directory (folder) I detached it into. How can I find it?

A If you have not changed the directory to which you saved other files that you have detached, open a memo with an attachment in it and double-click the attachment icon to view the Attachment Properties box. Select Detach. Your file should be located in the directory that opens when you select Detach. If you have already performed an operation that changed the directory in which you detached the file, open the memo containing the file attachment and note its filename below its file attachment icon. Use your operating systems file search (Start, Find, Files or Folders in Windows 95) capability to locate the filename you noted.

Preview of the Next Hour

Now that you know how to work with file attachments, it's time to work with some of the more advanced mail features such as automatically updating your Address Book with sender's names, creating letterhead and stationery, and working with the Out of Office Profile and Delegation Profile documents. The next hour's lesson teaches you to become a more advanced NotesMail user.

11

Hour **12**

Working with Advanced Mail Features

Goals for This Hour

Now that you have learned the basics of working with NotesMail, it is time to learn a few of the more advanced mail features that can make working with Notes much more efficient. In this hour, you will learn to:

- ☐ Add a sender's name to your address book
- ☐ Use the Out of Office Profile form
- ☐ Create letterhead
- ☐ Create stationery
- ☐ Use the Delegation Profile
- ☐ Work with Mail-In databases

Task 12.1: Adding a Sender to Your Address Book

You can add a sender to your Personal Address Book while you are reading mail from the sender. For example, if you received mail from Samuel Hatter, you could add Samuel's email address to your address book. Simply choose Actions, Mail Tools, Add Sender to Address Book while you have the mail message open.

You can also add a sender to your address book when you are in a folder or view by highlighting the document in which the sender's name is associated and then selecting Actions, Mail Tools, Add Sender to Address Book.

If you want to add multiple senders' names to your Address Book at the same time, click next to their respective documents (a check mark appears next to each document you have selected), and then select Actions, Mail Tools, Add Sender to Address Book.

Task 12.2: Using the Out of Office Profile

If you have used email before—particularly if you work for a large organization—you probably are aware of what happens when you go on vacation or must be out of the office for an extended period: Your email piles up because people send you email not knowing that you are gone. When you return, your mailbox is full, and your messages have not been responded to.

If you are going to be out of the office for an extended period, you can create an Out of Office Profile as shown in Figure 12.1. That way, others are notified of your absence.

You enter a Leaving Date and a Returning Date in the Out of Office Profile, and Notes fills in a default subject and message that you can edit. Within the time frame defined in this document, Notes will generate a response to all email messages you receive. The response informs others that you are out for the specified time period and gives them any other information that you define in the section entitled My Out of the Office Message for Most People. In addition, in the field People/Groups, you can define a special message for certain people who should receive a special message; you also can define a list of people and groups who should receive no message at all.

After you enter the appropriate information, click the Enable Out of Office Profile button. When you are asked which server is to run this agent, be sure to select your home/mail server.

On your scheduled return date, you will receive a Welcome Back message, and the Out of Office Profile will automatically be disabled.

Figure 12.1.

An Out of Office Profile gives Notes instructions on how to handle your mail while you are out of the office for an extended period of time.

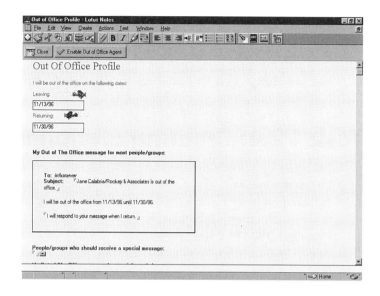

Task 12.3: Creating Letterhead

You can select predesigned letterhead, which adds a personal flair to your mail memo form. To change your letterhead, open your mailbox and choose Actions, Mail Tools, Select Letterhead. Notes displays the Choose Letterhead dialog box shown in Figure 12.2.

Figure 12.2.

The Choose Letterhead dialog box enables you to select a design for your Mail memo. Once you select a letterhead, you can change it by returning to this dialog box and choosing another letterhead or by selecting None to return to the standard Notes Mail Memo form.

12

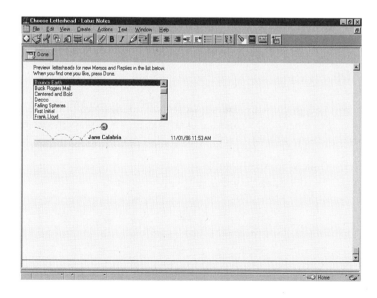

The Choose Letterhead dialog box displays a list of all of the available letterheads in your mailbox. Simply select one, and this new letterhead is applied to all your email messages. The From the Desk Of letterhead is the default letterhead used in all Mail forms.

You can change your letterhead at any time by choosing Actions, Mail Tools, Select Letterhead and selecting a new letterhead.

Task 12.4: Creating Stationery

Notes also lets you create stationery, which is an email message whose format and recipients list you will use again. This is particularly useful if you frequently send an email message to the same people or if you repeatedly send the same message out to many users—like a training class attendance confirmation letter. For example, if you send a weekly sales report to your sales team, you can create stationery that is well suited for this purpose and defines the recipients list. Use this stationery to send the weekly mail.

To create stationery, open your mailbox and choose Actions, Mail Tools, Create Stationery. This launches the Create Stationery dialog box, shown in Figure 12.3.

Figure 12.3.

The Create Stationery dialog box enables you to pick from two different templates for your stationery. You can create stationery for various events, such as a weekly report.

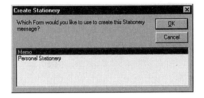

This dialog box contains a list of the currently defined stationery: Memo or Personal Stationery. Select one and click OK. Notes displays the selected stationery, and you can edit it appropriately.

You can base your stationery on one of two default templates: the Memo template, which is the Mail Message form, and Personal Stationery, which contains two more rich text fields than the Memo form. This second template enables you to add logos, graphics, and so on to your form in the fields provided for you at the top and bottom of the stationery form. Figure 12.4 shows a stationery form built from the Personal Stationery template in Edit mode.

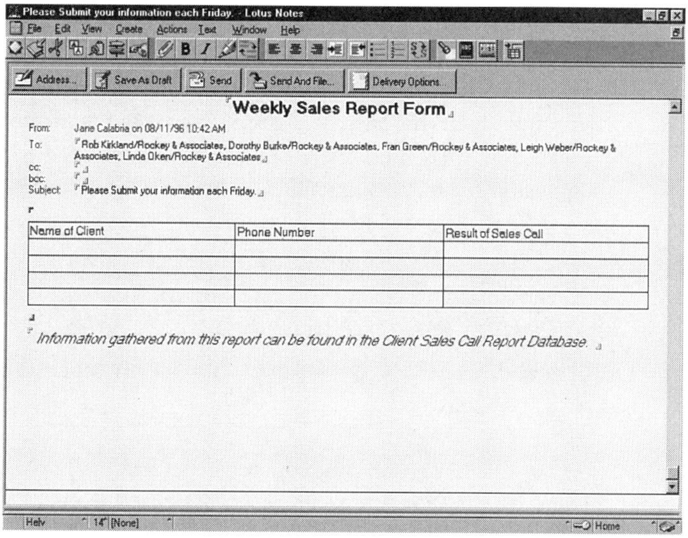

Figure 12.4.

This personal stationery has a table that's ready to be completed, so that the sales staff can fill in the sales call information.

When you finish editing the stationery's appearance, complete the recipient list, add any necessary text to the stationery, and then send the message. You are then asked if you want to save the message as stationery. If you choose Yes, you are prompted for a name for the new stationery. Enter a name and click OK. The Save As Stationery dialog box appears, as shown in Figure 12.5. Enter a name for the new stationery and click OK.

Figure 12.5.

Type the name for your stationery in the Save As Stationery dialog box. You can create many versions of stationery, reusing them time and time again.

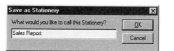

12

Notes tells you that the new stationery has been saved in the Drafts folder. To compose a new email message using the stationery you just created, open the Drafts view, highlight the name of the stationery you want to use, and then select the Use Stationery Action bar button. Notes opens up a new memo form based on the design of the stationery you selected. If you originally addressed the message to certain users, included company logos, or perhaps even placed a graphic with your signature into the design of the stationery, you will see those features again when you select the stationery for another message.

Task 12.4: Using the Delegation Profile

Though you typically want to protect your Mail database from "prying" eyes, you can let other people open your mail database and read your mail, send messages for you, edit existing messages, and delete messages. Typically, this feature is used by an executive whose secretary is responsible for managing email communication. However, you might take advantage of this feature if you want someone to manage your email database for you while you on are vacation or are otherwise unable to get to your mail.

If you add someone to your Delegation Profile, that person can send mail directly from your mail database as if he were you by selecting Create, Memo. If he wants to create a message from himself while he's in your mail database, he must select Create, Mail, Memo.

> Giving another user access to your mail database also gives him or her access to your Notes calendar and to public documents in other databases, if you have any. Keep in mind that whomever you delegate access to can see everything but encrypted documents in these databases.

To delegate the responsibility of your mail database to others:

1. Choose Actions, Mail Tools, Delegation Profile. The Delegation Profile opens (see Figure 12.6).

Figure 12.6.

You can use the Delegation Profile to give others access to your mail database.

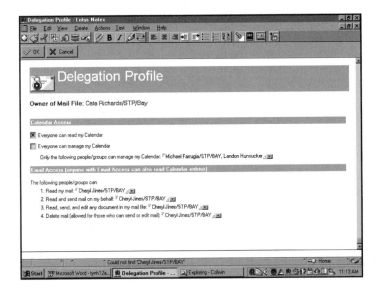

2. If the document is not in Edit mode, (the brackets are not open for you to type in), double-click anywhere in the document to place it in Edit mode.

3. In the E-Mail Access section of the profile, do any of the following:

   ☐ To let other users read your mail, enter their names in the Read My Mail field.

   ☐ To let other users read your mail and send mail on your behalf, enter their names in the Read and Send Mail on My Behalf field.

   ☐ To let other users read your mail, send new messages, and edit existing messages, enter their names in the Read, Send, and Edit Any Document in My Mail File field.

   ☐ To let other users delete messages, enter their names in the Delete Mail field. Notes will ask if you want to let them delete your messages or only the messages they create themselves. Indicate your preference.

4. Select OK to exit and save your entries.

> Only users who can send or edit your mail can delete your messages.

If you later decide that you want to modify your Delegation Profile, simply select Actions, Mail Tools, Delegation Profile again to access and edit your Delegation Profile.

> You will notice that there are entries available in the Delegation Profile for granting access to your calendar. You will learn about granting access to your calendar in Hour 18, "Working with Advanced Document Features."

12

Task 12.5: Working with Mail-In Databases

One of the advantages that Notes offers over other email packages is that the entire application is based on databases—including your mail database. Because of this, you can send mail to any database that is so enabled. This feature is helpful when sharing information between databases that do not replicate. For example, a suggestion box database could receive email messages, or a workflow application might route documents to people in an approval process.

If a database is designed to receive messages, it is listed in the Public Address Book under Mail-In Databases and Resources (see Figure 12.7). To send mail to the database, address your mail message to the database entry found in the Public Address Book. For example, suppose your Notes administrator has placed an entry in the Public Address Book titled Company Suggestions to define the database. If you wanted to send a suggestion to the Company Suggestions database, you would simply type Company Suggestions in the To: field of your memo. When you send the memo, Notes delivers it to the Mail-In database called Company Suggestions.

Adding entries to the Public Address Book is often a task that is restricted to certain users in a company. If you need to add or modify an entry in the Public Address Book, you will most likely have to contact your Notes administrator and ask her to do so.

Using Mail-In databases is a great way to take advantage of the mail-enable features of Lotus Notes and enables you to do more than just send memos from your email database to a Mail-In database. Database designers can build custom mail forms that you can access by selecting Create, Mail, Other. These forms are often used when the person who's going to use the information needs the data in a particular format—like Human Resources Benefit Enrollment forms.

Database designers can also build databases in which you create documents directly in the database, but when you exit to save, Notes automatically sends email a message out to one or more users or databases. An example of this would be a Sales Force Automation application in which you create a Trouble Report that needs to automatically let the Sales Executive know when there is a problem or concern with the account. When you save the form, Notes saves a copy of the Trouble Report directly in the database for history tracking, but it also sends a copy directly to the Sales Executive's mail database for quick notification. In these types of form designs, the developer generally creates the form to automatically address the document to whomever is listed as the Sales Executive of the particular account in which you are working.

Regardless of the method in which an email message is sent, Notes makes sure the document(s) are delivered to whatever user or database is defined as the recipient of the message—whether you can see the recipient's name or it is only defined by Notes. Because Notes can mail-enable every database, you can potentially create some very interesting and helpful database designs! If you are unsure whether a form is email-enabled, you can watch the status bar at the bottom of your Notes window. If you save a mail-enabled form, Notes indicates how many users it sent the form to. If you are still in question as to where messages are going, contact the database designer for additional information.

Figure 12.7.

The Public Address Book lists Mail-In databases under the category Databases. If your company has rooms and resources available for calendar and scheduling functions (see Hour 10), you will also see those listed under Mail-In Databases.

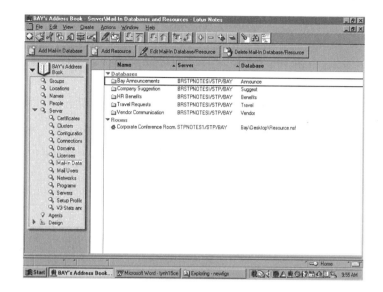

Workshop

In this hour's lesson, you learned how to take advantage of Notes' more advanced email features. Let's review some of the key terms you have learned. This workshop also reviews some of the common questions users have when working with the advanced email features.

Key Terms

Review the following list of terms:

☐ *Out of Office Profile*   A profile document provided by Notes in which you can create a message that will be sent automatically to anyone who sends you mail while you are away. Those who send you email will receive a message from you indicating the dates in which you will be out of the office and the date you expect to return.

☐ *Delegation Profile*   This lets you grant other Notes users access to your email database. This profile provides multiple levels of access to help refine the access you grant to other users.

☐ *Mail-In database*   Any database that the database designer created to be email-enabled and for which there is a corresponding Mail-In database document located in the Public Address Book.

12

Common Questions

Q **I am trying to send a memo to the Company Suggestion database, but I keep getting a delivery failure. Why?**

A Check to make sure you have spelled the name of the Mail-In database correctly and that the database is defined in the Public Address Book. If you continue to have difficulty, contact the database manager or the Notes administrator for assistance; access to the database may have been disabled.

Q **I just found out that several people have access to read and send mail from my database. How can I change that?**

A Open your Delegation Profile by selecting Actions, Mail Tools, Delegation Profile. Check to make sure the entries in the E-Mail Access section are correct for those individuals that you want to have access to your mail database. If they are correct, exit the Delegation Profile and select File, Database, Access Control. Check the list of users in the Access Control List to make sure users were not added via this method. If you have any questions regarding who is listed in these entries and who has access to your database, or if you cannot determine how someone gained access to your mail database, contact your Notes administrator for assistance.

Q **I'm going to create a memo that I will send out each month to the same recipients, and only some sales figures within the body of the memo will change. What is the easiest way to do this?**

A Create a Personal Stationery document by selecting Actions, Mail Tools, Create Stationery, Personal Stationery. Add the information you want in the message, and then save the document. When you want to use that message, open your Drafts view in your email database, highlight the name of the Personal Stationery document you created, and then select Use Stationery. Notes will open up a new message with the information you created already present. Edit the information as needed, and then send the message as you would any other memo.

Preview of the Next Hour

Now that you have learned how to use the Advanced Mail features, it is time to turn your attention to some special features of the Address Book that may help you work faster in Notes. The next hour introduces you to the Notes Address Book.

Hour 13

Using the Personal Address Book

Goals for This Hour

As a Notes user, you will get used to using two address books: the Public Address Book and the Personal Address Book.

The Public Address Book is stored on all the Notes servers in your domain and is administered by your Notes administrator. It actually defines your Notes domain, containing information on all users and servers and how the servers communicate with one another and with other organizations outside of your domain. As a user, you will primarily use the Public Address Book to address email messages by looking up individual names and resolving groups.

The Personal Address Book resides in your own Notes data directory. Its default title is *UserLastName's* Address Book, and its file name is NAMES.NSF. The address book can include five kinds of documents, each of which has a corresponding view:

- ☐ Business Card documents (the equivalent of Person documents in the Public Address Book) appear in the Business Card view.
- ☐ Group documents appear in the Groups view.
- ☐ Location documents appear in the Advanced/Locations view.
- ☐ Cross-Certificate documents appear in the Advanced/Certificates view.
- ☐ Connection documents appear in the Advanced/Connections view.

Of the listed documents, Location and Connection documents are the most important because they define how your copy of Notes functions. Cross-certificates enable you to communicate with servers in other Notes domains. Business Card and Group documents are useful for streamlining the addressing of mail. Business Card documents are useful if you use the Personal Address Book as your actual personal address book.

This chapter explains how to use the Personal Address Book by teaching you about the following:

- ☐ *Location documents*   Location documents define the values of many variables that might change as you and your computer move to another location.
- ☐ *Connection documents*   Connection documents tell your copy of Notes how to connect to Notes servers.
- ☐ *Cross-Certificate documents*   Notes uses Cross-Certificate documents to verify that you are accessing other organizations' databases under your identity.
- ☐ *Business Card documents*   Business Card documents make it easy to access people with whom you frequently communicate.
- ☐ *Group documents*   You can group several Notes users or other groups to perform actions that affect each member of the group.

Task 13.1: Understanding Location Documents

Location documents are important if you are constantly on the move, carrying Notes around with you on a laptop computer. Location documents define the values of a host of variables that can change as you and your computer move from one location to another, including the following:

- ☐ Which ports are available for connecting to other computers
- ☐ The identities of your home/mail server, passthru server, and InterNotes server
- ☐ Whether and how you can browse the World Wide Web within Notes
- ☐ Dialing rules (applicable if you are using a modem)

☐ Your current mail file's name and location

☐ Address book lookup characteristics

☐ Mail delivery settings

☐ Database replication scheduling

☐ Time zone information

☐ Java applet security information

The information on configuring the web retriever is covered in Hour 22, "Understanding the Web Navigators."

Task 13.2: Understanding Connection Documents

Connection documents (also known as Server Connection documents) tell your copy of Notes how to connect to Notes servers. If you work solely on your office LAN, you probably won't ever need to create a Connection document. Notes can usually locate LAN-connected servers without the benefit of a Connection document. However if you have to connect to a Notes server via a modem or by some other remote connection, you will need a Connection document. Creating Connection documents is covered in Hour 22.

Task 13.3: Understanding Cross-Certificates

If your company as a whole wants to be able to communicate with other Notes organizations, you will need Cross-Certificate documents. A process called cross-certification allows users and servers in one organization to be granted access to another organization's Notes servers. However, if you are the only one who needs access to the organization, your Notes administrator may decide to cross-certify only you. In that case, your administrator would add a cross-certificate to your Personal Address Book, and it would appear in the Advanced/ Certificates view. This would function as a key, allowing you to access another company's Notes servers.

13

Task 13.4: Working with Business Cards

Although it has a different name, the Business Card document in the Personal Address Book essentially fulfills the same task as the Person document in the Public Address Book. First, when you are addressing email, Notes looks up addressee names in your Personal Address Book and the Public Address Book as you type them. Notes looks up the names in the

Business Card, Person, Group, and Mail-In Database documents that it finds. It verifies that you have entered the names correctly, and if you have not disabled the Type-Ahead feature, it conveniently finishes entering the names for you as you type. Second, you can use your Personal Address Book as a more general address book. In addition to the email information fields, which are directly useful to Notes, the Business Card form has mailing address, phone, and other personal information fields that are of use only to you—not Notes.

Initially, the Public Address Book includes a Person document for every person registered in your Notes domain, and your Personal Address Book has no Business Card documents in it. As long as you work at a computer that is connected to the office LAN and has constant quick access to a Notes server, this state of affairs is acceptable. However, if you are a mobile user, disconnected from the LAN, and it is not feasible for your system to hold a replica of the Public Address Book locally (because of size), you will want to set up Business Card documents in your Personal Address Book so that you can use the Type-Ahead feature to help resolve email addresses.

You can add addresses and information to your address book in several ways. First, you can copy Person documents from the Public Address Book to your Personal Address Book. To do so, follow these steps:

1. Open the Public Address Book to the People view.

2. Scroll down through the view and select the people that you want to copy to your Personal Address Book. You select a person by clicking in the leftmost column of the People view. A check mark then appears in that column. You can select several contiguous names by dragging down through the leftmost column while pressing the left mouse button. To select several noncontiguous names, press and hold the Shift key and click in the leftmost column beside each individual name.

3. When you have selected everyone you want, choose Edit, Copy. Notes copies the selected documents to the Clipboard.

4. Close the Public Address Book and open your Personal Address Book. It doesn't matter which view opens.

5. With your Personal Address Book open to any view, choose Edit, Paste. Copies of the Person documents that you selected in the Public Address Book appear in your Personal Address Book's Business Card view. When you open them, you will see them through the Business Card form.

You can also add one Business Card document at a time in two different ways. First, whenever you receive email from someone who's not in your Personal Address Book, you can choose to have Notes create a Business Card document for that person. While the email is open on your screen, choose Actions, Mail Tools, Add Sender to Address Book.

Second, you can add Business Card documents manually. In general, you will add a Business Card document manually only if you are adding a non-Notes user to your address book. (For Notes users, you should paste in the Person documents from the Public Address Book or let Notes add the Business Card document for you.)

To add a Business Card document manually, from your Personal Address Book's Business Card view, click the action bar's Add Card button or choose Create, Business Card. A blank Business Card form opens (see Figure 13.1).

Figure 13.1.

A blank Business Card document opens in the Personal Address Book when you click the action bar's Add Card button or choose Create, Business Card.

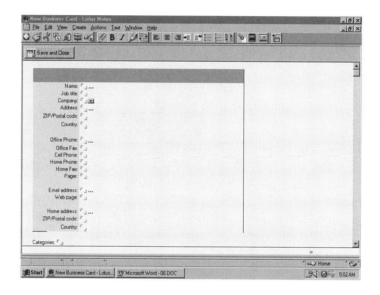

In certain fields, Notes will attempt to parse the information you type into appropriate fields. As you type in a name, Notes will attempt to split it up into the individual components of Title, First Name, Last Name, and Suffix. Click the entry helper (the small downward-pointing triangle) to the right of the Name field to see how Notes has assigned each component to the fields. You can then make any necessary corrections. Figure 13.2 shows an example of this.

If you start to fill in a Company Name, Notes will attempt to match what you are typing with the name of a company you have previously entered and will fill out the rest of the company name for you. Alternatively, you can click the arrow to the right of the field and choose from a list of previously entered company names. If you select a previously entered company, Notes will copy the address information from that entry to this new Business Card document.

13

Figure 13.2.

Notes parses the name you enter into its component parts.

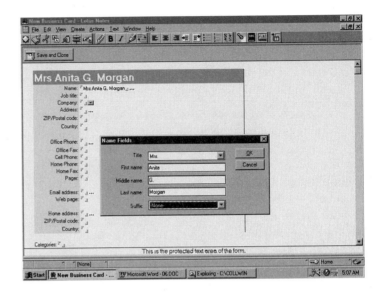

The section of the Business Card document that contains the telephone information is actually dynamic. You can change the field labels to reflect any information you want. Click the entry helper to the right of the Office Phone field to bring up the Phones dialog box. You may have no need, for example, to record this person's pager number, but instead maybe you would like to record his or her birthday. Simply edit the label, and then enter the birthday on the right (see Figure 13.3).

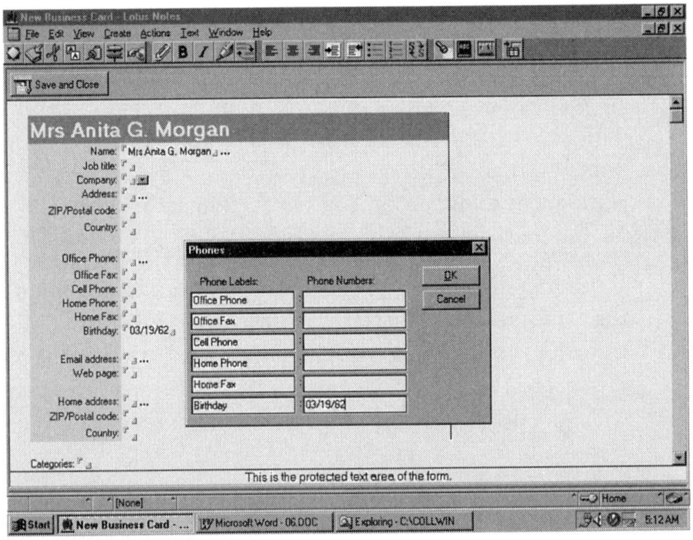

Figure 13.3.

You can change the field labels to show any information you choose.

If the user is someone with whom you will be corresponding by email, you can enter the person's email address in the Mail Address field. You can either enter the email address manually, or click the entry helper next to the field to invoke the aid of the Mail Address Assistant. The Mail Address Assistant displays a series of dialog boxes that prompt you for the information needed to form a correct email address for several mail systems. The first dialog box prompts you for the email system that your correspondent uses (see Figure 13.4).

Figure 13.4.

Select your correspondent's email system in the Mail Address Assistant dialog box.

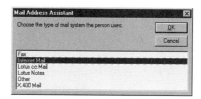

Select the correspondent's email system and choose OK. The second dialog box prompts you for the appropriate information to form a legal mailing address under the chosen mail system (see Figure 13.5).

Figure 13.5.

The Mail Address Assistant's second dialog box prompts for Internet mail information.

Enter the appropriate information in the fields, and then choose OK. The Mail Address Assistant then compiles the information that you entered and inserts it in the Mail Address field in the correct format (see Figure 13.6).

After you have completed the information in this part of the Business Card document, you may want to enter further information by expanding the More Info section that is collapsed at the bottom of the document.

After saving the new Business Card document, you can address mail to the person by entering whatever names you entered in the Business Card document's Name fields (or by using the nickname you entered in the More Info section).

You can send mail directly from the Business Card view by selecting the user or users you want to send to and clicking the Write Memo button. Notes creates a new memo and fills in the To field with the email addresses of those people you selected in the view. You can also schedule a meeting from your Business Card view by selecting the people you want to include and clicking the Schedule Meeting button. And if you have entered a web home page address

13

for a person or a company in the Business Card view, you can select the user and click the Visit Web Page button to open your chosen web browser in Notes and retrieve the page.

Figure 13.6.

The Mail Address Assistant formed the address in the Mail Address field by drawing from information you entered in the two Mail Address Assistant dialog boxes.

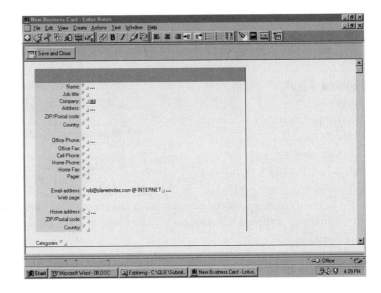

If you want to refer to someone by a nickname, you can enter the nickname, along with any other name, in the Full User Name field. To see this field, you have to expand the More Info section at the bottom of the Business Card document. For example, if you have a Business Card document for a colleague whose name is John Rumpelstiltskin but you call him "Pooky," you can add Pooky to the Full User Name field so that its contents appear as follows:

John Rumpelstiltskin; Pooky

You can then send email to "Pooky," and Notes will resolve it to John Rumpelstiltskin.

Task 13.5: Using and Creating Group Documents

A Group document collects a list of Notes servers, Notes users, and other Notes groups under a group name and functions similar to a mailing list. When you want to do something that affects every member of a group, you can assign the action to the group. For example, if you want to send a message to every member of the group, you can address the message to the group instead of to its individual members. Notes then automatically substitutes all of the member names for the group name.

When you create a Group document, you must give the group a name, which will be the name that you use when you refer to the group thereafter. The group will also appear under that name in the Groups view.

You can add members to the group by using the Members field. You can add the members' names manually or, if you click the button next to the Members field, you can select member names from the list in the Names dialog box.

You can also describe the group and define its purpose. Any group that a Notes user creates in his or her Personal Address Book almost certainly is a mailing list group. Therefore, you can either choose Mailing List in the Group Type field or just leave it as a multipurpose group.

Workshop

In this hour, you learned that the Personal Address Book is a very important tool in your interaction with Notes. You learned what Location, Connection, and Cross-Certificate documents are used for, and you set up Business Card and Group documents to help with sending email.

Here are some of the words you should be familiar with and some common questions you may have.

Key Terms

Review the following list of terms:

- [ ] *Type-Ahead* A feature to help address email. As you start to type an email address, Notes uses the Type-Ahead feature to look at the Private and Public Address Books for a match with the characters you have entered so far. If Notes finds a match, it fills in the found address in the addressing field. If the match is correct, simply stop typing; if not, just keep typing and Notes will try again.

- [ ] *Mailing List* A group set up to aid in email addressing. Instead of typing each name individually, you can enter the name of a group, such as Marketing. Notes ensures that the email is sent to all members of the group.

- [ ] *Nickname* If you call someone by a nickname or if a person has a name that's very difficult to spell correctly, you can enter his or her nickname in the mail addressing field. Notes will resolve the nickname to the actual address when you send the email.

13

Common Questions

Q   **Why would I want to copy Person documents from the Public Address Book into my Personal Address Book instead of just having a local replica of the Public Address Book on my computer?**

A   Having a local replica of the Public Address Book is the ideal method. But if your organization is very large, it might be impractical to carry around your large Public Address Book when you are mobile. If you only send mail to a few people regularly, you might find the space on your hard disk can be better utilized in some other way. Also, large Public Address Books tend to be modified frequently, so you might find replicating these changes via a modem connection to be a lengthy process.

Q   **Do I have to have either a replica of the Public Address Book or Business Card documents in my Private Address Book to be able to send mail?**

A   Absolutely not. If you can live without the Type-Ahead feature and are fairly sure you know the spelling of the names of the people to whom you are sending email, you can just type the names into the address field. When the mail is sent to the server, the server checks to see if the address is valid. If it can't deliver the mail, it will return the mail to you with an "Unknown Recipient" error. You can amend the address and resend the mail.

Preview of the Next Hour

A complete change now. In the next hour, you will look at working with text in your documents. You will learn to modify the appearance of text with font, size, and color changes and to manipulate the position of text on the page by changing alignment, tab, and margin settings.

Hour 14

Working with Text

Goals for This Hour

Though not as powerful as commercial word processors, the Notes editor enables you to control the appearance of your text in many ways. Here are some of the things you will learn in this hour:

- [ ] *Cut and paste text*   Notes enables you to perform various standard editing actions to move, copy, or remove selections of text.
- [ ] *Work with rich text fields*   In rich text fields, you can enter text, objects, and formatting information.
- [ ] *Use the Permanent Pen*   This feature of the Text menu enables you to mark revisions to a document.

If you have previously used a word processor—anything from Word Pro to WordPerfect—you're used to rearranging, highlighting, and manipulating text. Notes includes a sophisticated text processor that provides many of the same features that you have come to appreciate in word processors. If you're familiar with Windows-based word processors such as Microsoft Word, Word Pro, or WordPerfect, you will find that many of the Notes text processor's keystrokes are the same.

As you go through this hour, keep in mind that Notes provides you with a quick mouse trick to display a list of some of the most popular formatting selections, as well as the Text properties box. If you right-click once anywhere in the Notes document, Notes displays the context-sensitive menu shown in Figure 14.1. This shortcut gives you quick access to a wealth of text and paragraph settings to enhance your documents.

Figure 14.1.

You can quickly make formatting selections by right-clicking your mouse button anywhere in the document.

Task 14.1: Selecting Text for Editing

Some of the most powerful editing and formatting operations involve a two-step process. You first must identify the text that you want to affect and then tell Notes what to do with that text.

To select a section of text, place the pointer at the beginning of the text, hold down the left mouse button, move the mouse pointer to the end of the text, and release the mouse button. If you prefer to use the keyboard, position the insertion point at the beginning of the text that you want to select, hold down the Shift key, and move the insertion point to the end of the text using your keyboard's directional arrows. By using either method, you can select any amount of text.

After you select the text, it appears in reverse video—that is, the text appears in a lighter color with a dark box surrounding it.

You can select just one word quickly by double-clicking while the pointer is on the word. This is a great time-saver if you want to check the spelling or change the font attributes of just that one word.

After you select the text, you can tell Notes what you want to do to that text.

One of the simplest and most common operations is to delete the selected text, which you can do by pressing the Delete key. Other ways to delete selected text include selecting Edit, Clear, clicking the Edit Clear SmartIcon, pressing the Spacebar, or typing over a selected section of text with new text.

Be careful that you don't accidentally type text while you have text selected. If you type new text while old text is selected, Notes thinks that you want to replace the old text with the new text. Many users have experienced a momentary panic at seeing a large block of selected text disappear because their fingers accidentally brushed a letter or a digit. If you make such a mistake, choose Edit, Undo Typing before you type anything else or perform any other function.

Task 14.2: Using the Clipboard

The Clipboard is a storage area shared among Notes and other Windows, Macintosh, and OS/2 applications. It serves as a temporary holding location for data that you are moving or copying between Notes and word processors, spreadsheets, and many other programs. You can use the Clipboard to cut text, bitmaps, or other inserted objects (such as spreadsheets and other graphics files) from a Notes document and then paste the cut objects into a document of another application.

The Clipboard is a *temporary* storage location. You can store data there only during a single Windows or OS/2 session. If you turn off your PC or exit Windows or OS/2, you clear the Clipboard and lose the data permanently.

When you copy new data to the Clipboard, you erase whatever data the Clipboard was previously storing, unless you are appending text to the Clipboard.

14

Task 14.2.1: Moving Text

As you type your text, you might decide that your thoughts make better sense in a different order, and you might want to move text from one place to another. This process is called cutting and pasting. As the technique's name implies, cutting and pasting is really a two-step process: You remove the text from its old location (cut it) and insert it into its new location (paste it). You must be in edit mode to cut and paste data.

To cut and paste text, follow these steps:

1. Select the text that you want to move.
2. Press Ctrl+X; press Shift+Delete; choose Edit, Cut; or click the Edit Cut SmartIcon. Notes removes the text from your document.
3. Position the insertion point where you want to paste the text.
4. Press Ctrl+V; press Shift+Insert; choose Edit, Paste; or click the Edit Paste SmartIcon. Notes copies the text in the Clipboard into your document wherever you have placed the insertion point.

> The act of pasting copies text from the Clipboard into your document, but the text remains on the Clipboard, too. If you want to place another copy of the same text elsewhere, you need only move the insertion point to the new location and paste again. Thus, from a single cut or copy, you can perform as many paste operations as you want.

Task 14.2.2: Copying Text

Copying text is quite similar to moving text except that when copying text, you also want it to remain at its current location. You can be in read or edit mode to copy text, but you must be in edit mode to paste it.

1. Select the text that you want to copy.
2. Press Ctrl+C, press Ctrl+Insert; or choose Edit, Copy, or click the Edit Copy SmartIcon. The text remains in place.
3. Move the insertion point to a new position and paste as described in the preceding set of steps or by using any of the other methods described earlier. Notes copies the text from the Clipboard to the document in the new location.

Task 14.2.3: Appending Data to the Clipboard

Usually copying to the clipboard destroys any data that was already there. Notes gives you the opportunity to copy data from multiple locations and append them to the clipboard.

1. Use the usual key combination—Ctrl+C—to copy the first piece of text to the Clipboard.

2. For a subsequent piece of text, press Ctrl+Shift+Insert. Notes copies the selected text to the Clipboard; however, instead of replacing the Clipboard's existing contents, Notes appends the new text so that the Clipboard contains both pieces of text.

You can also hold down the Shift key and choose Edit, Copy or Edit, Cut for each piece of text that you want to add to the Clipboard.

> When you copy more than one noncontiguous section to the Clipboard, Notes does not insert a space between the last character of the first section copied and the first character of the next, unless you copy a space or blank line at the same time that you copy the text. Instead, Notes simply adds the text at the end of the section that you have previously copied.
>
> This appending might create a messy copy on the Clipboard, so you might have to spend time "cleaning up" when you paste the information into a new document. If keeping paragraphs, sentences, or words separate is important to you, make sure that you highlight the spaces you want to copy, as well as the text.

Place your cursor wherever you want to paste the copied text and then press Ctrl+V, Shift+Insert (or choose Edit, Paste). Notes pastes the entire contents of the Clipboard into the new location.

Task 14.2.4: Pasting Text into Dialog Boxes

Often, you might want to copy (or cut) and paste information into a dialog box, but the Cut, Copy, and Paste commands are not available to you because you cannot choose Edit. Don't worry; you can press Ctrl+C to copy (or Ctrl+X to cut) the information to the Clipboard, and then press Ctrl+V to paste the information. This alternative method is particularly helpful when you are trying to enter information into a dialog box—where the Edit command is not available from the menu bar.

Task 14.3: Undoing Changes

Whenever you perform an operation that modifies a section of text—delete, cut, copy, or paste—Notes offers you a chance to change your mind. You can reverse, or undo, the effects of the last operation by choosing Edit, Undo, pressing Ctrl+Z, or clicking the Edit Undo SmartIcon.

14

The exact wording of the first option on the Edit menu varies, depending on the last operation that you performed. If you last used a cut operation, the first item on the menu is Undo Cut; if you last did a paste, the command is Undo Paste. If you choose the command, Notes undoes the last operation by restoring the deleted text, removing the pasted text, or reversing whatever action you performed.

Notes also enables you to change your mind about Undo. If you undo an operation such as boldfacing text and then decide that you want to perform that function anyway, choose Edit, Redo. The bold text then reappears. As with the Undo menu command, the exact wording of the Redo menu command changes, depending on the action that you are performing.

Undo is useful only if you recognize your mistake immediately after making it, because you can undo only the most recent operation. Suppose that you delete a piece of text and then perform another operation (for example, typing another character, or copying another piece of text to the Clipboard). If you realize then that the deletion was a mistake, you're out of luck; your deleted text is gone for good.

You cannot use the Undo command to bring back entire documents that you have deleted from a database.

Task 14.4: Understanding Rich Text Fields

The most common type of field that you encounter in most Notes documents is a text field. You can enter any kind of text into such a field—words, sentences, names, and so on. In Notes, however, you encounter two types of text fields: plain text fields and rich text fields.

The body of your Notes email memo is an example of a rich text field, and the Subject field in the memo is a plain text field.

In a rich text field, you can enter text, objects, and formatting information. Associated with any portion of rich text is a particular color, type style, justification, and line spacing, as well as many other characteristics.

In the following sections, you learn how to make the most of text attributes. In Hours 16, "Working with Basic Document Features," and 18, "Working with Advanced Document Features," you learn how to insert objects like tables, document links, and buttons.

Rich text fields are the only fields in which you can change the font attributes, format paragraphs, and insert graphics, embedded objects, attachments, tables, document links, pop-up boxes, and other special objects. These fields are also the only ones in which you can import data from othe. applications. If you are trying to use one of these features but the menu command is not available to you, your cursor is not located in a rich text field.

Information entered in rich text fields, however, cannot display in views. Text and other field types are used when the information must display in a view or be used for calculations.

How can you tell whether a field is plain text or rich text? You cannot tell by looking at an empty field, but you can try to use some of the features described in this section. If Notes doesn't let you change the field's style—by adding color or changing the type style—the field is plain text. Also, with your cursor located in the field, you can look at the Text section of the status bar at the bottom of the Notes window. If the type and size of the font appear, you are in a rich text field; otherwise, you are not.

Finally, you can distinguish between the two types of text fields by placing the insertion point anywhere within the field and pulling down the Text menu. If the insertion point is on a plain text field, most of the menu choices, such as Bold, Italic, and Underline, are grayed out, which indicates that they are not available.

Task 14.5: Changing the Appearance of Rich Text with the Text Menu

The Notes Text menu gives you control over text characteristics, such as text attributes (boldface, italic, underline), fonts, justification, and spacing (see Figure 14.2).

You must be in edit mode to type text and change the font attributes.

Figure 14.2.

To change text attributes, use the Text menu to change one attribute at a time, or you can open the Text Properties info box to change them all at the same time.

14

Task 14.6: Selecting Text to Modify

To control the characteristics of *new* text that you are about to type, follow these steps:

1. Position the insertion point wherever you want to type the new text.
2. Choose Text, Text Properties, or press Ctrl+K.
3. Choose the characteristic that you want to change (such as font or size).

The new text that you type at that location takes on the characteristics that you selected.

You also can change characteristics for existing text. Suppose that you already have typed the sentence *This task is critical to our success* and then decide that you want critical in bold red. Follow these steps:

1. Select the text that you want to change—in this example, the word *critical.*
2. Choose Text, Text Properties. The Text properties box appears.
3. Choose Red in the Text Color drop-down list and select Bold from the Style list box.

The text that you highlight remains in reverse video when you choose OK to change the font attributes. Click the mouse button once anywhere in the document to view your font changes.

> If you like using the keyboard, another shortcut to opening the Text properties box is to press Alt+Enter. This will not only bring up the property box relevant to wherever your cursor is, but it also is a toggle. So, when you're done with the info box, press Alt+Enter to close it again.

Task 14.7: Setting Margins and Tabs with the Ruler

Notes provides two methods for indicating how you want to set the margins and tabs: You can access the Text properties box, as discussed in the next hour, or use the ruler. Whether you use the ruler method for setting margins and tabs or the Text properties box, you might want to display the ruler so that it can guide you in making your settings.

The Notes ruler is a bar near the top of the screen, marked off in inches like a ruler but with special marks indicating your margin and tab settings (see Figure 14.3). The ruler helps you visualize distances in your document and provides a simple means for setting margins and tabs.

To display the ruler, choose View, Ruler (or click the View Ruler SmartIcon if it is present in your current SmartIcon group). Along with measuring the document in inches, the ruler shows margins and tabs. Notes displays tabs as arrows pointing up and the left margin as a pentagon arrow. Choose View, Ruler again to hide the ruler.

Figure 14.3.

Use the ruler to help guide you in setting margins and tabs.

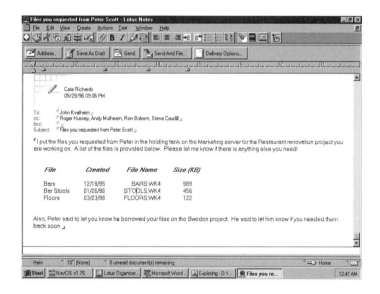

 The ruler indicates table column settings with a marker that looks like a T. You learn more about creating tables in Hour 16, "Working with Basic Document Features."

In addition to changing margins, you can use the ruler to set tabs, as the next section describes.

To use the ruler to change the first line's left margin, click the top pentagon arrow and drag it to its new location. If you want to adjust the paragraph's left margin to indicate a setting other than the one set for the first line, click the bottom pentagon arrow and drag the arrow's bottom portion to a new location.

By specifying a different left margin for the first line and all other lines, you can create the paragraph styles shown in Figure 14.4.

You also can use the ruler to set tabs. Display the ruler if it isn't already showing and then select the paragraphs that you want to change. You can then change a margin's position by dragging the corresponding triangle to a new position. Recall that the upward-pointing triangles are tabs. Figure 14.5 shows all four types of tabs that you can define.

14

Figure 14.4.

You can use the ruler to define margin settings in your documents.

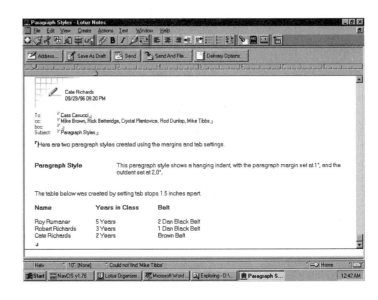

Figure 14.5.

You can define four types of tab stops by clicking within the ruler.

To set a new tab, place the mouse pointer on the ruler at an empty position and click. A tab arrow appears to mark the tab stop. To change the tab setting, click and drag the corresponding tab arrow to a new position and release the mouse button. To clear an existing tab, click the corresponding tab arrow.

As discussed earlier, you can place four types of tabs in your documents. To use the ruler to place these tabs, perform one of the following:

- ☐ Left tab—Left-click at the tab location.
- ☐ Right tab—Right-click at the tab location.
- ☐ Center tab—Press Shift+right-click at the tab location.
- ☐ Decimal tab—Press Shift+left-click at the tab location.

(Refer to Figure 14.5 for examples of each of these tab settings.)

Using the ruler to set margins and tabs is one of the few Notes operations that require a mouse; there are no corresponding hotkeys. If you don't have a mouse, you must choose Text, Properties and use the properties box's Pages/Tabs page to set margins and tabs.

Setting Margins Quickly with the Keyboard

Notes provides several keystrokes for changing margins quickly. After selecting the paragraphs that you want to affect, you can do the following:

- ☐ Press F7 to indent the first line by a quarter of an inch. By pressing this key several times, you can indent the first line by any multiple of a quarter of an inch. Press Shift+F7 to outdent the first line by a quarter of an inch.

- ☐ Press F8 to indent every line by a quarter of an inch. Pressing Shift+F8 outdents every line by a quarter of an inch.

You can create a *hanging indent* (that is, a paragraph in which the first line is farther to the left than the other lines) by pressing F8 to indent all lines one or more times and then pressing F7 to outdent the first line.

Task 14.8: Working with the Permanent Pen

The Permanent Pen option enables you to use revision marking to quickly add comments that stand out in a document. When you use the Permanent Pen, you don't have to reset the font every time that you move somewhere different in the document. For example, if you are answering questions in a document and want to write all your answers in a bold, red font, you can set up your Permanent Pen to use these font attributes.

Before you use your Permanent Pen, you might want to change the font attributes. To do so, choose Text, Properties and then, in the Text properties box, select the font, size, style, and color that you want to assign to the Permanent Pen. After selecting your settings, press the Set Permanent Pen Font button to save your selections.

To use the Permanent Pen, use the following steps:

1. Choose Text, Permanent Pen.
2. Click once at the beginning of the section in which you want to add a comment.
3. Type your text. The text that you type will be in the style, size, and color you specified for the Permanent Pen.
4. Move your cursor to the next position at which you want to use the Permanent Pen. Type your comments.
5. Continue using the Permanent Pen until you have entered all your comments.

14

6. Reselect the Permanent Pen by choosing Text, Permanent Pen to disable this option. The Permanent Pen will also be disabled when you exit the document.

If you want to change the font characteristics for the Permanent Pen, choose Text, Text Properties. In the Text properties box, make all the necessary font, size, style, and color selections that you want to use. Then select the Set Permanent Pen Font button. Notes redefines the Permanent Pen font characteristics until you repeat this process.

Task 14.9: Using Special Characters

Occasionally, you might have to use special characters that don't appear on your keyboard, such as currency, copyright, and trademark symbols. With Notes, you can enter hundreds of special characters into a document by pressing special key combinations.

To type a special character, press Alt+F1 followed by the code that represents the special character. Each code consists of one or two keys reminiscent of the special character. To type the symbol for the Japanese yen (¥), for example, press Alt+F1 and then type **Y =**.

Using this feature, you can enter letters that belong to non-English alphabets, enter fractions, international currency designations, and more.

Your Notes administrator should be able to furnish you with a table of codes that you can use.

Workshop

In this hour, you learned how you can modify the way text appears in rich text fields in Notes documents. Following are some of the words this hour introduced you to and some common questions that you might have.

Key Terms

Review the following list of terms:

☐ *Rich text field*   A special field type in Notes that can contain any data type, such as text, graphics, spreadsheet files, and file attachments.

☐ *Dialog box*   A box that appears on the screen when input is expected from the user, such as requesting a filename to open or a piece of text to be used in a search.

☐ *Undo*   Being able to revert back to what the document looked like before your last action. Undo can recover from a variety of situations if you have performed an action in error.

Common Questions

Q **I composed a Notes document, but users complain that the font is really difficult to read. It looks fine to me, so what's the problem?**

A When composing a Notes document you have to bear in mind the intended users. They might not have the "Pristine Sigma Elite" font you used to create the document, so another font might have been substituted. Try and stick to the standards like Times and Helvetica to ensure you get your message across.

Preview of the Next Hour

Now that you've completed some of the basic actions of working with text, the next hour will focus on the Text Properties Box, which you use to change things like font, alignment, tabs and other such things.

14

Hour 15

Using the Text Properties Box

Goals for This Hour

Now that you've done some basic work with text, this hour takes a detailed look at using the Text properties box. The first selection from the Text menu, Text Properties, enables you to control the appearance of the characters that make up a section of text. In the Text properties box, you can control the characters' size, color, type style, and other attributes (see Figure 15.1). The Text properties box consists of five tabs:

- ☐ *Font* controls the font sizes, styles, and colors. You also use this page to adjust the font attributes used by the Permanent Pen.

- ☐ *Alignment* controls how the text in a paragraph aligns in relation to the left margin. The options on this page also include automatic bulleting and numbering for text and the line spacing for the text in a paragraph.

☐ *Pages/Tabs* controls the pagination and tab settings for the paragraph. This page also contains the right margin setting for printing purposes.

☐ *Hide* controls when Notes displays a paragraph. Notes enables you to hide text under several conditions.

☐ *Style* enables users to define frequently used paragraph styles. The styles defined through this page are available for selection in the Style section of the status bar at the bottom of the Notes window.

Figure 15.1.

You use the Text properties box's Font page to change the font style, height, color, and other attributes of your text.

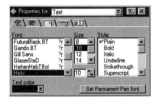

By the time you complete this hour, you should know how to use each of those settings to accomplish desired results. Specifically, you will learn the following:

☐ *Use different font styles, sizes, and colors*   Notes enables you to enhance your text's appearance in a variety of dazzling ways. The Text menu makes it easy.

☐ *Work with bulleted and numbered lists*   Notes can automatically indent your text and insert bullets or numbers to help you format lists in your documents.

☐ *Work with tabs, margins, and other page settings*   The Notes ruler makes it easy to add and adjust page-formatting features.

Task 15.1: Using the Font Settings

In the Font page of the Text properties box, you can select the font type (Figure 15.2 shows Helvetica selected), the size of the font, the color, and the type style.

You can change the text style to highlight portions of your text in various ways. The style includes characteristics (such as text color and font) and attributes (such as boldface and italic). Different text styles can emphasize important phrases and give your document a more interesting appearance.

The following sections describe the different text attributes available in the Text properties box and suggest some possible uses.

Task 15.1.1: Changing the Fonts

You can choose one of many fonts. The default font is determined by your operating system. Helvetica 10-point is typically Notes' default font (except in Macintosh, for which Geneva is the default font). The following are three examples of typefaces:

Helvetica

```
Courier
```

Times Roman

You can also display text in the monospace Typewriter font, which looks similar to the following:

```
Typewriter
```

To do so, choose File, Tools, User Preferences and select the Typewriter Fonts option. This option tells Notes to display all information (including database titles, views, and documents) in a monospace font, in which all letters take up the same amount of space. You might find this option useful for checking the width of columns. If a column is wide enough in a monospace font to display the entire contents of the column, it probably will be wide enough when you switch back to a proportional (non-monospace) font.

Task 15.1.2: Changing the Point Size

You can choose from any of the font sizes in the Size list box or type an entry in the box below the list. By clicking the up and down arrows next to the Size text box, you incrementally increase or decrease the text size.

Task 15.1.3: Changing the Color

When you click the down arrow next to the Text Color selection box, Notes presents a list of 16 colors. Click the desired color to select it.

Task 15.1.4: Changing the Text Style

In addition to the text styles with which you are probably already familiar (bold, italics, and so on), Notes provides the following text enhancements. Note that these styles are for display only and will not print with these attributes.

☐ *Shadow* creates a gray shadow effect behind each letter. This feature is typically used in the titles of forms or sections to jazz up a document's appearance.

☐ *Emboss* creates a three-dimensional raised effect that highlights text. This attribute is especially appealing to use on text that is shown in three-dimensional layout regions.

☐ *Extrude* creates a three-dimensional, sunken look to your text. This attribute is especially appealing to use on text displayed in three-dimensional layout regions.

You also can enlarge and reduce the size of text one point size at a time. To do so, use the Text menu commands or the following function keys:

☐ *Enlarge Size*   Press F2 or choose Text, Enlarge to enlarge text by one point size. Pressing F2 repeatedly makes the text repeatedly larger.

☐ *Reduce Size*   Press Shift+F2 or choose Text, Reduce Size to reduce text by one point size. Pressing Shift+F2 repeatedly makes the text smaller.

You also can change fonts and font sizes quickly by clicking the font name or font size portions of the status bar at the bottom of the Notes window. The available font types and sizes display in a pop-up list when you choose the status bar option (see Figure 15.2).

Figure 15.2.

You can quickly change the font and size by using the status bar options.

Task 15.2: Using the Alignment Settings

As with any good word processor, you can set margins if you want part or all of your document to have margins different than the one-inch default. You also can use tabs to indent text to predefined positions that you select. The following sections explain how to set margins.

Although some characteristics, such as type style or size, can apply to any portion of text, other characteristics, such as justification, apply only to whole paragraphs—that is, a section of text that ends with a carriage return. You cannot have part of a paragraph with one kind of justification while another part of the same paragraph has a different type. If you change the justification of any portion of a paragraph, the whole paragraph changes.

For these paragraph-only characteristics, Notes provides a shortcut. If you want to adjust a characteristic for a single existing paragraph, you don't have to select the paragraph; just place the insertion point anywhere within that paragraph. Then, from the Text properties box's Alignment page, choose the characteristic that you want to adjust. If you want to adjust more than one paragraph, however, you must select the paragraphs as you would any section of text.

> A paragraph is the text between hard carriage returns. Hard carriage returns are made when you press the Enter key.

To change the attributes for paragraphs, you can open the Text properties box by choosing Text, Text Properties. To set paragraph alignment, bulleted lists, numbered lists, margins, and line spacing using the Text properties box, click the Alignment tab (see Figure 15.3). The following selections are available:

- ☐ Alignment
- ☐ First line
- ☐ List
- ☐ Left margin
- ☐ Spacing

Figure 15.3.

You can change para-graph settings in the Text properties box's Align-ment page.

Task 15.2.1: Aligning Text

The Alignment page's Alignment setting controls how Notes aligns each line of text along the left and right margins. To set alignment, select the text-alignment icon that represents the type of alignment that you want to use in the info box . The following are the available types of alignment:

- ☐ *Left Alignment* aligns each line of text at the left margin.
- ☐ *Center Alignment* centers text between the left and right margins.
- ☐ *Right Alignment* aligns each line against the right margin but not the left, resulting in a ragged left paragraph.

□ *Full Alignment* aligns each full line of text along the left and right margins. By adding tiny, almost imperceptible amounts of space between words, Notes manages to make each line exactly the same length.

□ *None* displays each paragraph as a single long line. If a paragraph is longer than Notes can display on the screen, you must use the scroll bars or left- and right-arrow keys to view the rest of the line. You will often see this alignment setting when importing text into Notes. Usually, you will want to change it to left justification after the import.

Task 15.2.2: Indenting or Outdenting First Lines

The First Line group of icons tells Notes how to treat the first line of text in a paragraph. You use these settings to indent or outdent the paragraph, as follows:

□ *Standard* does not indent or outdent the paragraph; instead, Notes aligns the first line of text with the rest of the paragraph-alignment setting.

□ *Indent* indents the first line of the paragraph. In the text box that appears to the right, type the amount that you want to indent the text. The default setting is .25".

□ *Outdent* outdents the first line of the paragraph. In the text box that appears to the right, type the amount that you want to outdent the text. The default setting is .25".

Figure 15.4 shows an example of these settings.

Figure 15.4.

Add pizzazz to your documents by indenting or outdenting paragraphs.

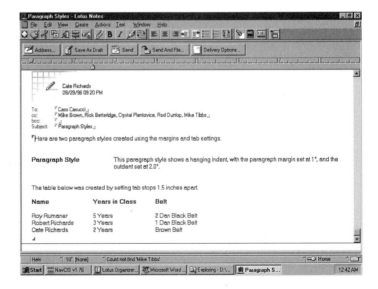

Task 15.2.3: Adding Bullets and Numbers

Notes automatically indents and inserts bullets and numbers in documents when you select the Bullets and Numbers buttons in the Alignment page's List section.

You can also insert bullets and numbers by choosing Text, Bullets and Text, Numbers as needed from the menu command list (see Figure 15.5).

Figure 15.5.

You can add impact (and sometimes fun) to your documents by using the bullet and numbering features.

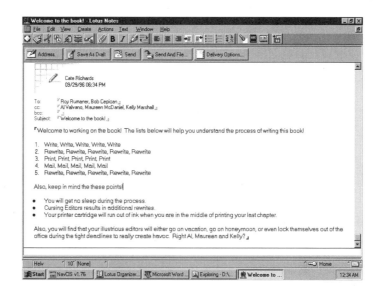

Select the bullet or number styles before typing your text. Entering text is then easier because, as you type, Notes automatically adds the next bullet or the next consecutive number in the list. Then, you can more easily concentrate on your text's substance rather than its format.

Task 15.2.4: Setting Left Margins

To enter a paragraph's left margin setting, you can use whole numbers and decimals. The standard paragraph left margin setting is 1". The maximum limit for this setting is 22.75"—but you should ensure that the margins display on-screen so that readers of the document can see the paragraph.

You can select the top, bottom, left, and right margin settings for the entire document by choosing File, Page Setup. The Page Setup dialog box appears, in which you can alter global document settings.

Task 15.2.5: Setting Line Spacing

The spacing options in Notes control the amount of space between paragraphs and between the lines of text in a paragraph. The following selections are available:

☐ *Interline* controls how many blank lines Notes inserts between lines within each paragraph.

☐ *Above* controls how many blank lines Notes inserts before each paragraph.

☐ *Below* controls how many blank lines Notes inserts after each paragraph.

When you click the down arrow next to each of these options, Notes displays a selection list, asking for the number of blank lines. Notes uses the same type of notation that you might have encountered when adjusting the spacing setting on a typewriter:

☐ Single (no extra blank space)

☐ $1^1/_2$ (half a line's worth of blank space)

☐ Double (a full-line's worth of blank space)

If you choose Below and then Double, for example, an extra line of blank space follows each paragraph.

If you select options for both Above and Below for a paragraph, you might be left with as many as four lines between paragraphs. If this is not your intention, select one option or the other.

Task 15.3: Using the Pages/Tabs Settings

As you work with Notes, you sometimes will want to specify where to insert a page break rather than letting Notes automatically insert it after filling up a page of text. You might also want to adjust tab settings and set the right margin for printing purposes. To perform any of these functions, highlight the paragraph that you want to affect and then open the Text properties box. Click the Pages/Tabs tab to display the page shown in Figure 15.6.

Figure 15.6.

In the Text properties box's Pages/Tabs page, you can specify settings that affect the printed version of your document.

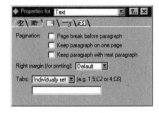

Task 15.3.1: Inserting Page Breaks

Select one of the following to specify where the page break occurs:

- [ ] *Page Break Before Paragraph* inserts a page break before the selected paragraph.

- [ ] *Keep Paragraph on One Page* keeps the selected lines of text together when printing. Notes breaks the page either before or after the selected paragraph but not within the text.

- [ ] *Keep Paragraph with Next Paragraph* keeps the selected paragraph on the same page as the following paragraph. Notes breaks the page before the selected paragraph if it does not fit on the same page as the following paragraph.

> You also can set a page break by pressing Ctrl+L or choosing Create, Page Break. The Ctrl+L key combination is a toggle for setting page breaks—pressing Ctrl+L once enters a page break and pressing Ctrl+L again removes the page break.

A line appears across the page to indicate any page breaks that you specify.

Task 15.3.2: Removing a Page Break

If you decide that you want to remove a page break before a paragraph, place your cursor in the first line of the paragraph immediately following the page break and choose Create, Page Break. Notes then removes the page break—unless you are at the natural end of a page and you have selected View, Show, Page Breaks from the menu commands. You also can press Ctrl+L to remove a page break, as mentioned in the previous Tip.

Task 15.3.3: Setting the Right Margin for Printing

Use the Right Margin (for Printing) option to specify the right margin. This option applies only to the printed document; the right side of the screen is always the right margin when you display a document, so make sure that you specify this setting based on the paper size. Keep in mind that many printers (such as lasers) do not print any closer than one-fourth of an inch from the edge of the paper—regardless of the margin that you specify.

Task 15.3.4: Setting Tabs

You can set tab spacing for your text by using the Text properties box's Pages/Tabs page. To set tab stops for one or more paragraphs, enter specific tab stops in the text box provided. Setting tab stops is a two-step process. You must first indicate how you want to set the tab stops and then specify the factor that Notes is to use in setting the tabs. Follow these steps to set tabs:

1. Click the down arrow next to the Tabs text box. You have two options from which to choose:

   □ *Individually Set* enables you to specify the locations at which to place tab stops. You can enter numbers in inches or centimeters (for example, **.5"** or **.5 cm**). If you enter more than one tab stop, separate them with semicolons (for example, **.5"; 1.35"; 4"**).

   □ *Evenly Spaced* specifies that Notes is to space tab stops evenly based on an interval setting that you provide. For example, you can tell Notes to set a tab stop every .45".

   Notes offers four types of tab stops that you can set. To set one of these tab stops, you can either type its corresponding letter before the tab stop or click the ruler. (See "Setting Margins and Tabs with the Ruler" later in this chapter for more information on using the mouse.) The following are the types of tab stop, their corresponding letters, and the corresponding tab indicator that the ruler displays:

   □ *Right* is represented by the letter R before the tab stop in the Tabs text box. Right tabs align text flush right at the tab stop. You often use this setting when aligning currency values.

   □ *Left*, the standard tab entry, is represented by the letter L before the tab stop in the Tabs text box. Left tabs align text flush left at the tab stop. They are the standard tab entry.

   □ *Decimal* is represented by the letter D before the tab stop in the Tabs text box. Decimal tabs align text according to a decimal point located in the text. This setting is ideal when aligning numbers in a list.

   □ *Center* is represented by the letter C before the tab stop in the Tabs text box. When you select Center, Notes centers your tabs within both sides of the tab stop. This option is ideal for displaying a list of items to the reader.

2. After selecting the tab type, specify the interval for the tab settings in the text box below this selection list. If you are specifying the tab stops individually, type the exact location for each tab, using semicolons to separate multiple entries. If you want Notes to space the tab stops evenly, type the interval space between each tab setting.

You do not have to enter semicolons to separate multiple entries (as the following example demonstrates). If there is a space between the number settings, Notes inserts the semicolon when you save your selections. However, inserting the semicolon helps delineate the individual tab stops when you review your settings—which decreases the chance of misreading your numbers and ending up with an incorrect setting.

You have flexibility when setting tab stops. To set tabs at 1.5, 2, and 4 inches, for example, type the following:

1.5 2 4

or

1.5;2;4

You don't need to type the double quote (") after the number, becauseNotes automatically adds the character to all numbers that represent inches.

> Notes always uses semicolons to display the current tabs in the tab setting text box, even if you used spaces when entering the tabs.

If you prefer to measure a specific tab stop in centimeters, you can type cm after a number, as in the following example:

1 2.3 10cm 15cm 6

In this example, Notes sets five tabs. The 1, 2.3, and 6 represent inches, and the 10 and 15 represent centimeters.

If you chose Metric measurements as your default measurement (see Hour 3, "Specifying Your Notes Preferences"), Notes assumes that all measurements you enter are in centimeters unless you enter a double quote to indicate that a measurement is in inches. Suppose that you set your default to Metric and set tabs at the following positions:

5 10 6"

Notes sets a tab at 5 and 10 centimeters and at 6 inches.

After you set tabs, you can press Tab to move to the next tab stop in your document. If the insertion point is already past the last tab stop, pressing Tab causes Notes to tab at the default intervals.

Task 15.4: Using the Hide Settings

Notes enables you to hide text within a document during particular functions. Database designers typically use this feature when designing forms. This section discusses this feature only briefly.

With the Text properties box open, click the Hide tab. The Hide page appears, as shown in Figure 15.7.

Figure 15.7.

You can hide text in documents, depending on how you are working with the document. You make the "hide-when" selections in the Text properties box's Hide page.

Notes provides the following options:

☐ *Previewed for Reading* keeps the hidden information invisible when users read documents in the Preview pane. Users can, however, read the text if they open the document for reading or editing.

☐ *Opened for Reading* hides any text selected when users open a document for reading. Users can, however, read the text if they have rights to edit the document.

☐ *Printed* tells Notes to print everything but the highlighted text. You can use this option when you want to omit portions of sensitive text when printing a document for someone else to read or otherwise limit the text that prints.

☐ *Previewed for Editing* enables readers of the document to see the text when reading but not when composing or editing a document when readers are viewing the document in the Preview pane.

☐ *Opened for Editing* enables readers of the document to see the text when reading a document but not when composing or editing a document.

☐ *Copied to the Clipboard* tells Notes to ignore text that it is copying to and from the Clipboard. This setting also affects text when a database forwards a document; the text marked for hiding does not appear in a message that the database has forwarded. This option does not affect entire documents that are copied and pasted at the view level.

☐ *Hide Paragraph If Formula Is True* enables database designers to enter a qualifying formula in the Formula window and thus set conditions specifying when to hide the text. (Writing formulas is beyond the scope of this book.)

Task 15.5: Using the Style Settings

You can define and save combinations of paragraph and text properties that you use regularly as named paragraph styles. This is a handy way to define particular styles that you frequently use so that you do not have to continuously set the attributes individually through the Text properties box. To set up a named paragraph style, follow these steps:

15

1. Place your document in edit mode by double-clicking anywhere within the document.

2. Select a paragraph and specify all the attribute settings that you want. In the following steps, you will save this paragraph style. For example, if you want to create a style to use as a response to other memos with indented, bold, and read text, create these settings for the existing paragraph.

3. Choose Text, Text Properties and then click the Style tab. The Style page appears (see Figure 15.8).

Figure 15.8.

If you want to copy a style and reuse it, highlight a paragraph that uses the style and then click the Text properties box's Style tab.

4. Select the Create Style button. The Create Named Style dialog box appears (see Figure 15.9).

5. In the Style Name text box, enter a name for the paragraph style. For example, name the style **Bold Read Response**.

6. Select the Include Font in Named Style check box, which is the default, if you want to include all font settings as well as paragraph settings.

Figure 15.9.

In the Create Named Style dialog box, provide a descriptive name to make your style's use easier to remember.

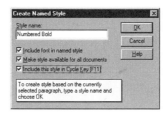

7. Select the Make Style Available for All Documents check box if you want to have this style setting available regardless of the document in which you are working. Selecting this check box adds the style name to the status bar pop-up selection list at the bottom of the Notes window.

8. Select the Include This Style in Cycle Key [F11] check box if you want this style to appear when you press the F11 key to cycle through the available styles.

9. Choose OK.

After defining the style name, you can highlight a paragraph and select the setting by returning to the Text properties box's Style page or by choosing Text, Named Styles and then clicking the name of the style that you want to apply. If you elected to display the style when pressing F11 to view the cycle key, you can select the style through those options, as well. You can also select styles by clicking the Styles option on the status bar to display the list of currently defined styles, as shown in Figure 15.10.

Notes 4.6 predefines the following three styles that you can select from the Text, Named Styles menu:

- *Headline* displays the selected text in bold, purple, Helvetica 12-point font.
- *Bullet* displays the selected font in bullet style.
- *Basic* changes the selected font size to Helvetica 10-point but maintains any other text-formatting options previously defined.

You can use the Redefine Style button in the Text properties box to redefine a named style, based on the current paragraph selection. Alternatively, you might want to "clean house" periodically and get rid of old styles by clicking the Delete Styles button and then selecting the style to delete.

Figure 15.10.

You can quickly change the style of a paragraph by clicking the Style option of the status bar and then selecting one of the defined styles in the pop-up menu.

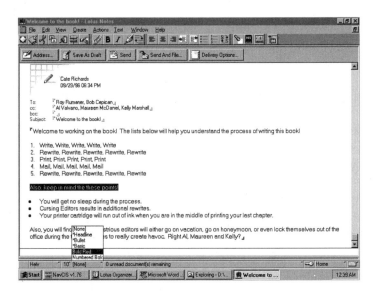

Workshop

Now that you have completed the previous hour and this one, you should feel comfortable working with text to achieve a desired result. Just like using a word processor, you have control over font size and style and text alignment and positioning in the document, as well as things like tabs, hiding, using indents, and so on.

Key Terms

Review the following term:

☐ *Page breaks*   A page break where the printer will start printing on a new page. Most word processing programs automatically insert page breaks when you have filled the page of text. However, you can also manually add new page breaks if you want to leave part of a page blank for notes or other such things.

Common Questions

Q I've noticed that sometimes when I type in 10-point size, it's smaller than other times I type in 10-point size. Why is that?

A When changing fonts and font sizes, keep in mind that some fonts naturally appear smaller to the reader. For example, the default font, Helvetica 10-point, is relatively easy to read onscreen. If you change the font type to Script and leave the font size at 10, however, the text becomes difficult to read. For the Script font to be readable onscreen, you must increase the font size.

Also, although the Helvetica 10-point font is easy to read onscreen, some people often find it difficult to read text printed at this font size. You might want to increase the font size to 12 or greater if you are printing the document or if you are fairly sure that the reader will want to print the document.

Preview of the Next Hour

Having worked with the text in this hour and the previous one, you'll be working with the documents in the next. You will learn how to perform a spell check, work with read/unread marks, and copy and paste documents.

Hour 16

Working with Basic Document Features

Goals for This Hour

Lotus Notes 4.6 has a wide variety of document features that help make it a robust environment for communicating with others. You can add or apply these features directly to a rich text field within a document that already has been designed. Some of these features, as you will learn in this hour, also can be built into the design of the database forms. In Hour 14, "Working with Text," you learn how to use text to enhance your use of Lotus Notes. This hour covers features that enable you to use the power of Notes to enhance your documents, such as the following:

- ☐ Using the Notes spell checker
- ☐ Searching for text and phrases
- ☐ Working with read marks
- ☐ Copying and pasting documents

Task 16.1: Checking Your Spelling

No matter how professional your document appears or how insightful your message, you will not impress readers if misspellings litter your document. Notes includes a spell checker that looks for misspelled words and other common mistakes.

To check the spelling of a document, position the insertion point anywhere in the document. Then choose Edit, Check Spelling. If Notes finds a misspelled word or detects some other irregularity that it regards as a mistake, it displays the dialog box shown in Figure 16.1. In this example, the word "developed" is misspelled.

 Your document must be in edit mode to check spelling. If you do not see open brackets around the fields in your document, then you are not in edit mode. To put your document in edit mode, select Actions, Edit document, double-click your mouse anywhere in the document, or select the Edit SmartIcon.

At the bottom of the dialog box is the Status field, which describes the problem Notes found with each word or phrase that it highlighted. For example, in Figure 16.1, the Status field displays Unknown Word. (That is, the word isn't one that Notes recognizes as correctly spelled.) Notes highlights the offending word within your document and displays the word in the Replace text box. At this point, you need to choose among the following options:

☐ If the word is misspelled, as in this example, you can fix the word in the Replace text box and then choose the Replace button. Notes replaces the misspelled word in the document with the fixed word. If you misspelled the same word in the same way elsewhere in the document, Notes fixes the word in only one location at a time and asks you what to do each time it encounters the misspelled word.

☐ If you agree that the word is misspelled but don't know how to spell it correctly, you can view the guesses that Notes makes. Notes searches its dictionary for words similar to the misspelled word and displays them in the Guess list box. Figure 16.1 shows the guesses that Notes produced for "developped."

Figure 16.1.

Use the Check Spelling option to find misspelled words and other common errors in documents.

Often, the first word in the Guess list box is the correct spelling. In this example, Notes guessed the correct spelling as "developed." Select the correctly spelled guess and then choose Replace. Alternatively, you can double-click the correctly spelled word. Notes replaces the misspelled word in the document with the correctly spelled word.

☐ You might want to prompt Notes to accept an incorrectly spelled word or phrase deliberately. For example, if you intentionally misspell a word or phrase, such as *Ye Ol' Shoppe*, but want Notes to point out similar misspellings later that might be unintentional, you can choose Skip to skip just this one instance of the spelling or Skip All to always skip this misspelling during this spell-checking session.

This feature is most useful for acronyms, names, or technical terms that occur several times throughout the document that you know are correct but that you don't want to add to your dictionary.

☐ If you know that you have spelled the word correctly and that you use the word often, choose Define. Notes adds the word to your personal dictionary so that Notes considers the word valid any time you check spelling in the future, whether in this document or another.

☐ If you want to exit the spell checker before Notes prompts you that it is complete, choose the Done button. Notes stops checking spelling at that point and returns you to your document.

Along with catching misspelled words, Notes watches for other common errors, such as unusual capitalization and repeated words (such as I saw the the dog). As with misspelled words, you can tell Notes to ignore the problem, or you can tell Notes how to fix it.

After displaying all the questionable words, Notes displays a final dialog box telling you that it has finished checking spelling. Click OK to close this dialog box.

Although a wonderful aid for producing error-free documents, the spelling checker cannot replace proofreading. The spelling checker cannot catch grammatical errors, incorrectly used words, or many names that you use. Worst of all, it doesn't catch words that are used incorrectly. For example, if you meant to write *I hear that we have hired ten new people*, but mistakenly omit the *a* in *hear*, Notes doesn't catch the resulting *her* as a misspelled word. Likewise, if you spell the word *here*, Notes doesn't recognize it as an error, even though it's not the correct usage.

16

Task 16.2: Searching for Text in a Document That You Are Reading

Notes makes it simple to find (and replace if you're in edit mode) a word or phrase in a document. You can search for a word or phrase anywhere within a field by choosing Edit, Find and Replace. Notes displays the Find and Replace dialog box (see Figure 16.2). In the Find text box, enter the word or phrase that you want to find (you don't have to type in a word to replace it with when you just want to search for a word or phrase).

Figure 16.2.

Finding and replacing text is easy when you use the Find and Replace feature in Notes.

If the phrase that you want to find or replace is onscreen, you can select the phrase so that it appears as the phrase to find when you perform a find or replace operation. Suppose that your screen is displaying a paragraph discussing money market funds and you want to find other places in the document that also discuss them. Select the phrase money market fund; when you choose Edit, Find and Replace (or Edit, Find Next), the phrase money market fund already appears in the phrase to find.

After you enter the search phrase (if it differs from the one that Notes displays), you can choose any of the following check box options in the dialog box's Match section to change the way that Notes performs its search:

☐ *Whole Word*   Normally, Notes looks for the search phrase without regard to word boundaries. If you search for cat, for example, Notes stops not only on the word cat but also on scat and catalog because they both contain the letter sequence cat. If you are searching for especially short phrases, however, you can choose Whole Word to tell Notes that you are interested only in the word cat, not these three letters within any word.

☐ *Accent*   When searching text, Notes normally ignores diacritical marks for the purposes of finding phrases. If you choose this option, Notes considers diacritical marks when searching for text. Suppose that you are writing a document that includes the name Björn. If you want to search for this word and you don't choose Accent, Notes finds the word if you enter only Bjorn. If you choose Accent, however, Notes finds only Björn if you enter it with its umlaut.

☐ *Case* If you choose this option, Notes looks only for phrases capitalized exactly the way you typed the search phrase. During a search for cat, for example, Notes won't stop on Cat or CAT.

Choose Find Next to begin the search. Notes searches for the phrase from the current insertion point position and repositions the insertion point on the next occurrence of the phrase. If Notes reaches the end of the document without finding the phrase, it displays a dialog box telling you that it cannot find the phrase.

Often, the first occurrence of your phrase that Notes finds isn't the one that you want. Choose Edit, Find Next or press Ctrl+G to repeat the last search. Notes searches for the same phrase, using the same combination of selected options. By pressing Ctrl+G enough times, you can find each occurrence of the phrase throughout the document.

Task 16.3: Replacing Text

Occasionally, you might have to change a phrase that occurs several times throughout a document. For example, suppose that a particular function that your company's Denver office formerly performed transfers to Atlanta, and you need to find all instances of Denver within a document and change them to Atlanta. You can use the Find feature to find and change each occurrence individually, but Notes provides a related feature—Replace—that makes this kind of wholesale replacement easier.

To perform a replace, you must be in edit mode. Press Ctrl+E to switch to edit mode if you're now in read mode (brackets appear around each field if you are in edit mode). Position the insertion point at the top of your document and choose Edit, Find and Replace. Notes displays the Find and Replace dialog box (see Figure 16.3).

Figure 16.3.

To find and replace text quickly, use the Find and Replace dialog box—but first, make sure that you are in edit mode.

The Find and Replace dialog box offers exactly the same check boxes as the Edit Find dialog box, and you use them the same way. After you enter the phrase to find and the replacement phrase, choose any options that apply and then choose Find Next. Starting at your cursor's current location, Notes looks for the first occurrence of the search phrase, highlights the occurrence, and waits for you to choose one of the following buttons:

- ☐ If you choose *Find Next*, Notes leaves the current occurrence of the phrase unchanged and finds the next one.

- ☐ If you choose *Find Previous*, Notes searches for the occurrence directly before the current one (or the cursor location if you are just beginning your search).

- ☐ If you choose *Replace*, Notes replaces the current occurrence with the replacement phrase.

- ☐ If you choose *Replace All*, Notes replaces every occurrence of the search phrase with the replacement phrase.

> Think carefully before choosing Replace All. If you make a mistake, you cannot undo the operation with the Edit, Undo command. The Replace All button makes it much too easy to make incorrect changes to your document that will take you hours to fix. If, for example, a female replaces your male personnel manager, you might want to revise a certain memo by changing he to she. If you forget to select the Whole Word option, however, Notes changes other to otsher, there to tshere, and similarly messes up all other words that include the letters he.
>
> When you select Replace All, Notes prompts you with the following: `Replace All cannot be undone. Would you like to proceed?` Answering Yes to this query begins the search and replace of text you have identified.

- ☐ If you choose *Done*, Notes stops the search, leaving the current occurrence of the search phrase unchanged.

> Save your document (choose File, Save) before using Replace All. If you make an error in your editing, you can always exit the current document without saving and then reopen the saved version of the document.

Task 16.4: Working with Document Read Marks

You have seen that Notes displays a star next to documents that you haven't read. In databases such as your mailbox, these markers can serve as important reminders that you need to read certain documents. Sometimes, however, you might decide that you don't want to read certain documents in a database or in your mailbox at a particular time.

Suppose that your company maintains a database of important scheduled events, and you want to keep abreast of these events. Someone in your company, however, routinely adds notices about the company softball team, which just doesn't interest you. After a long vacation, you return to your desk and find 14 softball announcements in the database. You really don't want to read them, but they all have the stars next to them, screaming, "Pay attention to me!"

You can use the Unread Marks operation to tell Notes to remove the stars and make the documents appear as though you have read them. To mark documents as read, open the database and choose Edit, Unread Marks. The Unread Marks menu appears, enabling you to select one of the following four options (see Figure 16.4):

☐ *Mark Selected Read* marks all selected documents as read.

☐ *Mark All Read* marks all documents in the database as read.

☐ *Mark Selected Unread* marks all selected documents as unread.

☐ *Mark All Unread* marks all documents in the database as unread.

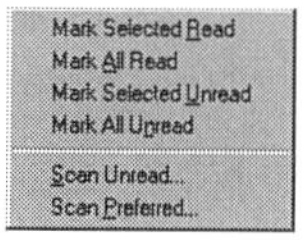

Figure 16.4.

You can mark documents as read to indicate that you have already read them or as unread to draw your attention to those documents later.

Note that the last two choices enable you to mark read documents as unread; that is, you can read a document and then tell Notes to mark it as though you hadn't read it. At first glance, this capability might seem like a useless feature, but you actually might find it useful, especially if you keep old memos in your mailbox that you think might be important later.

> You can use your keyboard's Insert key to toggle the read/unread marks on and off for a document.

When you open your mailbox, you probably look for the stars that call attention to newly arrived mail. Suppose, however, that you read a message just before quitting time one afternoon and realize that the memo will require significant attention tomorrow. If you close the message, Notes now considers it one of the many previously read messages and removes its attention-grabbing star. You can put the star back, however, by marking the document as unread so that it will again attract your notice the next time you read your mail.

Task 16.5: Scanning for Unread Documents

Many people work with several different databases and must constantly be on the lookout for new documents showing up in those databases. Suppose your company has several databases that contain status reports from different departments, and one of your jobs is to monitor those status reports for customer problems. You might find it cumbersome to check each database several times a day to see whether new documents have appeared. Instead, you can use the Scan Unread feature in the Edit, Unread Marks menu to tell you about new documents.

Task 16.5.1: Scanning Preferred Databases

You can use the Scan Unread feature in several ways, but the most common—and most useful—method involves a two-step process. In the first step, you tell Notes which databases you want to watch for unread documents; these databases are known as your preferred databases. Then, at any time, you can ask Notes whether any unread documents are in any of your preferred databases.

To supply Notes with your list of preferred databases, choose Edit, Unread Marks, Scan Preferred. The Scan Unread dialog box appears, as shown in Figure 16.5. Select Choose Preferred. The Scan Unread Preferred Setup dialog box appears (see Figure 16.6).

Figure 16.5.

You can use the Scan Unread dialog box to begin setting up preferred databases to scan.

Figure 16.6.

You must select, individually from the list, each database that you want to mark as preferred. you cannot select workspace page names.

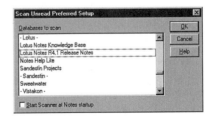

Notes lists all the databases on all your workspace pages. To indicate the workspace pages, Notes encloses the names with dashes, as in the following example:

- Lotus-

Select the databases that you want to scan for unread documents. You must click each database title individually. Choose OK to save your selections.

> The Scan Unread Preferred Setup dialog box includes the check box Start Scanner at Notes Startup. If you select this check box, Notes automatically scans your preferred databases for unread documents each time you start Notes.

After selecting your preferred databases, you can scan them for unread documents by making sure no databases are selected on the workspace (click anywhere in the workspace's blank gray portion) and choosing Edit, Unread Marks, Scan Preferred. Notes displays the Scan Unread dialog box (refer to Figure 16.5).

The dialog box displays the name of the first of your preferred databases and shows the number of unread documents in the database. You can choose any of the following actions:

- [ ] *View First Unread* opens the first document in the first database. You can then read the unread document. Press Tab to move to the next unread document in the database. Press Esc to exit the current document and open the database view.
- [ ] *Mark All Read* tells Notes to assume that you don't want to read the documents and mark them as read from this database only. This selection does not affect all the other databases that you are scanning.
- [ ] *Skip This Database* displays the name of the next preferred database and the number of unread documents in that database.

After scanning all databases, Notes loops back to the first and begins scanning again. When you see the same databases appearing again, choose Done to exit scanning.

Task 16.5.2: Scanning a Single Database

To scan a single database for unread documents, highlight the database that you want to scan by clicking the database icon once. Choose Edit, Unread Marks, Scan Unread. Notes opens the first unread document in the database. Press Tab to open the next unread document. Press Esc to end the scan and exit the document. You return to the database view.

Task 16.5.3: Scanning Multiple Databases

You can select multiple databases and then scan them. To do so, press the Shift key and then click each of the databases that you want to scan from the Notes workspace. Choose Edit, Unread Marks, Scan Unread. Notes opens the Scan Unread dialog box. Follow the procedures listed in the section "Scanning Preferred Databases," earlier in this section, to scan your selected databases.

Task 16.6: Copying and Pasting Documents

Not only can you use the Clipboard to copy pieces of text from one document to another, as described in the section "Copying and Pasting Text" in Hour 14, "Working with Text," but you can use almost the exact same technique to move or copy documents from one database to another. Follow these steps:

1. Open the database in which the documents now exist.
2. Select one or more documents by clicking the left margin next to each document. A check mark appears next to selected documents.
3. If you want to copy the documents, choose Edit, Copy, press Shift-Insert, press Ctrl+C, or click the Copy SmartIcon. If you want to move the documents, choose Edit, Cut, press Shift+Delete, press Ctrl+X, or click the Cut SmartIcon.
4. Close the current database and open the database in which you want to place the documents.
5. Choose Edit, Paste, press Ctrl-Insert, press Ctrl+V, or click the Paste SmartIcon.

Notes inserts the documents into the new database. This procedure works best if both databases contain the form that you used to compose the documents. If, for example, the documents were composed with a form called Client Information and both databases contain that form under that name, Notes can move or copy the documents easily. Otherwise, Notes must rearrange the fields within the documents to conform to the default form in the receiving database—in which case Notes might not display some or all of the text—depending on how successfully Notes figures out how to display the information.

> If you try to copy documents into a database that does not contain a copy of the form in which they are created, Notes might be incapable of displaying any of the information in the form or might display the information in a way that is difficult to read.

Often, depending on the database's design, your copy of the document appears slightly indented below the original document as a response document if you highlighted the original document before pasting. (When designing the form, your database designer might have precluded your need to do this by selecting one of the following options in the Form Properties box: New Versions Become Responses, Prior Versions Become Responses, or New Versions Become Siblings.

If you are highlighting a document when you paste documents that have been created by using the Response type of document, your documents will become responses to the document you have highlighted. If you do not intend to make the documents responses, then make sure you do not highlight a document in the view.

Workshop

In this hour, you learned how to spell check your documents, search for information in your Notes documents, by searching views and documents and by utilizing the powerful full text index. You also learned how to manage your read/unread marks and copy and paste documents. As follows are some common questions you might have.

Key Terms

Review the following term:

☐ *Encrypted Field*   For extra security you can encrypt selected fields in Notes documents. You create an encryption key and distribute it to the people you want to be able to read the document.

Common Questions

Q How can I spell check just one word instead of taking time to spell check the entire document?

A Highlight the word or words and then choose Edit, Check Spelling.

Q I noticed that I can now open documents from the Preview pane, but how do I get Notes to mark that as a read document?

A If you want to make sure that documents you read in the Preview pane are also marked as being read, choose File, Tools, User Preferences. In the Basic settings, select Mark Documents Read When Opened in Preview Pane in the Advanced options section. Notes then marks any documents that you open through the Preview pane as being read, as well as those that you open directly through the view.

Preview of the Next Hour

This hour has introduced you to some of the basic document features, such as spell checking and finding and replacing text within a document. Next, you will learn about the more sophisticated method of searching and indexing databases.

Hour **17**

Searching for Documents in Databases

Goals for This Hour

In the course of your daily work, you probably encounter more documents than you need and many documents that you don't think you need, but eventually do for some reason or other. When that happens, you want to find the document you need quickly and easily. In this hour, you will explore different ways to search for a document. Specifically, you should expect to learn how to do the following:

☐ Use a full-text search in a database

☐ Index a database to make searching possible, including how to index attachments, stop files, and so on

☐ Delete an index

☐ Perform searches by using different criteria, such as date, name, author, and so on

☐ Refine your search results to a manageable amount

Notes provides a very powerful search mechanism known as a full-text search. By using this search feature, you can search for documents that contain several phrases rather than a specific single phrase. Perhaps you want to find documents that discuss stock prices and quarterly earnings, for example. This type of search also enables you to search an entire database or even more than one database at a time, displaying all the documents that meet your search criteria in a view.

To use a full-text search, the database must be indexed for full-text searches. The indexing process creates a special file that enables Notes to determine quickly which words or phrases a document contains. If a database isn't indexed, you can perform only limited searches by choosing Edit, Find, as previously discussed.

Task 17.1: Indexing a Database

 You must have Manager-level access to a database to be able to index, update an index, or delete an index.

You can index any databases that you create on your local hard disk. Only someone with designer access or above, however, can index a database that is shared with other individuals on a server. You can index a database in one of two ways:

☐ Choose File, Database, Properties to display the properties box. Select the Full Text tab and then choose Create Index to display the Full Text Create Index dialog box shown in Figure 17.1. In this dialog box, you control how Notes indexes the database.

Figure 17.1.

To index a database, open the Full Text Create Index dialog box in the Database properties box.

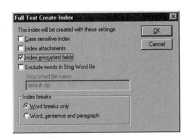

☐ When in a database not already indexed, choose View, Search Bar. This tells Notes that you want to index the database. Notes opens the search bar, which provides a Create Index button. If you click this button, the Full Text Create Index dialog box opens to begin the process, as shown in Figure 17.1.

In the Full Text Create Index dialog box, you usually should accept the default selections, as shown in Figure 17.2. These selections provide the most compact (small) index possible— except for the Exclude Words in the Stop Word File selection (as you will learn later in this hour), which does typically reduce the index size. The following sections describe the indexing options.

Task 17.1.1: Making the Index Case-Sensitive

The Case sensitive index option enables you to indicate whether or not you want Notes to distinguish between uppercase and lowercase letters. For example, you can tell Notes to recognize cat, Cat, and CAT as different entries. If your index doesn't need to be case-sensitive, as is usually the case, don't select this option, because it can greatly increase the index's size and exclude documents that you actually want to find. Use this option only if case-sensitive searches are required, such as when you index a database full of C programming concepts and structures.

Task 17.1.2: Indexing Attachments

By choosing the Index attachments option, you can indicate whether or not you want Notes to index any attachments containing text that are inserted in a document. If you choose this option, you can search the database for words or phrases stored in Notes documents and any files attached to the documents. For example, if you attached a Word Pro document to a document stored in a database that maintains this selection in its indexing setup, you can search the Notes text and the Word Pro text when you query the database. Choosing this option, however, can significantly increase the length of time that it takes to index the database, as well as the amount of space that the index takes up on the hard drive. Notes cannot highlight the words in the search phrase in the attached document but, instead, highlights the attachment icon in the document.

Task 17.1.3: Indexing Encrypted Fields

If you want to include text in encrypted fields in a full-text index, choose Index Encrypted Fields. You can index encrypted fields only if you have the appropriate encryption key, and only people with the encryption key can search the fields. Using this option increases the size of an index by the number of encrypted fields in a database and the amount of text that they contain.

17

Task 17.1.4: Using Stop Word Files

The Exclude Words in Stop Word File option tells Notes not to search for extremely common words (the, and, if, it, and so forth). These common words are called stop words and are defined in the field located just below this selection. You probably should choose this option, as it limits the number of selected documents to only those that match the remainder of your search criteria.

Task 17.1.5: Working with Index Breaks

The Index Breaks section has two options: Word Breaks Only and Word, Sentence and Paragraph. You normally will choose the Word Breaks Only option unless you are trying to perform fancier searches. If you choose the Word, Sentence and Paragraph option, Notes enables you to perform more complex searches that specify that all the search words must be in the same sentence or paragraph. This requirement can lengthen the time of your search and also can take up a large amount of space. Because most documents that you search are fairly short (particularly in your email database), choosing Word, Sentence and Paragraph is not necessary.

Task 17.1.6: Completing the Indexing Process

When you have completed your selections, Notes tells you that it has queued the database's indexing if the database is located on the server. If you index a database on your hard drive, Notes informs you that it is performing a local index. If the database is located on the server, you can continue working in other databases while Notes indexes the database, but you cannot work in the database that the server is indexing until it is finished. Notes doesn't tell you when it has finished indexing, but you know that it is done when you can open the database. If the database is local, you cannot continue working in Notes until the indexing is complete. In local indexing, you know that indexing is complete when the Indexing Database status box disappears.

> If you are running short on hard disk space, don't index your database. If you begin indexing a database and run out of disk space before indexing is complete, you will not be able to use the index. You must delete the index, clean up space on your hard drive, and then create a new index on the database.

If you add, delete, or change any documents in a database that has been indexed, the index will no longer accurately reflect the database; the index will omit new words and continue to contain words no longer in any document. For this reason, your searches will behave unexpectedly if you are searching for words that have changed. You have to update a database index periodically by selecting File, Database, Properties and then selecting the Full Text tab. Select Update Index to update the index of the database.

Task 17.1.9: Deleting an Index

You can delete a full-text index if you no longer want to index a particular database. You also should delete the index and then re-create it if you are experiencing full-text index problems or if you want to change index options. In the latter two cases, create a new index after deleting the original. Do not delete the index from the index subdirectory directly; instead, use the following procedure when you delete an index:

1. Select the database from the Notes workspace page and then choose File, Database, Properties.

2. Select the Full Text tab in the Database properties box.

3. Select the Delete Index button. Notes displays the dialog box shown in 17.6.

Figure 17.2.

To conserve disk space, delete database indexes that you no longer use.

4. Choose Yes when prompted to delete the index.

Notes deletes the database's index and removes the subdirectory created for this index from your hard drive. If you want to reindex the database after selecting new indexing options or if the index was experiencing problems, follow the procedures to create a full-text index described in the earlier section, "Indexing a Database."

Task 17.2: Performing a Full-Text Search

If a database has been indexed for full-text searches, choosing View, Search Bar causes Notes to display the search bar across the top of the document window, as shown in Figure 17.3, which is quite different from the Find dialog box that you saw earlier. The search bar consists of two areas into which you can enter one or more phrases.

Figure 17.3.

Use the search bar to perform queries against indexed databases.

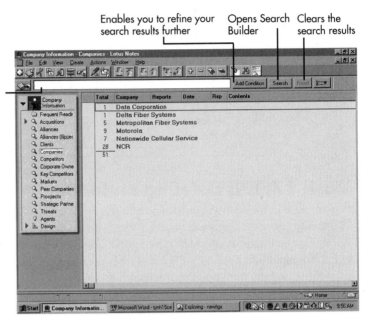

Enables you to refine your search results further

Opens Search Builder

Clears the search results

Enables you to enter search text directly

If you are performing a simple search for just a word or phrase, you can type it in the text box to the left of the Add Condition button and then click Search or press Enter. Notes searches the database's documents and displays the results in the view according to how you elect to see them. You can work with the documents displayed in the view; if you exit the database while doing so, however, you clear your search's results. You also can clear the search's results by selecting the search bar's Reset button. (You learn more about how Notes displays query results in the next few sections.)

Occasionally, you might find that a search returns no documents (or fewer than you expect), despite the fact that you know the database contains documents that match your criteria. In these situations, look at the *View* you are using for the search. Would that view normally contain the missing documents? A full-text search cannot display documents that would not normally appear in the selected view. It is always a good idea to use an *All Documents* view, if one exists, for the basis of your search. If there is no All Documents view, try selecting different views to see if the missing documents show up.

If you want to perform a more detailed query, you can select the Add Condition button to add further detail on the query that you want to build in the Search Builder. When you finish building a query, select Search, which tells Notes to display the results of your query in the view according to how you elected to see them. This section walks you through the process of building a query, selecting viewing options, and interpreting your view results.

> You can create complicated, extensive search queries by using any of the search techniques described in the following sections. You also can use a combination of any of these search methods to refine your search query further. For example, you can define a search for a particular author's documents by selecting the By Author search, making your selections, and then clicking OK to save your entry. You can then select another condition and input words or phrases that you want the document to contain, enhancing your query further.

Task 17.2.1: Searching for Specified Text

In the previous examples, you learned how to search for a single word or phrase in a database. If your database is full-text indexed, however, you can use the Search Builder to find documents that contains a list of words and phrases that you provide.

Before you begin the search, make sure that the database is open to the view that you want to search. Then, perform the following steps:

1. If the search bar is not visible, choose View, Search Bar.
2. Click the Add Condition button.
3. In the Condition drop-down list, accept the default value Words and Phrases.
4. Choose All to have Notes display only documents that contain all of the words or phrases that you enter into the Search Builder. If you choose Any, as described later in this section, Notes displays documents that contain any of the words or phrases that you type.
5. Type a word or phrase in as many of the numbered text boxes as you want. The Search Builder searches for documents that contain all your specified words and phrases (see Figure 17.4).
6. Choose OK. Notes displays the query that you have built in the Search Builder's text box. Between entries that you create in the fields, Notes inserts the word AND to signify that these words and phrases must all be in the document before Notes can display it in the results.
7. Click the Search button in the search bar.

Figure 17.4.

By typing words or phrases into each text box, you can narrow your search results so that only a few documents meet all of your criteria.

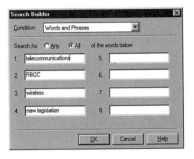

 If you want to include more than eight words and phrases in your search, repeat steps 2 through 6 until you have entered all your criteria.

Figure 17.5 shows a query that searches a product marketing database for all documents that contain the words telecommunications, RBOC, and wireless, and the phrase new legislation.

Figure 17.5.

This view displays the results of a full-text query against a database.

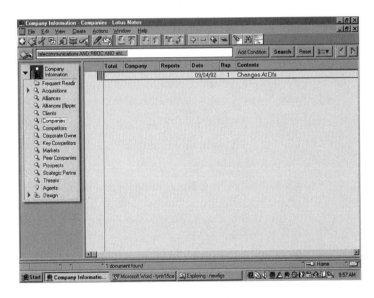

The results from this query are any documents in the database that contain all the words and phrases entered into the text boxes. In this example, only one document, as shown in Figure 17.5, contains all the specified words and phrases.

When you open the document in the view, red boxes highlight all the words and phrases defined in the query, as shown in Figure 17.6. To move through the document finding all occurrences of the searched-for text, press Ctrl-+. As you do this, the next occurrence of the searched-for text is displayed, and the color of the box surrounding the word or phrase changes from red to green.

Figure 17.6.

When you open a document from an indexed database after running a query, Notes uses red boxes to highlight defined words and phrases.

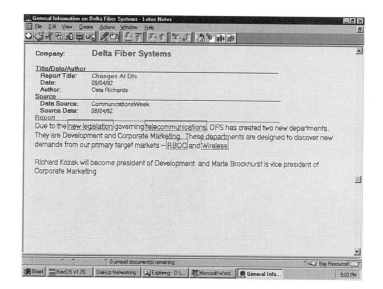

To find documents that contain any of your specified words or phrases, choose Any in step 4. Between each entry that you created in the fields, Notes inserts the word OR to signify that at least one of these words or phrases must be in the document if it is to appear in the results.

Notes displays this query's results in the view, as shown in Figure 17.7. In this example, 10 documents meet the query's defined criteria.

Task 17.2.3: Searching Portfolios

Searching a Portfolio is similar to searching a database, except now you can search multiple databases at one time. Follow these steps:

1. Open the Portfolio.

2. Perform a full-text search, as usual.

3. To see the results of the search, click the database icons in the Portfolio Navigator on the left. As you do so, the documents displayed on the right change to display the found documents in the last-used view in that database.

4. To check other views in the selected database, click the twistie to the left of the database icon to expand it and then click the desired view.

Figure 17.7.

If two or more documents meet the search query, Notes lists them in the view according to your defined criteria.

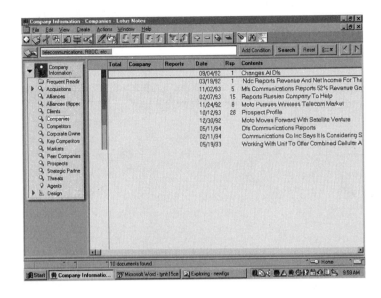

Before carrying out your search, it is a good idea to make sure that each database in your Portfolio actually has a full-text index. If not, create one. Also make sure that for each database in the Portfolio, you have selected to display the search bar (View, Search Bar); otherwise, when you click a database that does not have it displayed you will lose the search criteria in *all* the databases in the Portfolio and will have to start over.

Task 17.2.4: Searching by Author

If your database is indexed, you can define a query to search a database and display all documents composed by a specific author or group of authors.

Before conducting such a search, make sure that the database is open to the view that you want to search. Then perform the following steps:

1. If the search bar is not visible, choose View, Search Bar.

2. Click the Add Condition button. The Search Builder appears (see Figure 17.8).

3. In the Condition drop-down list, select By Author.

4. In the Search for Documents Whose Author drop-down list, select Contains if you want documents created by the authors that you select, or Does Not Contain if you want to exclude documents created by a specific author.

Figure 17.8.

When you query a database for documents written by a particular author, Notes changes the dialog box's appearance.

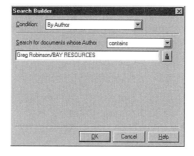

In any query that you build, if you exclude an entry based on a selection or term that you enter, Notes inserts the word NOT before the phrase to indicate that Notes should exclude any documents that contain that entry. You can achieve the same effect by typing the entry directly before any word or phrase. For example, if you want to exclude documents authored by anyone named Larry, enter **NOT Larry** in the By Author search formula.

This principle works for all search queries that you build, including By Author searches.

5. Perform one of the following:

   ☐ Type the name of an author in the text box. To include more than one name, separate the names with commas.

   ☐ Click the Author icon (its graphic looks like a person) and select the names of the authors you want from the Name & Address Book displayed (see Figure 17.9). If you are working on the network, Notes displays the Public Name & Address Book. If you are working remotely (off the network), Notes displays your Private Name & Address Book. If you have more than one Address Book available to you, you can switch between them as usual.

Figure 17.9.

You can select the authors for whom you want to search from your Address Book. This way, you ensure that your query spells the author's name correctly.

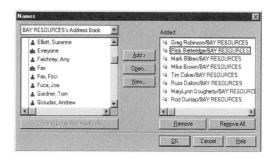

☐ Select a name from the address list by highlighting the author's name (group names have no effect in this search) and then choosing Add. Notes adds your selected name to the list on the right side of the dialog box. Continue to select names until your query includes all the author names for which you want to search.

6. Choose OK in the Names dialog box. Then choose OK again in the Search Builder dialog box.

7. Click the Search button on the search bar.

> You can search by author in all databases created by using Notes Release 4.x, as long as the database's design includes an author field. However, you might have trouble searching databases created in versions earlier than Release 4.x. You cannot search by author in anonymous databases (which are databases that conceal the identity of a document's author).

Task 17.2.5: Searching by Date

If your database is indexed, you can search for documents based on the date when they were created or modified. Before conducting the search, make sure the database is open to the view that you want to search. Then perform the following steps:

1. If the search bar is not visible, choose View, Search Bar.

2. Click the Add Condition button.

3. In the Condition drop-down list, select By Date. Notes alters the dialog box to appear, as shown in Figure 17.10.

Figure 17.10.

This query searches for documents created after November 19, 1995.

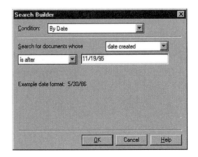

4. In the Search for documents whose drop-down list, select Date Created or Date Modified.

5. In the next drop-down list, select how the date for which you are searching is related to the documents for which you are searching. For example, select Is After if you want to find only those documents created or modified after a particular date.

6. Type a date in the date text box. If Notes displays two text boxes, type dates in both of them. Wh-n typing your dates, make sure that you use the format indicated below the list box. The required date format depends on your operating system.

7. Choose OK. (Repeat steps 2 through 7 if you need to include more dates in your search.)

8. Click the Search button on the search bar.

After searching the database for all documents that meet your date criteria, Notes displays the documents in the view.

Task 17.2.6: Searching by Field Contents

If a database is indexed, you can search for documents that have a specific entry in a particular field. For example, in a Marketing database, you might want to find documents that contain the word Competitor in the ClassificationR field (a field in the design of the database used in this example).

Before conducting the search, make sure that the database is open to the view that you want to search. Then perform the following steps:

1. If the search bar is not visible, choose View, Search Bar.

2. Click the Add Condition button.

3. In the Condition drop-down list, select By Field. Notes displays the dialog box shown in Figure 17.11.

Figure 17.11.

This query looks for the word Competitor in the ClassificationR field of the database.

4. In the Search for documents where field drop-down list, select the field that you want to include in the search. This drop-down list box contains all the fields in the database's design.

5. In the last drop-down list, make a relationship choice: The field either does or doesn't contain the entry.

6. In the text box (or text boxes), type the text, dates, or number for which you want to search. For example, type **competitor**.

7. Choose OK. (Repeat steps 2 through 7 if you need to include more fields in your search.)

8. Click the Search button on the search bar.

If you are not familiar with the database's design and do not know the name of the field that you want to use in your query, you can review the field design information by highlighting a document in the database view that you are searching and choosing Edit, Properties (or right-click and choose Document Properties). Notes displays the Document Properties info box for the document. Select the Fields tab. A list of all the fields appears in the left list box, as shown in Figure 17.12. As you select a field name, Notes displays in the right list box the design and contents of the field for the document that you selected. Reviewing this information should assist you in finding the appropriate field to use in this query.

Figure 17.12.

You can view the form's field design in the Fields page of the Document properties box for the document.

Task 17.2.7: Searching by Criteria in a Form

If your database is indexed, you can search for documents by entering criteria into any database form—as long as the database designer indicates that the Search Builder can display the form.

Before starting the search, make sure that the database is open to the view that you want to search. Then complete the following steps:

1. If the search bar is not visible, choose View, Search Bar.

2. Click the Add Condition button.

3. In the Condition drop-down list, select By Form. Notes displays the dialog box shown in Figure 17.13.

4. In the Form drop-down list, select the form that you want to use in the search; in Figure 17.13, the standard Memo form is used. All forms in the database appear in the drop-down list, unless the database developer specified that the forms not appear in the list.

Figure 17.13.

This query checks for the word WorldCom *in the memo's Subject field.*

5. In the selected database form, type entries (consisting of text, numbers, and so on) in as many defined fields as you want to include in the search. Your entries in each field define your search criteria. You type your entries into the form's fields just as if you were typing in a regular Notes document.

6. Choose OK.

7. Click the Search button on the search bar.

Notes searches for documents that include all the criteria that you entered in the fields.

Task 17.2.8: Searching for Documents Created with a Certain Form

If a database is indexed, you can use the Search Builder to find documents that were created by using a specific form. For example, you can create a query in a Marketing database to find only documents created using the Company form. Typically, you use this type of search when you know that a particular word or phrase appears in many different documents in a database, but you are interested only in information that one particular type of form might contain. For example, the word hotel might appear many times in a company travel database, but you are interested only in the instances of the word appearing in a Trouble Report form in the database, if you are preparing a report on all problems with hotels reported by employees.

Before conducting the search, make sure that the database is open to the view that you want to search. Then complete the following steps:

1. If the search bar is not visible, choose View, Search Bar.

2. Click the Add Condition button.

3. In the Condition drop-down list, select By Form Used. Notes displays the dialog box shown in Figure 17.14.

4. In the Forms list box, select one or more forms; a check mark appears next to each selected form.

5. Choose OK.

6. Click the Search button on the search bar.

Figure 17.14.

*This selection indicates
that you want to search
in the Company Profile
and Activity Report
forms.*

Task 17.3: Refining Your Search Results

Notes provides many ways to view and alter the results that you receive when you run a search
query. You can alter the order in which documents are displayed, use synonyms in your
search, change the maximum number of entries displayed, and save a search formula. You
make these settings through the search bar's Options button. When you refine your searches
by selecting the Options button before running the query, the menu in Figure 17.15 displays.

Figure 17.15.

*Clicking the search bar's
Options button enables
you to change the way
that Notes displays your
results.*

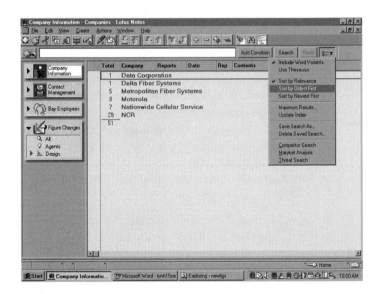

The following options are available in this drop-down menu:

☐ *Include Word Variants* tells Notes to include any words that have a base part that
matches your search criteria. For example, if you enter `training` as the search
criteria, Notes also finds any documents containing the word `train`. If you enter
`train`, Notes also displays `training`, `trained`, and so on.

☐ *Use Thesaurus* enables you to include synonyms of search words in your search. For example, if you search for documents that contain the word `doctor`, Notes also finds documents that contain the word `physician`. This selection remains active until you reset the Search Builder or exit the database.

☐ *Sort by Relevance* displays search results based on relevance—that is, the more times Notes finds the word or phrase in a document, the higher up in the list the document displays. By default, Notes uses this order to display search results in databases queried with the Full Text Search feature. You can ascertain the document's relevance in the search by looking to the left of the documents in the view. A vertical bar displays to indicate the relevance of each document to the search criteria (see Figure 17.16). The darker the portion of the bar, the more relevant the document.

☐ *Sort by Oldest First* displays the documents found in the search according to their compose date, displaying the oldest documents first. This sort order is ideal if you want to read a discussion on a topic from beginning to end.

17

Figure 17.16.

By default, search results are displayed in the view according to relevance.

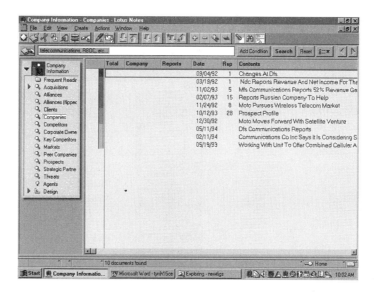

☐ *Sort by Newest First* displays the documents found in the search according to their compose date, with the newest documents displayed first. This sort order is ideal if you are looking for the latest information regarding a particular topic. For example, you might select this option when reviewing a database of customer contact reports to see the current report for a particular customer.

☐ *Maximum Results* enables you to determine the maximum number of documents that a search will accept in its results. The default setting is 250 documents, which is usually adequate. If you are interested in receiving only those documents that best suit your query and want to speed up the search process, reduce this setting.

☐ *Update Index* immediately updates the full-text index with any new documents added since the index was last updated.

☐ *Save Search As* enables you to save a search formula so that you can use it whenever you use the database in which you created it. If you have designer or manager access to the database on a server, you also can make the search formula available to anyone who uses the database. To do so, choose Shared Search in the Save Search As dialog box, as shown in Figure 17.17. Saved search formulas appear at the bottom of the Options menu in the search bar, as shown in Figure 17.18.

Figure 17.17.

You can save search formulas in the database in which you used them.

Figure 17.18.

Saved searches display at the bottom of the Options menu in the database in which you saved them.

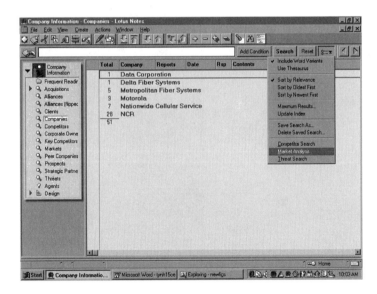

☐ *Delete Saved Search* enables you to remove saved search formulas. When you select this option, Notes displays the Delete Saved Search dialog box (see Figure 17.19). Select the saved search name that you want to remove and then choose Delete.

Figure 17.19.

To keep your menu list from becoming cluttered, you should delete old, saved queries that you no longer use.

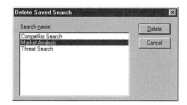

Notes displays a check mark next to selected items. After making your selections, click the Search button on the search bar to begin searching the database.

In addition to the methods that you have learned in the preceding sections for refining your queries, you also can use the following terms in your query field entries to further enhance your query capabilities.

If you choose Word, Sentence and Paragraph as Index Breaks when you create the full-text index, you can use the proximity operators to increase the relevance ranking of words that are close to each other. The following Proximity operators are available to you:

☐ *Near* specifies that the closer the words or phrases are to each other, the higher Notes ranks their relevance in the sort view. For example, if you enter Competitor near Threat in a query field, Notes sorts the documents in which these terms are closer to each other.

☐ *Sentence* works much the same as Near, but all the words or phrases must be in the same sentence. For example, if you enter **Competitor sentence Threat** in a query field, Notes sorts the documents that include both of these terms in the same sentence.

☐ *Paragraph* also works much the same as Near, but the words or phrases must all be in the same paragraph. For example, if you enter **Competitor paragraph Threat** in a query field, Notes sorts the documents with both of these terms in the same paragraph.

Workshop

In this hour, you have learned how to search for information in your Notes documents and databases by searching views and documents and by utilizing the powerful full-text index. You should be comfortable indexing your databases to make searching easier.

Key Terms

Review the following term:

☐ *Stop Word File* A list of words and numbers that you do *not* want to be included as part of the full-text index. DEFAULT.STP works well for most users, but you might want to consider adding your own name and company name to it, as these occur so often in your documents, it is a waste of time to search for them.

Common Questions

Q I replicated a database down from the server to my PC, but the full-text index is missing. What happened?

A Full-text indexes are not replicated. Each individual database must be indexed separately.

Q I entered a document in a database on the server and then immediately searched for it with the full-text index. It didn't find the document. What happened?

A Even though the indexing option on the server might be set to "Immediate," the server cannot stop everything else it does to index documents, or it would be doing very little else. The document will be added as soon as possible when higher-priority tasks have been completed. This could be a few seconds or a few minutes.

Preview of the Next Hour

In the next hour, you will continue to work with documents, this time learning about more advanced features, such as pop-ups, hotspots, horizontal rules, background images, and organizing your documents with folders.

Hour 18

Working with Advanced Document Features

Goals for This Hour

Continuing from the last hour, you are going to look at other tools that are available to help you manage your Notes documents. By the end of this hour, you will learn

- ☐ How to link documents, views, and databases
- ☐ How to use pop-ups and hotspots
- ☐ How to add horizontal rules and graphical backgrounds
- ☐ How to use folders to organize your documents

Task 18.1: Linking Documents

You often want to guide readers to other areas that contain information related to the topic about which they are currently reading. This could be a few pages down in the same document, or it could be in another document in another database. For example, if you are discussing the health benefits of broccoli, you might want to create a link to another document that contains a recipe for actually making the stuff edible! The link need not be in the same database, or even on the same server, as the document that you are reading.

The following types of links are available:

- ☐ *Document Anchors*   In a long document, you can set a Document Anchor to allow the reader to navigate to another part of the document (say, from the Table of Contents at the top of the document down to the particular chapter she is interested in). This much-requested feature (common on web pages) is new to version 4.6.

- ☐ *Documents*   Commonly known as *doclinks,* these take the reader to another document, which might be in another database and on another server.

- ☐ *Views*   These take the reader to a specific view in a database.

- ☐ *Databases*   Database links are often used in email to give users immediate access to new databases or to send a list of useful databases to a new employee.

Links look like pages of paper with their corners folded down, as shown in Figure 18.1. Associated with each link is a location, called the *link point,* within the link document. When the user clicks the link, Notes displays the link anchor, document, view, or database. When the user closes the link document, Notes returns to the original document that contained the link. This is not true, however, when a user clicks an anchor link that points to some other part of the *same* document. There is no way for Notes to backtrack to the position the user was in when he clicked the anchor link.

Creating a Document Anchor is slightly different from creating the other types of links. Because you can have several Document Anchors in the same document, you have to add these links and save the document you are linking to. Follow these steps to create a Document Anchor:

1. Open the document in Edit mode (Ctrl+E) and scroll through the document until you find the point you want to link to.

2. Choose Edit, Copy as Link, Anchor Link.

3. In the Anchor dialog box, accept the default name for this link or change it to something that's more meaningful to you. Click OK, and the Document Anchor icon appears in your document.

4. If you want to reference this anchor in the *same* document, skip to step 5; otherwise, save and close this document and open in Edit mode the document where you want to reference the anchor.

Figure 18.1.

Notes can link a document to other documents, views, or databases or to other parts of the same document.

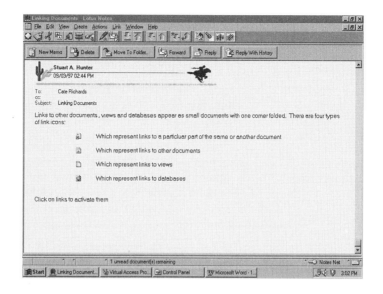

5. Scroll through the document until you reach the place where you want the link to appear.

6. Choose Edit, Paste or press Ctrl+V.

7. Save the document.

To create a document, view, or database link, complete the following procedure:

1. Start with one of the following:

   □ *For a document link,* open the link document (the document to which you want to link, which does not have to be in the same database) or highlight the link document in the view. Then select a link point by clicking within the document you want Notes to display when the doclink is activated.

   □ *For a view link,* open the view to which you want to link (the view does not have to be in the current database).

   □ *For a database link,* highlight the database to which you want to link by clicking its icon once.

2. Choose Edit, Copy as Link, and then specify whether the link you are creating is a Document link, View link, or Database link. Notes puts a link on the Clipboard that corresponds to the link point that you selected. In the status bar at the bottom of your Notes window, Notes indicates that it has copied the link to the Clipboard.

3. Open the document in which you want to insert the link. (You must open the document in Edit mode.)

18

4. Paste the link into any rich text field in the document just as you would a section of text. (Choose Edit, Paste or press Ctrl+V.)

5. Save the document.

Under the following circumstances, the links might not work for you when you try to use them:

☐ If the database ID or document ID referenced in the doclink is changed, the link will have to be re-created. This circumstance often occurs if a user copies a database to another server (instead of making a replica copy) and then deletes the original database. It can also happen if a user cuts the document from the linked database and then stores it in another database.

☐ If the user does not have access to the database, server, or directory on the server in which the referenced database is located, the link will not work. The user must have at least Read access.

☐ If the user does not have access to read the document referenced in the link, the link will not work. The database designer assigns the access when creating the form. The default read setting is All Users (meaning all users who have access to the database).

☐ If the user does not have the view access necessary to read the linked view, the link will not work. The database designer creates the access level for reading a view. The default is All Users (meaning all users who have access to the database).

☐ A remote user cannot use the link unless the referenced database is located on his hard drive or he is dialed out to a server hosting a copy of the database.

☐ You cannot create an anchor or document link from a document you are currently creating (both options will be grayed out in the Edit, Copy as Link menu). At that point the document has not been saved and, therefore, has no identity that the link can use to reference it. Save the document first, and then you can create a link from it.

If you click a link when working on the network, and the referenced database is not located on your workspace, Notes searches the servers to which you have access and adds the database icon to your workspace, opened to the link point.

Because a link is simply a set of numbers referencing the database ID and document ID, you can use a link in a message to have the recipient add a new database to her desktop and open the database to the referenced link point. When the recipient closes the database to which she has been linked, she will notice that Notes has added the database icon to her desktop. The database icon remains on the workspace page until the reader removes it.

Links offer an ideal way for database managers to assist users in accessing new databases. You might receive several messages that prompt you to click a link to add a new database when it is first deployed in a company.

Task 18.2: Adding Pop-Up Hotspots

If you want text to pop up whenever a user clicks and holds down the left mouse button on a particular hotspot, you can define a text pop-up hotspot. To do so, complete the following steps:

1. Make sure that the document is in Edit mode.

2. Select the area where you want to add the hotspot. (This might be text that you have typed or a graphic that you have pasted in from the Clipboard.) If you forget to highlight something before you create a pop-up hotspot, Notes prompts you to do so.

3. Perform one of the following actions:

   ☐ Choose Create, Hotspot, Text Popup and enter the text that you want to pop up. For example, suppose the developer of the database elected to include help information in the Field help line located at the bottom of the window. Although the help information is displayed when your cursor is in a particular field, sometimes the instructions are too long to fit in the Field help line. In such a case, you might type the information about that particular field in the Popup text box to appear over the field itself when your cursor is there. For an example of pop-up text, open the Connection document in your Personal Address Book. Although nothing looks out of the ordinary, if you click and hold your mouse button over any of the field labels, you will see some descriptive pop-up text.

   ☐ Choose Create, Hotspot, Formula Popup. In the programmer's pane, enter a formula that sets the text that you want to pop up. For example, you can set a formula that displays the reader history of the current document whenever the hotspot is selected. Try using @Username (which will display your name) or @Now (which will display the current date and time).

> If you have already entered the desired text in another Windows or OS/2 document, you can highlight the text and choose Edit, Copy to copy the text to the Clipboard. Then, with your cursor in the pop-up text field, press Ctrl+V to paste the text from the Clipboard. (The Edit, Paste command is not available when you are in a dialog box.) This technique offers a quick way to place a large amount of text in a pop-up. Note, however, that you cannot apply formatting and font attributes to pop-up text.

18

As mentioned previously, database designers most often use pop-ups to include additional help or reference information in a form's design. However, you can take advantage of the pop-up feature in the body of documents to limit the amount of information that a reader has to filter through to get to the information he needs.

For example, suppose you are working on a proposal and have been exchanging information about it (close dates, dollar amounts, and so forth) with your team. However, you also want to define some of the contract's terms for the readers, so you create a pop-up that defines the terms. If a reader needs a definition, he or she can access it; otherwise, the reader does not need to waste time reading through the definition and can continue reading the rest of the document.

> The online help database provides some great examples of the use of pop-up hotspots in documents and navigators.

Task 18.3: Adding Link Hotspots

You can add a hotspot that enables users to switch to another document, view, folder, or database. These link hotspots lead to other documents (as do the links you learned about in "Linking Documents," earlier in this chapter). The difference between a link and a link hotspot is in the appearance of the "trigger" that initiates the link.

When you create a link, you paste into a document an object that looks like a document. When you create a link hotspot, any area that you highlight serves as the trigger for making the link. For example, you could highlight a graphic of an airplane to have Notes link you to a policy on airline travel in another database.

To create a link hotspot, complete the following steps:

1. Perform one of these actions:

    ☐ In the View pane, click the document to which you want to link.

    ☐ In the Navigator pane, click the view or folder to which you want to link.

    ☐ In the workspace, click the database to which you want to link.

    ☐ In a document, click anywhere within the document to which you want to link.

2. Choose Edit, Copy as Link.

3. Open the document to which you want to add the hotspot. (Make sure that the document is in Edit mode.)

4. Highlight the area to which you want to add the hotspot. (This area can consist of text or a graphic).

5. Choose Create, Hotspot, Link Hotspot.

Task 18.4: Adding Action Hotspots

You can add a hotspot to an area of a document (such as text or a graphic) that enables users to perform a Notes action. For example, you can add a hotspot that creates a document you can type and send, such as a registration form in a training database. Although only applications developers typically use this feature, this section presents the steps for the process in case you find the urge to try it yourself.

Many of the Notes Release 4.x navigators provide good examples of action hotspots. They enable users to click a graphic to open a navigator, view, or document to read. Other examples in the help database include the action hotspots that are programmed for each of the book icons in the Navigator pane. Clicking a book opens another navigator and view for quick access to the information that you need the most.

To create an action hotspot, follow these steps:

1. Make sure that the document is in Edit mode.

2. Highlight the area to which you want to add the hotspot. (The area that you select can consist of text or a graphic.) If you don't highlight something before you try to create a hotspot, Notes prompts you to do so.

3. Choose Create, Hotspot, Action Hotspot. The Programmer pane appears, as shown in Figure 18.2.

18

Figure 18.2.

To create action hotspots, you must work in the Programmer pane.

4. In the Programmer pane, perform one of the following options:

☐ Specify a preprogrammed action that Notes includes by clicking the Simple Action(s) option button and clicking Add Actions. Then select an action, specify any settings that Notes needs in order to perform the action, and choose OK.

☐ To enter a formula that performs an action, click the Formula option button and enter the formula. The formula that you use can be a simple one (such as one that closes the database), or it can be quite complicated.

☐ To enter a script that performs an action, click the Script option button and enter the script. The script that you use can be a simple one (such as one that composes a document), or it can be quite complicated.

> Writing formulas and other development features is beyond this book's scope. If you want to learn how to develop applications, obtain a book on Notes application development, such as Que's *Special Edition Using Lotus Notes and Domino 4.6.*

5. Click anywhere within the document to close the Programmer pane and continue working.

You can remove the green border that surrounds a hotspot by highlighting the hotspot while you are in Edit mode or in the Programmer pane and choosing Edit, Properties. The Hotspot Button properties box appears, as shown in Figure 18.3.

Figure 18.3.

Use the Hotspot Button properties box to control how the document or form displays the hotspot.

Deselect the Show Border Around Hotspot check box. By making the appropriate selections in the hotspot's properties box, you can also change fonts, colors, and other text attributes; hide the hotspot; and specify paragraph formatting options.

To use a hotspot, click anywhere within its borders—unless you are using a pop-up hotspot. To use a pop-up hotspot, click anywhere within its borders and hold down the left mouse button. The text remains displayed as long as you hold down the mouse button.

Task 18.5: Computed Text Hotspots

Computed Text Hotspots allow you to display a piece of text in a document based on a formula. For example, suppose you're sending a piece of mail to 50 different people, but you would like it personalized so that when each of them opens the mail, it greets them by name. Computed Text recalculates every time you open the document so that what you see may be different every time.

To create a Computed Text hotspot, complete the following steps:

1. Make sure that the document is in Edit mode.
2. Position your cursor in the text where you want the Computed Text to appear.
3. Choose Create, Computed Text. The label "<Computed Text>" appears in your document, and the Programmer pane appears.
4. Enter a formula in the Programmer pane (see Figure 18.4).
5. Click anywhere within the document to close the Programmer pane. The Computed Text evaluates immediately.

Figure 18.4.

Entering a formula to create Computed Text.

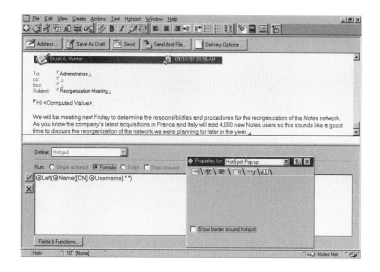

18

If you want to edit the Computed Text after you close the Programmer pane, click anywhere inside the Computed Text. Choose Hotspot, Edit Hotspot to open the Programmer pane so you can change your formula.

The Hotspot menu also allows you to change the properties of the Computed Text hotspot and to delete it. Note that if you delete the hotspot, the text in your document remains intact, it just ceases to be a Computed Text hotspot.

Task 18.6: Adding Horizontal Rules to Your Documents

If you are used to working with the World Wide Web, you have probably seen horizontal rules used on the screen to break up a document into sections. You can now add horizontal rules to your Notes documents (see Figure 18.5). To do this, carry out the following steps:

1. Make sure the document is in Edit mode.
2. Click in your document at the point where you want the rule to appear.
3. Choose Create, Horizontal Rule, and Notes inserts the default horizontal rule.
4. Double-click the rule, or right-click and select Horizontal Rule Properties to change the default settings (see Figure 18.6).
5. Save the document.

Figure 18.5.

You can display different kinds of horizontal rules in your document.

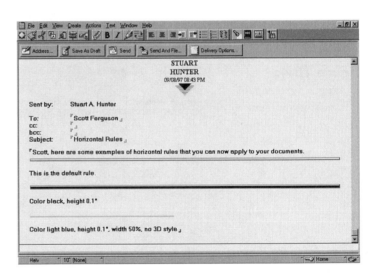

If you have Fit to Available Width selected and set to 100% (the default), when you resize the document window, Notes automatically resizes the rule to the width of the window.

To delete a rule you have placed in a document, click to select it and press the Delete key.

Figure 18.6.

You can change the height, width, color, and style of the horizontal rule.

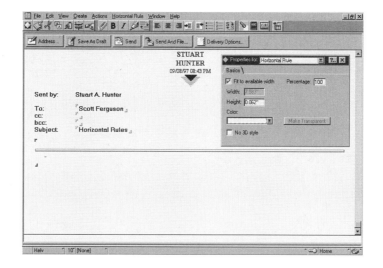

Task 18.7: Adding Backgrounds to Your Documents

Another feature added to Notes because of the influence of the World Wide Web is the capability to change the background color of a Notes document or to allow the use of background images. This feature may not be available in some databases because the application developer may have disabled it in order to present a uniform interface. However, you should be able to use this feature in your own mail file.

When you are creating or editing a document, click the Properties SmartIcon or select File, Document Properties. Then select the Background tab (see Figure 18.7).

To change the background color of the document, click the Background Color drop-down menu and select the desired color. If you are not satisfied with the color you choose, you can repeat the process to choose another color, or you can click the Reset to Form Color button to restore the document's original background color.

You can add a background graphic to your document in two ways. If you have previously copied a graphic to the Clipboard, you can use the Paste Graphic button to add the graphic to your document. Alternatively, if you have an image on disk that you want to use, you can click the Import Graphic button and select the file from the Import dialog box. You can choose between BMP, GIF, JPEG, PCX, and TIFF file types. When you've made your selection, click the Import button to add the image to your document. If you are unhappy with your choice, choose another image to import or click the Remove Graphic button. Figure 18.8 shows a mail message with a background image added.

Figure 18.7.

Changing the background properties of the document.

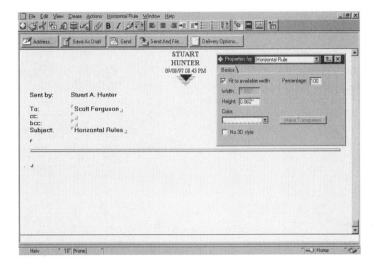

Figure 18.8.

A mail message enhanced with a background image.

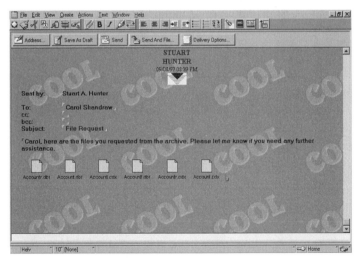

Task 18.8: Using Folders to Organize Your Documents

You can use existing folders in a database or create your own folders to organize your documents in a manner that makes sense to you. For example, in your Mail database, you might create a folder called "Hot Topics" to store memos on issues of great importance to you. (Creating such a folder is similar to selecting a category for the mail memo in Lotus Notes 3.x.)

When you find a document in a view that you want to store in your folder, simply click the document and drag it to the folder. When your mouse pointer is over the appropriate folder (when selected, the folder is highlighted by a box), release the mouse button, and Notes moves the document into the folder. If you click the folder, you can see that your document is in it. The following section continues your exploration into using folders.

Task 18.8: Creating Folders

Folders can take on the characteristics of views in the sense that you can copy the column design of the views so that they appear the same in a folder. For example, you can create a folder called "Executive Correspondence" and base the folder design on the database's People view, which sorts documents according to people's names.

To create a new folder, follow these steps:

1. Select or open the database in which you want to create the folder.

2. Choose Create, Folder (or Create, Design, Folder if you are not working in a view, as Notes will "hide" the Folder option if it thinks you don't need it). The Create Folder dialog box appears (see Figure 18.9).

18

Figure 18.9.

You can enter or edit the name of a folder in the Create Folder dialog box.

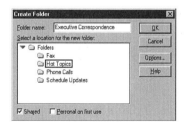

3. Enter a name for the folder in the Folder Name text box. The name should be descriptive and can contain any characters; however, the text box limits the number of characters that you can type (the maximum is between 14 and 26 characters, depending on the capitalization you use).

4. If you want to place the folder inside another existing folder, click that folder in the Select a Location for the New Folder list. This list varies depending on whether you create a private folder (the default) or choose the Shared check box (as discussed in the following note).

> If you have been granted appropriate access by the developer, you have the option of choosing the Shared check box to tell Notes that you want everyone who uses the database to have access to this folder.

5. Choose OK. Notes creates the folder and displays it in the navigator according to your selected options.

If you want to select a view or folder on which to base the folder's design, follow these steps:

1. Perform steps 1 and 2 of the previous instructions. In the Create Folder dialog box, select the folder you want to affect and choose the Options button. The Options dialog box appears (see Figure 18.10).

Figure 18.10.

Select the view design that you want your folder's design to inherit.

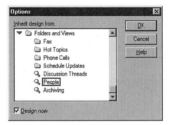

2. Click a view or folder in the Inherit Design From list. If you want to change the folder's design as soon as the folder is created, choose the Design Now check box. When you choose OK to create the folder, Notes automatically opens its Design pane.

3. Choose OK.

Task 18.9: Deleting Folders

Occasionally, you might find that you no longer need a particular folder in your database and don't want it cluttering up your navigators. You can easily delete a folder (if you have the appropriate access) by performing the following steps:

1. In the Navigator pane, select the folder that you want to delete.

2. Choose Actions, Folder Options, Delete Folder.

3. Click Yes when prompted to delete the folder.

Notes removes the folder from your navigator but does not delete the documents that were stored within the deleted folder. To see these documents, you can switch to any view designed to display them.

You can also delete a folder by highlighting the folder's name in the folder navigator, pressing F6, and then pressing the Delete key. Click Yes when prompted to delete the folder.

Task 18.10: Renaming Folders

Occasionally, you might want to rename a folder to better define its contents. You can do so by selecting the folder that you want to rename and then choosing Actions, Folder Options, Rename. The Rename dialog box appears, as shown in Figure 18.11. Type the new folder name in the Name text box, and then choose OK.

Figure 18.11.

You can also open the Rename dialog box by selecting the folder you want to rename, pressing F6, and choosing Actions, Rename.

18

Task 18.11: Moving Documents In and Out of Folders

You can move a document to a folder by clicking the document in a view and dragging the document to the folder in which you want to store it. Alternatively, you can select all the documents that you want to move to the folder by clicking in the left margin next to the documents' titles (a check mark appears next to each one) and then choosing Actions, Move to Folder. Notes prompts you to select the folder to which you want to move the documents, as shown in Figure 18.12. Select the folder's name, and then choose Move.

Figure 18.12.

You select which folder you want to move documents into by highlighting the folder and choosing Move.

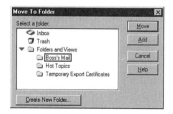

Moving a document to a folder does not remove the document from a view; if you return to the view that originally displayed the document, that view still displays the document.

You can remove a document from a folder by clicking the document and choosing Actions, Remove from Folder. To remove multiple documents, place a check mark next to each document in the marker column, and then choose Actions, Remove from Folder. Notes removes the selected documents from the folder, but it doesn't delete the documents from the database; if you switch back to a view designed to display the documents, you can still see them.

Do not select the documents and press the Delete key; do not send the documents to the trash; and do not choose Edit, Clear. All of these actions delete the documents permanently from Notes. Unlike selecting documents to remove from a folder, these actions permanently delete the documents from the database.

Workshop

Having completed this hour, you should feel comfortable creating links to documents, views, and databases. You have learned how to create pop-ups that make your documents more informative, and you know how to create and use folders to better organize your documents. Here are a few of the words you should be familiar with and some common questions that you may have.

Key Terms

Review the following list of terms:

☐ *Document Anchor* If you are a user of the World Wide Web, you are probably used to being able to click on an URL that takes you to another part of the same document (perhaps linking from a table of contents at the top of the document down to the desired section). Notes has always been able to link between *different* documents via doclinks, but now Notes has Document Anchors that you can use to perform the same type of linking you perform on the Web.

☐ *Hotspot* Although there are different kinds of hotspots, all hotspots have one thing in common: When you click a hotspot, something happens. Notes might display some pop-up text, perform a calculation, or display a view.

Common Questions

Q **Can I send a link to someone who doesn't have physical access to the server I created the link from?**

A This is one of the great things about Notes replication. If the user who receives the link has a replica copy of the database in question on her own server, yes, she will be able to retrieve the linked document, view, or database. If she does not have a replica copy, she will not be able to retrieve the link.

Q **I deleted a document from one folder, and it has also disappeared from other folders I had copied it to. What happened?**

A If you want to remove a document from a folder without affecting the document in any other folder, you have to use the Actions, Remove from Folder command. Remember, Notes does not store multiple copies of the same document; one document just appears in different folders. If you delete the document from any folder, it is gone and will not appear in any other folder or view.

Preview of the Next Hour

This hour you learned how to enhance the appearance of your documents by using horizontal rules and graphical backgrounds. In the next hour, you will discover how tables and sections can also enhance the appearance and functionality of your documents.

18

Hour 19

Utilizing Tables and Sections Within Documents

Goals for This Hour

In addition to the advanced document features you have just read about, there are two more useful features that deserve special attention. Tables enable you to present structured data by using rows and columns and lines and colors that help make sense of the information. Sections enable you to collapse blocks of text under a meaningful heading that the reader can expand if it is considered relevant.

In this hour, you should expect to learn about the following:

- ☐ Creating a table
- ☐ Adding, deleting, and appending rows and columns
- ☐ Using borders and colors
- ☐ Splitting and merging cells
- ☐ Creating a section
- ☐ Changing a section title
- ☐ Deleting a section

Task 19.1: Creating Tables in Documents

To create a new table, position the insertion point in the rich text field where you want the table to appear and then choose Create, Table. Notes opens the Create Table dialog box shown in Figure 19.1.

Figure 19.1.

In the Create Table dialog box, enter the number of rows and columns for your table.

In the Create Table dialog box, enter the number of rows and columns that you want your table to include. Notes immediately creates a table in your document with the specified numbers of rows and columns. Also, the menu bar at the top of the Notes window adds a new Table menu command. Use this menu command to control the attributes of the table that you are creating.

At any time, you can add and delete columns and rows from a table or change the cell widths, borders, and other table attributes. The following sections provide details.

Task 19.2: Adding and Deleting Columns in Tables

If you need to add a single column to the right side of the table, select Table, Append Column. To add a new column inside your existing table, click where you want to add the column and then choose Table, Insert Column. Notes adds another column to your table to the left of your cursor location.

Figure 19.2.

When you choose Table, Insert Special, Notes enables you to add multiple columns or rows to your table at one time.

If you want to add multiple columns to your table, click where you want to add the columns and choose Table, Insert Special. Notes displays the Insert Row/Column dialog box shown in Figure 19.2.

In the text box, type the number of columns you want to add. Then, choose Column(s). Next, choose from among the following options:

☐ *Insert* adds the specified number of columns to the left of the current location of the cursor.

☐ *Append* adds the specified number of columns to the table's far-right side.

☐ *Cancel* enables you to exit the dialog box without adding any columns.

☐ *Help* accesses the Notes online help.

You also can delete columns from your table by placing your cursor in a column that you want to remove and choosing Table, Delete Selected Column(s). Notes prompts you to confirm that you want to delete the column. Choose Yes.

You also can delete multiple columns by placing your cursor in the first column of the table that you want to delete and then choosing Table, Delete Special. Choose Column(s) and specify how many columns you want to remove. After making your selections, choose Delete. Notes removes the current column and any additional columns to its right, according to the number of columns you specified.

Task 19.3: Adding and Deleting Rows in Tables

If you simply need to add a single row to the bottom of the table, select Table, Append Row. To add a new row inside your existing table, click where you want to add the row. Choose Table, Insert Rows. Notes adds another row above your current cursor location. If you want to add multiple rows to your table, click where you want to add the rows and choose Table, Insert Special. In the text box, type the number of rows that you want to add and then choose Row(s). Next, choose from the following options:

☐ *Insert* adds the specified number of rows above the current location of the cursor.

☐ *Append* adds the specified number of rows to the bottom of the table.

19

    ☐ *Cancel* enables you to exit without adding any columns.

    ☐ *Help* accesses the Notes online help.

You can delete rows from your table by placing your cursor in the rows that you want to remove and choosing Table, Delete Selected Rows(s). Notes prompts you to confirm that you want to delete the row. Choose Yes.

You also can delete multiple rows by placing your cursor in the first row that you want to delete and then choosing Table, Delete Special. Choose Row(s) and specify how many rows you want to remove. When you have made your selections, choose Delete. Notes removes the current rows and any additional rows below the current one, according to the number of rows you specified.

Task 19.4: Changing Table Attributes

You can change your table's appearance by changing border attributes, the column width, the spacing between the columns and rows, and cell colors, by splitting or joining cells or by adjusting the margin settings. To change these attributes, place your cursor in the first column or row that you want to modify—or, if you want to modify multiple cells, select the first cell, click and hold down your left mouse button, and drag the cursor over all the cells that you want to modify—and choose Table, Table Properties. The Table properties box's Borders page displays, as shown in Figure 19.3.

Figure 19.3.

By changing your table's borders in the Table properties box's Borders page, you can add pizzazz to your table and highlight important information.

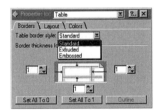

You can specify border widths ranging from 0 (no border) to 10 (thickest border) for each side of the cell's border. You can also specify whether you want the table border to be one of the following:

    ☐ *Standard*, which is a plain black line

    ☐ *Extruded*, a "pushed-in," three-dimensional effect

    ☐ *Embossed*, a raised 3-D effect

To change border settings (the thickness of the lines and the appearance surrounding your table's cells), complete the following steps:

1. Select the cell(s) you want to modify.

2. In the Table properties box's Borders page, do one of the following:

   ☐ To change the Table border style, click the drop-down arrow selection indicator and select Standard, Extruded, or Embossed. This selection affects all cells of the table, not just the cells that you have highlighted.

   ☐ To set the border on one or more sides, select the up/down arrow next to each Border Thickness for Current Selection Setting option and increase or decrease each border's width.

   ☐ To set the border on all sides to single, click Set All To 1.

   ☐ To remove the border from all sides, click Set All To 0.

   ☐ To set the outline of the cells that you have highlighted to a particular thickness or style, click Outline and then select any of the other available options.

3. If necessary, select another cell in the table and repeat steps 1 and 2 until you have all the cell's borders as you want them.

4. Close the dialog box.

> To change borders for the outer sides of the table only, select the entire table by dragging your mouse over it and then clicking the Outline button in the Table properties box. Then, select the border styles and settings for each side of the table. This feature makes framing your table with a special border setting easy. You also can highlight the entire table and remove the border or select border styles that affect the entire table, including each individual cell's borders.

19

To adjust the margins, column width, and spacing between rows and columns, click the Layout tab while viewing the Table properties box. Notes displays the Table properties box's Layout page, as shown in Figure 19.4.

Figure 19.4.

Adjusting margins, spacing, and column width adds impact to your tables.

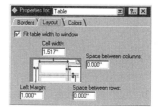

The following are the settings that you can control:

☐ *Fit Table Width to Window* tells Notes to always adjust the column widths proportionately to fit within the current size window. This setting enables the table's readers to easily see all the columns, regardless of the current window size.

> Large tables can sometimes be difficult to read unless you select the Fit Table Width to Window setting, because the user has to scroll back and forth in the window to see all the information.
>
> Also, tables can sometimes be difficult to read on different platforms, screen sizes, or resolutions. When creating tables in documents, keep in mind other users who might want to read the documents in which you have created tables.

☐ *Left Margin* enables you to indent your table beyond the default margin of the field you are creating your table in. You simply enter a larger number in this field. Notes moves the left margin of the table accordingly.

☐ *Space Between Rows* and *Space Between Columns* enable you to specify how much blank space Notes displays between the text and the cell's borders. The default is zero.

☐ *Cell Width* enables you to specify the width of the cells in each column. You can make the setting for the current cell's column and then click another cell to adjust its width.

To add color to any of the cells in your table, highlight the cells and click the Colors tab in the Table Properties box. The Colors page then appears, as shown in Figure 19.5. Select the color from the Background Color drop-down list. Notes fills the cells with your selected color. Click the Apply to Entire Table button if you want the selected color to fill all the table's cells. You also can click Make Transparent to remove the color from any selected cells.

Figure 19.5.

Notice that Notes has filled in the table's top row of cells with black to emphasize the table's column headings. This example is just one use for adding color to your tables.

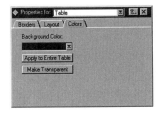

When you have made all your adjustments, close the Table Properties box to continue working with your table.

 Large tables in documents tend to slow down the PC's response time when reading and printing documents. Keep this in mind when deciding to insert a table.

Task 19.5: Merging and Splitting Cells

Joining and splitting cells provide you with the capability to create online forms that look more like the paper copies you might be used to. Joining a group of cells across the top of the form, for example, enables you to create a title for the table that can be centered across the table. The capabilities also enable you to more accurately duplicate in Notes the design of many simple paper forms.

To merge cells, follow these steps:

1. Highlight the cells that you want to join.
2. Choose Table, Merge Cells, as shown in Figure 19.6.

Figure 19.6.

You can join cells to highlight portions of your tables.

19

 You must highlight more than one cell before the Merge Cells menu command is available for you to use.

Notes merges the cells into one. If you have text in any of the cells, Notes displays the combined text from the single cells in the new cell created.

To split cells, follow these steps:

1. Place your cursor in the cell that you want to split.

The cell that you want to split must be a previously merged cell before the Split Cells command is available for you to use.

2. Choose Table, Split Cell.

Notes splits the highlighted cell into two cells and copies any text in the merged cell into one of the new cells.

Task 19.6: Entering Data in a Table

Suppose that you need to represent revenue figures for each of the four quarters and for each of your company's three business units, along with totals. At first, you might think that you want a table with four columns and four rows, but an extra row and column would enable you to label each month and business unit. Therefore, you enter **5** as the number of rows and **5** as the number of columns. When you click OK, Notes creates the table.

You can enter data in the new table just as you can anywhere in the document. Figure 19.7 shows what the table might look like after you enter data into the cells (but before adjusting its characteristics to make it more attractive). In this example, the data was typed individually into each cell, including the totals. If the table had been part of the form's design, a formula could be designed to add the numbers automatically in the Total row.

Figure 19.7.

Although this table communicates information correctly, it is bland and does not highlight important information.

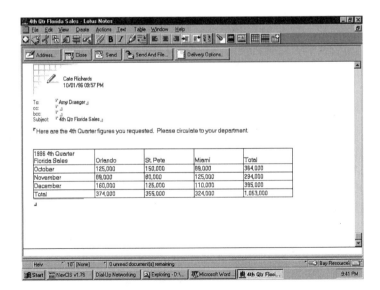

After designing the table set, you can adjust the borders, cell widths, and other text-formatting characteristics to add impact and highlight information to which you want to draw the reader's attention. Figure 19.8 displays the same table shown in Figure 19.7 but formatted to enhance the presentation of information. Notice that it is a little easier to read. You will see this table once again in Figure 19.10 with additional text enhancements to make it complete.

Figure 19.8.

You can use table settings to highlight text in a document.

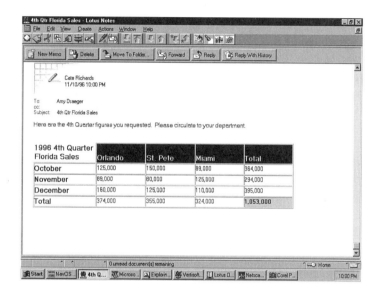

As you enter data into a table, keep the following points in mind:

☐ You can move around within a table by using the arrow keys just as you can move anywhere within the document. Within a table, however, you also can press Tab to move from one cell to the next and press Shift+Tab to move to the preceding cell (that is, the cell to the left or, if you are at the beginning of a row, the last cell on the preceding row).

☐ If you enter text that is too wide for the cell, the cell expands into as many lines as necessary to hold the text as the text wraps around when it meets the cell's width.

☐ If you enter a single word that is too long to fit in a cell, Notes expands the cell's height and splits the word. Notes never increases the cell's width to accommodate long words. If a word is too long to fit, type a hyphen and then press Enter to divide the word correctly. When you press Enter, Notes adjusts the cell's height to accommodate the additional line.

19

Task 19.7: Creating a One-Cell Table

You can highlight text in a document to emphasize a point by creating a table that has one cell and one column, as shown in Figure 19.9. In this example, the author created a one-cell table with the right and bottom borders defined as 2, while the top and left borders were left defined as 1. These settings yield a shadowing effect that adds some pizzazz to your documents.

Figure 19.9.

You can use a one-cell table as a border around text in a document.

After creating the one-cell table, you can enter text into the box. Notes will not put a box around text that has already been typed. Therefore, if you want to try this feature with previously entered text, you must first create the table and then cut and paste the text into it.

Task 19.8: Changing Table Text Characteristics

You can change many characteristics of the table text at any time, just as you can with any text. You can use the Text menu settings and the Text Properties box to change the color, size, and other font attributes for the table's text.

You can't set tabs in Tables directly. Rather, pressing the Tab key moves you from one table cell to the next.

You also can change the justification of an entire column or row. To do so, highlight the columns or rows for which you want to set justification, and choose Text, Align Paragraphs. You can specify whether the entire column or row should be left-justified, right-justified, centered, or full (you cannot specify None in tables). In Figure 19.10, the columns of numbers are right-justified so that the numerals line up properly.

Figure 19.10.

You can align text in tables and modify table settings to improve the table's readability. The information in this table is the same as that shown in Figure 19.8, but the text has been formatted to enhance its presentation.

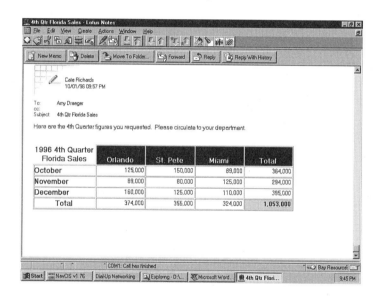

19

Task 19.9: Creating Sections in Documents

You can use sections to collapse one or more paragraphs in a document into a single line that is called the section title. To see more detail than that displayed on the section title, the reader can click the section indicator (down arrow) next to the section title to expand the section and reveal more information. Sections make navigation in large documents easier.

Readers can expand a section when they want to read its contents or can ignore the section if it does not apply to them. When designing forms, database designers can create hide-when formulas to provide logic that determines when Notes displays a particular section. In this section, you learn how to create sections in documents.

To create a collapsible section, you must be in a rich text field.

Figure 19.11 shows a document announcing an upcoming meeting. The document includes sections. One section, "Directions to Roy Rogers," has been expanded to display further information. The twistie to the left of the section title tells you that the section is collapsible.

Figure 19.11.

Collapsible sections can make navigating through documents easier for the reader.

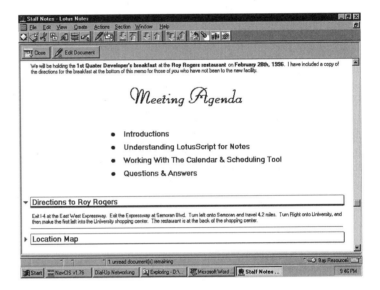

To create a section, perform the following steps:

1. Highlight the paragraphs, graphics, and other information that you want to collapse into a section.

2. Choose Create, Section. Notes immediately collapses the section and displays the first line of text as the section's title. If the first few lines that you highlighted were blank, your section heading will pick up the first line of text. If the block that you highlight contains no text at all, then the section will be headed "Untitled Section."

Task 19.10: Changing a Section's Title

If you want to edit the title of a collapsed section after creating or changing any of its other attributes, click anywhere within the collapsed section's title and choose Edit, Properties, or right-click in the section title and choose Section Properties from the pop-up menu. Notes displays the Section Properties box, as shown in Figure 19.12.

> If you do not see the Section Properties box when you choose Edit, Properties, click the section's title again in the document. Notes switches the open Properties box to display the section's information.

Figure 19.12.

You can change titles of collapsible sections in the Section Properties box.

In the info box's Title page, you can change the section title by clicking the Title text box and typing your section's title. You also can select the Formula option button and have Notes compute the section's title based on a formula that you enter. After entering the section's title, you can select the border style and color from the drop-down list boxes at the bottom of the info box.

Task 19.11: Controlling How Notes Displays the Sections

Notes also gives you control over the way the collapsible sections appear when you first open the document. With the Section properties box open, click the Expand/Collapse tab. Notes displays the Expand/Collapse page shown in Figure 19.13.

The Expand/Collapse page provides the following options for each mode that the document is in, whether Previewed, Opened for Reading, Opened for Editing, or Printed:

☐ *Don't Auto Expand or Collapse* displays the section in the state that you left it the last time that you saved the document.

☐ *Auto Expand Section* always expands the section.

☐ *Auto Collapse Section* always collapses the section.

Figure 19.13.

You can control how Notes displays the collapsible sections when you open or print the document.

You also can select the check box Hide Title when Expanded if you don't want the section title to display when the section expands. You also can select the check box Preview Only if you want the section feature active only when previewing a document. In any other mode, the expand and collapse capabilities are unavailable and the section title does not display. In fact, if the section is collapsed, you won't even know it is there!

> Selecting Auto Expand Section is often useful when printing, regardless of how you want documents viewed online. This selection ensures that your printout includes all the data on the form. Also, you should not include required fields (fields in which users must enter data before they can save the form) in sections that collapse automatically. Hiding such a field might frustrate users when they try to save the form and discover required fields of which they were unaware.

Task 19.12: Deleting Sections

Sometimes you might not want to keep the section setting in your document. For example, you may not want to keep the collapsible section that you created when you selected Reply with History in your email database; some users would rather see only the section's contents. If you decide that you don't want a collapsible section in your document, you can easily remove it—as long as it is not part of the form's design. To remove a section, click the section title and choose Section, Remove Section. Notes prompts you that this operation cannot be undone; select Yes. Notes removes the section but leaves all the text, graphics, and other objects in the document.

Workshop

Having finished this hour, you should be comfortable with the creation of tables and sections, both designed to make your documents easier to read and more informative. You have discovered how to manipulate your tables by adding and deleting rows and columns, and by changing the lines and colors of the cells within the table itself. You know how sections are created and how you can change their names or the way they look, and also how to delete them altogether. Following are some of the terms this hour introduced you to and some common questions.

Key Terms

Review the following list of terms:

- ☐ *Table* A grid made up of rows and columns for presenting tabular data.
- ☐ *Cell* The box that is formed where a column and row meet, usually used to store a single item of information.
- ☐ *Border* The lines that run around and define a cell.
- ☐ *Section* A block of text that can be collapsed and expanded under a section title.
- ☐ *Section Title* The text used as a header for a section. A twistie to the left of the section title allows you to expand and collapse the text within.

Common Questions

Q Can I change column widths by using my mouse?

A Yes, you can. Switch on the ruler by choosing View, Ruler. As you click in the cells of different columns, the column boundaries and the text margins appear in the ruler. Clicking and dragging the column boundaries (vertical bars) changes the boundary for the whole column. Clicking and dragging the text margins (triangles) affects only the current or selected cells.

Q Can I place tabs in a cell?

A Not directly. If you create text that contains tabs elsewhere in your document, however, you can copy that text to the clipboard and then paste it into a cell and the tabs will be honored.

Preview of the Next Hour

Next, you are going to learn about the powerful Calendaring & Scheduling functionality built into Notes. Keep yourself on-track with appointments, events and reminders. Invite others to meetings and check if they are free. Examine your commitments on a daily, weekly, or monthly schedule.

19

Hour 20

Working with Notes Calendaring and Scheduling

Goals for This Hour

For years, standalone personal information managers (PIMs), such as Lotus Organizer, have helped people better organize and schedule their time and priorities. However, the fundamental problem with these tools has been their inability to share information in a workgroup. To be truly effective, group scheduling has to be able to deal with people who are geographically disparate and not necessarily connected via the same LAN. If you've ever tried to schedule a meeting, particularly in a large company or with employees who are frequently on the road, you know the frustration of not being able to contact key people.

This hour covers the following:

- ☐ Creating calendar and delegation profiles
- ☐ Scheduling and viewing your appointments, invitations, events, reminders, and anniversaries

With the native Notes group C & S tools, Lotus revolutionizes the way your organization handles calendaring and scheduling. This chapter introduces the concepts of Group C & S and demonstrates how to use Notes for C & S in your workgroup.

Task 20.1: Creating a Calendar Profile

To maximize the usefulness and functionality of Notes C & S, you must create a Calendar Profile that defines how you want to use C & S. To create a Calendar Profile, open your Notes mailbox and choose Actions, Calendar Tools, Calendar Profile. Alternatively, if you attempt to create a Calendar Entry without first defining a Calendar Profile, you are prompted to create a Calendar Profile first. Figure 20.1, which represents three screens, displays a Calendar Profile document.

The first field on the form, Mail File Owner, tells Notes to whom this profile belongs. It defaults to the user name on the ID in use when the document is composed and enables you to choose a different user from the Public Address Book.

Below that there is a button called *Allow other users to view your calendar*. This button takes you to the Delegation Profile that enables you to decide who can access your calendar and what actions they can perform there. The Delegation Profile is described in the next section.

> Allowing others to see your calendar is very different from allowing others to see your free time. Be careful with this selection. If you allow others to see your calendar, they can see appointments you enter into your calendar, except for those you specifically mark as "Not for public viewing." You also can give people access to your mail; however, be careful when considering who can have this privilege.

The Scheduling Options section contains a number of fields that enable you to configure your scheduling defaults. The first field, *Default Appointment/Meeting Duration*, is for setting a default value for meeting length in minutes, meaning that for each new appointment you create, its length is set to the default value you enter here. It defaults to 60 minutes. The next field, *Enable Alarm Notifications*, is a check box that acts as a toggle switch for setting Alarms. When this feature is checked, it tells Notes to scan your calendar for appointments that have alarms so you can be notified. If you have checked the *Enable Alarm Notification* option, the *Automatically Set Alarm(s) for* option becomes enabled so that you can set alarms and set default values for each type of appointment. The usage of these fields is self-explanatory.

The Freetime Options section enables you to define who can access your free-time information and what days and time ranges should be considered when calculating your free time.

Figure 20.1.

You use the Calendar Profile document to define your usage of Notes C & S.

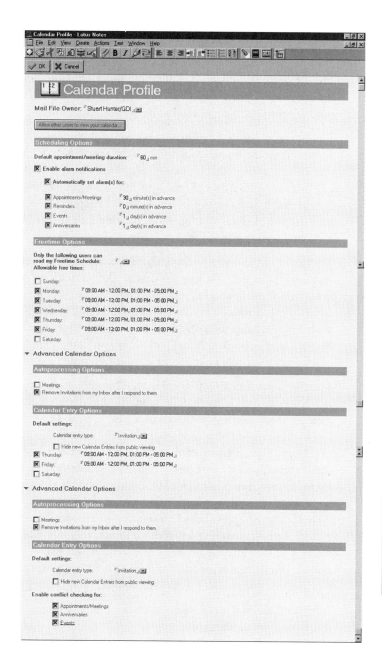

The first field, *Only the Following Users Can Read My Freetime Schedule,* is a keyword field that pulls up a dialog box, displaying users from your Address Book. Just select the users who should be able to access your free-time information. To enable a day for which a meeting can be scheduled, simply check its box and enter the times you are available. For example, if you don't want to be scheduled for Saturday meetings, do not check the Saturday check box.

The expandable section, *Advanced Calendar Options*, contains two additional sections, *Autoprocessing Options* and *Calendar Entry Options*, each of which enables settings that can make Group C & S more productive for you.

The Autoprocessing Options section contains options that enable you to automatically process items in your calendar. Currently, you can only autoprocess meetings. To do so, check the Meetings check box and choose the people you want to autoprocess from the keyword list Autoprocess Meetings Only from the Following People. You can click the Remove Invitations from My Inbox After I Respond to Them check box to tell Notes to automatically delete invitations from your mailbox after you have accepted the invitation to a meeting, saving you the time of having to look for invitations and delete them manually.

The final section, *Calendar Entry Options*, is subdivided into two categories: *Default Settings* and *Enable Conflict Checking For*. In the *Default Settings Options*, the *Calendar Entry Type* field enables you to choose from the different kinds of calendar entry so that each time you create a new appointment, it sets to the type chosen here. For example, if you tend to have more appointments than meetings, you might want to change the default from Meeting to Appointment. The *Hide New Calendar Entries from Public Viewing* check box tells Notes to enable only users explicitly named in your Delegation Profile to view your calendar entries.

The *Enable Conflict Checking For* section contains a series of check boxes that enable you to tell Notes to check for conflicts on certain types of appointments. Your choices are appointments/meetings, anniversaries, and events. To enable any of the options, place a check in the respective box and Notes checks for scheduling conflicts when you create any of these types of calendar entries. If a conflict is detected, a dialog appears, warning you of the conflict. You have the option to schedule the entry anyway, in which case the conflicting entries appear in the Calendar with a red bar to the left of the conflicting entries. You might be tempted to enable conflict checking for all calendar entry types, but you should consider this carefully for types such as Anniversaries and Events. For example, if you schedule an event because you are attending a two-day seminar, you will receive conflict warnings when you attempt to schedule the times for the lectures you will be attending during that two-day period. Likewise, a conflict warning would be inappropriate when scheduling a business meeting that happens to fall on your daughter's birthday.

After you have set your desired options, save the document, and your Notes client will begin using your new configuration.

After setting your options, save the document. Your Notes client then begins using your new configuration.

Task 20.2: Creating a Delegation Profile

If you travel much or work as part of a closely knit team, you often might need someone else to read and respond to your mail and schedule. Notes adds this capability through delegation, the feature that enables you to provide access to your mailbox to a user or group that you specify.

To enable delegation, you must create a Delegation Profile. To do so, open your Notes mailbox and choose Actions, Mail Tools, Delegation Profile. Figure 20.2 displays a Delegation Profile.

Figure 20.2.

In the Delegation Profile form, you tell Notes who can access your mailbox.

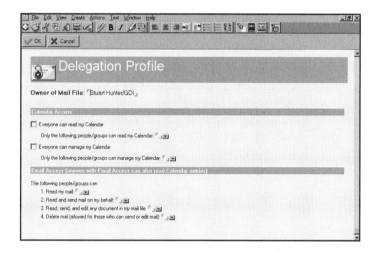

The first editable section, *Calendar Access*, contains calendar delegation options. If you'd like everyone to be able to read your calendar, click the *Everyone Can Read My Calendar* check box, which will hide the *Only the Following People/Groups Can Read My Calendar* field. If you want only specific users to access your calendar, use the *Only the Following People/Groups Can Read My Calendar* field to select people or groups who should have access. As you might expect, the *Everyone Can Read My Calendar* and the *Only the Following People/Groups Can Read My Calendar* fields are mutually exclusive.

You also can allow other Notes users to manage your calendar. If you'd like everyone to be able to manage your calendar (this is not recommended), click the *Everyone Can Manage My Calendar* check box, which will hide the *Only the Following People/Groups Can Manage My Calendar* field. If you want only specific users to access your calendar (this is the better choice), such as an assistant, you can use the *Only the Following People/Groups Can Read My Calendar* to select people or groups who should have access. As you might expect, the *Everyone Can Manage My Calendar* and the *Only the Following People/Groups Can Manage My Calendar* fields are mutually exclusive.

20

> There is a big difference between read and manage access to your calendar. If you grant manage access to everyone, anyone can add, edit, or delete your appointments. You should use that level of access judiciously.

The second section, *Email Access,* enables you to define people or groups that can access your mailbox. The first thing you should notice is that anyone you grant email access automatically has calendar access. You can use these four fields to control a number of email access options:

☐ *Read My Mail*   Used to select a list of users who can read mail in your mailbox.

☐ *Read and Send Mail on My Behalf*   When users or groups are named in this field, they will not only be allowed to read mail but also send mail on your behalf. It is denoted on the mail, however, that they sent the mail for you.

☐ *Read, Send, and Edit Any Document in My Mail File*   Enables users named in this field to not only read and send mail but also to edit any type of message in your mailbox. This is a very powerful delegation and should be given judiciously.

☐ *Delete Mail*   Enables you to name users who can delete mail from your mailbox. Notice that if you have given people/groups send or edit access, they receive this access by default.

> As long as your mailbox's access control list is set correctly, you will have no worries. Only the people you name in the Email Access section will have access. If you don't specify any users, only you can read your mail.

After you create a Calendar Profile and a Delegation Profile (if necessary), you are ready to begin using Notes Calendaring and Scheduling to manage your time and the time of your colleagues.

Task 20.3: Creating a Calendar Entry

When you are ready to schedule a meeting, open your mailbox and choose Create, Calendar Entry or from the Calendar view, click the *New Entry* button on the Action bar. This launches a new Calendar Entry form, as shown in Figure 20.3. The default type is *Invitation* unless you change this in your Calendar Profile.

> You also can create a calendar entry from any mail message that you have in your mail file. To do so, select a document in any view in your mail file, or open the document. Select Actions, Copy Into, New Calendar Entry.

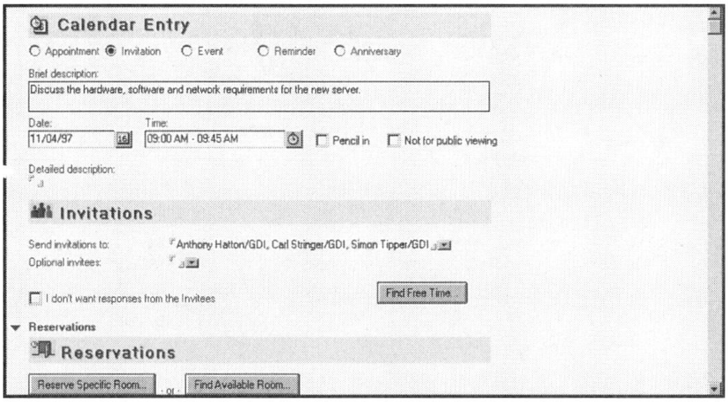

Figure 20.3.

*The Invitation-type
Calendar Entry with
invitees selected.*

The first thing you'll notice about this form is a series of five option buttons that you can use to choose the type of entry you'd like to create. As you work with the calendar entries, notice that each of the five form types has many overlapping fields, but each has fields specific to the purpose of the form. Because there are differences between the forms, each one is examined individually. Your choices are as follows:

☐ Appointments are used to add meetings to your schedule.

☐ Invitations enable you to create an appointment and invite other people/groups to the meeting. They will receive an invitation by email.

☐ Events are used to denote special meetings, such as a trade show or presentation, to your schedule.

☐ Reminders are added to your calendar to help you remember to do something. They can work hand-in-hand with anniversaries, for example, to help you remember to purchase an anniversary present for your spouse.

☐ Anniversaries are used to enter recurring events, such as birthdays, wedding anniversaries, and holidays, to your schedule.

Task 20.4: Scheduling Appointments

Creating an appointment is simple. Click the Appointment option button, and the Calendar Entry form displays the fields shown in Figure 20.4.

The first field, *Brief Description*, is used to enter the text that describes the appointment. It is displayed like a mail message subject in the views and folders in your mailbox, so it's important to enter a description that makes sense.

The *Date* and *Time* fields are relatively self-explanatory: They are used to store the date and time of the appointment. The *Date* field defaults to the current date, and the *Time* field defaults to the current time. However, pay special attention to these fields, as they implement two of the controls that Lotus has added from the award-winning Lotus Organizer—the Date control and the Time control.

Figure 20.4.

The Appointment form.

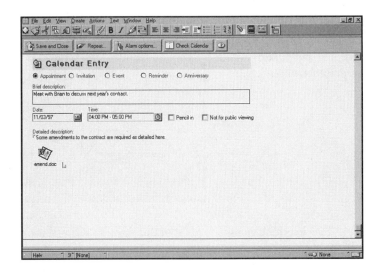

Notice that beside the Date field is a small button with a calendar graphic. When you click this button, it launches a graphical calendar control. You can move forward and backward a month at a time by clicking the small, black arrows in the upper corners of the control. When you find the date you want, simply click it, and it will be inserted into the Date field. Figure 20.5 displays the Calendar control.

Figure 20.5.

The Calendar control enables you to easily select date values.

Next to the Time field is a button with a clock graphic. Much like the new Calendar control, when clicked, this button displays a graphical time bar so that you can select the time range for your appointment. To select a time range, click and drag the clocks at either end of the time bar to the appropriate start and end times. If you need to see more of the time control, click the up and down arrows to scroll through the times. Figure 20.6 displays the new time control.

The *Not for Public Viewing* field is a check box that acts as a toggle to enable you to indicate that this appointment is confidential and should not be displayed to other users.

When checked, the *Pencil In* check box is just like penciling in something in your day timer. It just indicates that this appointment is tentative.

The final field, *Detailed Description* (indicated by the gray angle brackets), is a rich text field that you can use to enter a detailed description, add file attachments, or insert objects that help to additionally describe the appointment.

Figure 20.6.

The Time control enables you to point-and-click your way to setting the time of your appointment.

Also notice the *Save and Close, Repeat, Alarm Options, Check Calendar,* and *Help* buttons on the Action bar. When clicked, the *Save and Close* button saves the appointment and closes the current window.

If you'd like to make the appointment repeat without rekeying the information, click the *Repeat* button, which launches the Repeat Rules dialog box shown in Figure 20.7.

Figure 20.7.

The Repeat option enables you to quickly and easily schedule recurring appointments.

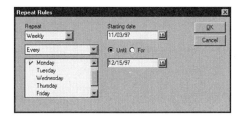

The Repeat Rules dialog box enables you to easily choose the repeat options. You can use the Repeat drop-down field to tell Notes how often this appointment will repeat from the following choices:

- [ ] *Weekly*   Choosing Weekly tells Notes to create an entry in your calendar each week on the dates and times you specify. An example would be your weekly staff meeting every Friday at 9:00 a.m.

- [ ] *Monthly by Date*   Choosing Monthly by Date tells Notes to create an entry in your calendar each month on the dates and times you specify. For example, you attend the monthly Notes user's group on the tenth of each month.

- [ ] *Monthly by Day*   Choosing Monthly by Day tells Notes to create an entry in your calendar each month on a specific day rather than on a date. For example, you might get paid on the last Friday of each month.

- [ ] *Yearly*   Choosing Yearly tells Notes to create an entry in your calendar each year on the date and time that you specify, such as an annual Marketing convention that you attend.

- [ ] *Custom*   Custom is the most powerful option. You tell Notes to enter entries based on criteria that you specify.

20

After you have made a choice for repeating your entry, use the other fields to define the specifics of the repeating appointments. For example, if you choose monthly on the second and that falls on a weekend, you have the option to move the meeting forward or backward on that one specific instance. This is a very powerful tool that can make scheduling recurring appointments easy.

The Alarm button launches the dialog box shown in Figure 20.8. From this dialog box, you can set the alarm parameters for this entry. The first field, When, is static text that displays the time and date of the entry.

Figure 20.8.

The Set Alarm dialog box is very handy when you need to remember important appointments.

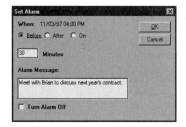

 If you have not enabled Alarms in your Calendar Profile, you will be prompted to enable this before the Set Alarm dialog box is displayed.

The next two fields work together to determine when the alarm process will notify you. The Minutes field enables you to enter a time in minutes that, when the *Before*, *After*, or *On* option button is set, causes you to be notified before, after, or on the appointment time and date.

The *Alarm Message* field enables you to enter a message that displays when the alarm is kicked off. This value defaults to the value of the Brief Description field, but you can enter any value you want.

The final field, *Turn Alarm Off*, is a check box that toggles the individual alarms off or on.

 If you enable alarms in your Calendar Profile, the Minutes and the Before, After, and On fields default to the values you entered for *Automatically Set Alarm for Appointments* field. You can override this on an individual basis by entering a new time for the alarms. To change this value permanently, edit your Calendar Profile.

After you enable an alarm for an entry, a dialog box pops up on your screen at the designated time to remind you of your scheduled appointment.

The *Check Calendar* button opens your Calendar view so that you can quickly check your schedule for available times. When you are finished, press Esc to return to your appointment. The final button on the Action bar is the *Help* button. When clicked, it displays a context-sensitive dialog box that explains how to complete the calendar entry you are creating.

> To make the C & S process as easy as possible, Lotus made the usage of the *Brief Description*, *Not for Public Viewing*, *Pencil In*, and the *Detailed Description* fields consistent throughout the five types of calendar entries, as is the usage of the date and time controls, which helps to decrease the learning curve and make Notes C & S more user-friendly and useful. In addition, the *Alarm* and *Repeat*, *Check Calendar*, and *Help* action buttons are consistent across all of the calendar entries.

Now that you know how to create an appointment, using the Calendar Entry forms is easy because of the overlapping fields. Rather than reiterate the same information for each of the forms, you can examine the divergence from the Appointment form in the remaining four forms.

Task 20.5: Sending Invitations

If you work in an organization with more than one person, you'll often want to schedule other individuals to attend a meeting, which is where the invitation comes into play. To create an invitation, create a new calendar entry and click the Invitation option button. Notice that in Figure 20.9, an invitation contains the same information as an appointment, but adds a subsection that enables you to define the invitees.

Figure 20.9.

The Invitations section enables you to schedule meetings with colleagues.

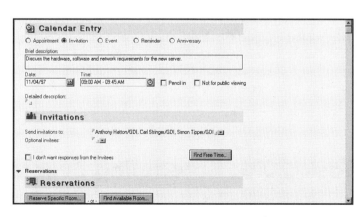

20

Because the invitation is identical to the Appointment, other than the Invitations subsection, only the Invitations subsection is examined here. The first field, *Send Invitations to*, is a keyword list that enables you to select a list of users or groups that you want to send an invitation to from the Address Book. The next field, *Optional*, is identical to the *Send Invitations To* field, except that people and groups selected here are not required to attend but could benefit from attending.

The *Find Free Time* button enables you to search the Freetime database for each of the named recipients to ensure they are available at the designated time (see Figure 20.10). The *I Don't Want Responses from the Invitees* check box enables you to tell Notes not to have the recipients send you mail responses regarding the invitation.

Figure 20.10.

The Free Time dialog box, showing a conflict for the desired meeting time.

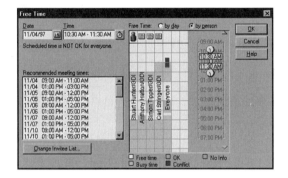

If you want to reserve rooms or resources for your meeting, click the *Reservations* twistie. Reservations is an expandable section that contains three subsections: *Reserve Specific Room*, *Find Available Room*, and Reserve Resources. The *Reserve Specific Room* button launches a dialog box that displays a list of available resources. When you select a room, Notes checks to see if it is available at the specified time and date; if so, it is reserved for your meeting. The *Find Available Room* button enables you to search the Resource Reservation database for any room that is available during the time and date you have specified for the calendar entry. The *Reserve Resources* button works in a way that is very similar to the *Reserve Specific Room* button: You can choose a resource from the list, and Notes will check to see if it is available; if it is, it will be reserved for your meeting.

The final field, *Chairperson*, is a display-only field that, when the document is saved, displays the common name of the Notes ID in use.

Task 20.6: Scheduling Events

If you want to schedule an event, such as a trade show or conference, create a new calendar entry and click the *Event* option button. This changes the appearance of the form slightly, as shown in Figure 20.11.

Figure 20.11.

Events enable you to schedule multi-day entries easily.

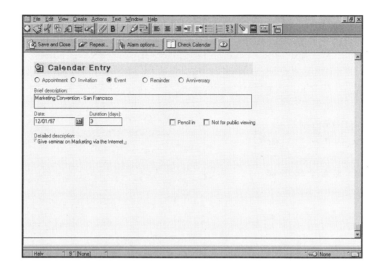

The primary difference between an Event and an Appointment or Invitation is that Events are entered on a daily basis rather than an hourly basis. This is why you have a *Duration* field in which you can indicate the number of days the event lasts. Notes creates an Event in your schedule for each of the days you indicate in the *Duration* field.

Task 20.7: Scheduling Reminders

Reminders are almost identical to appointments, except the *Time* field expects a discrete time rather than a time range. Figure 20.12 displays a Reminder.

Figure 20.12.

Create a Reminder for those important one-off events.

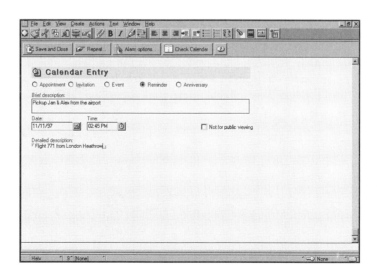

20

Task 20.8: Scheduling Anniversaries

The last type of Calendar Entry, Anniversary, enables you to keep track of important anniversaries such as birthdays, wedding anniversaries, Mother's Day, and so on. Figure 20.13 displays an Anniversary.

Figure 20.13.

Keep on your spouse's good side; use Anniversary to keep track of important dates.

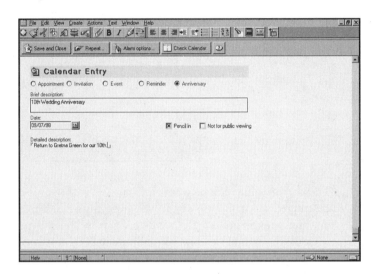

Task 20.9: Managing Tasks

Though you do not create Tasks from the Calendar Entry form, it is useful to include them here as you have the option to present them in your Calendar view. (The details are discussed later in this section.)

Chances are that in addition to attending those meetings for which you have been creating entries, you also will have to prepare some work for them. If you are working on specific projects you might be assigned tasks that have to be completed within a certain time frame. Task documents enable you to track these items and their status in a variety of views.

Tasks have their own view, which you can access by clicking the To Do "tile" at the bottom of your mail navigator. Figure 20.14 shows your mail file with the To Do view open.

The To Do view sorts your Tasks by urgency and priority. Tasks that are overdue come first, followed by tasks that are current but have not past their due date. Future tasks are next, and the least priority goes to tasks marked as Completed. Within each of these categories, the priority a task has been given (1-High, 2-Medium, 3-Low) determines its position in that category.

Figure 20.14.

The To Do view shows your Tasks sorted by urgency.

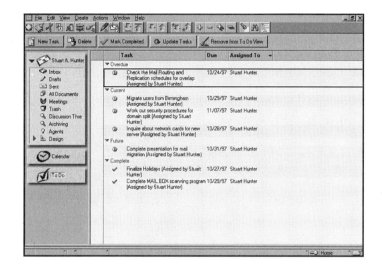

You can create a new Task in several ways:

☐ If you are not in your mail file, you can select Create, Mail, Task.

☐ If you are presently in your mail file, you can select Create, Task.

☐ If you are currently in your To Do view, you can press the *New Task* button on the Action bar.

☐ From any view in your mail file, or while looking at a specific mail document, you can select Actions, Copy Into, New Task. This creates a new Task with the Subject field of the selected or open memo copied to the Subject field of the new Task and the body of the original message included in the Additional Information field of the Task.

The Task form (see Figure 20.15) contains many fields in common with other calendar entry documents, but it contains two date fields for setting a *Start Date* and a *Due Date*. These fields affect how the Task is sorted in the To Do view. You also can display the Task in your Calendar view by selecting the *Display Task on My Calendar* button. In the Calendar view, the Task is displayed under its Start Date; there is no indicator on the Due Date. If you subsequently decide you don't want the Task in your Calendar, click the *Remove From Calendar View* button.

If you are managing a project, you can assign tasks to others working on the project. After filling in the details of the Task, click the *Assign to Others* button. *Assign To* and *CC* fields are where you can type in the names of the people to whom you want to assign the Task. You can use the *Address* button on the Action bar to select the names from the Public Address Book. When you save the Task, you are prompted to mail the Task to the Assignee.

20

Figure 20.15.

The Task form has two date fields between which the Task is "current."

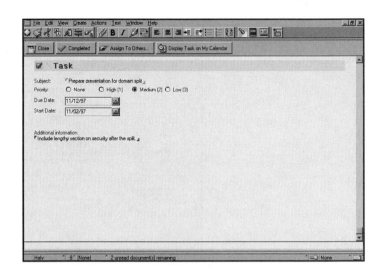

You can mark a Task as complete from the To Do view by selecting the Task and selecting the *Mark Completed* button or by accessing the Task document and choosing the *Completed* button on the Action bar.

The To Do view contains a button called *Remove from To Do view*. This button is useful for getting rid of Tasks that you have marked as Complete but do not want cluttering up the To Do view. These Tasks still appear in the *All Documents* view of your mail file.

Workshop

Wasn't that fun? At its simplest, Notes makes a great Personal Information Manager. You learned how to create Appointments, Events, Anniversaries, Tasks, and Reminders for yourself that should make you a lot more organized and productive. The real power of Calendaring & Scheduling, however, becomes apparent when you look at how it enables you to organize not just your time but that of others, as well. You learned how to create Invitations for others, check free time, and respond to meeting invitations. Here are some of the key terms to which you been introduced and some common questions you might have.

Key Terms

Review the following list of terms:

☐ *Personal Information Manager (PIM)*   A piece of software that helps organize your time and usually includes some form of contact management. C&S within Notes helps organize your time, and the Business Card documents in your Personal Address Book help you organize your contacts. Other Notes databases can be set up to track activities between you and your contacts.

☐ *Free time*   The availability of others to attend meetings. Notes C&S makes it extremely easy to find your colleagues' free time when you want to arrange a meeting.

☐ *Conflict*   If you try to create a meeting with someone when she is already committed to another appointment, you have a conflict. Notes C&S has tools to help you resolve this and move the meeting to a time when everyone is free.

Common Questions

Q Can I check users' free time when I am mobile?

A Yes you can, in two ways. If you are in a hotel room, you can dial into your Notes server, create appointments, and check free time as if you were back in the office. Second, you can replicate the free time database so that you can still check free time even when you cannot access your Notes server. Hour 24, "Working Remotely" explains how this works.

Q I have just upgraded from Notes 4.1 to Notes 4.6, but I can't see the Calendar view in my mail file. Where is it?

A The Calendar view is part of the standard Notes mail template that was introduced in Notes 4.5. Even though you have upgraded your Notes software, your mail file itself is not automatically upgraded. Ask your administrator to do this for you. The Notes 4.6 mail template has the filename MAIL46.NTF.

Preview of the Next Hour

Now that you know how to schedule appointments and meetings, the next Hour covers viewing your calendaring and scheduling appointments.

20

Hour **21**

Viewing Calendaring and Scheduling

Goals for This Hour

Now that you are familiar with the basic calendaring and scheduling features of Notes, this hour takes you through viewing your calendar. Specifically, you should learn the following:

- ☐ Viewing your appointments, invitations, events, reminders, and anniversaries
- ☐ Using the Calendar view to view your calendar entries in a layout that resembles that of a day planner
- ☐ Responding to a meeting invitation
- ☐ Printing your Calendar view

Task 21.1: Viewing Your Calendar Entries

After you have created calendar entries or been invited to appointments, you obviously need to be able to view, edit, and delete them, and Lotus makes it easy to do so. To find your standard appointments, you can use the Meetings view, Calendar view, or All Documents view.

Task 21.1.1: Understanding the Meetings View

The Meetings view, shown in Figure 21.1, displays all of your appointments and is a quick and easy way to manage your schedule.

Figure 21.1.

The Meetings view displays all of your calendar entries in a basic format for ease of use.

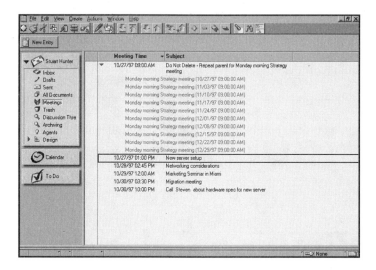

The first column, *Meeting Time*, is sorted in ascending order, based on the meeting time and date. Notice the down arrow on the column header, which indicates that the column can be re-sorted in descending order.

The second column, *Subject*, displays what the user entered for the brief description of the meeting.

Task 21.1.2: Understanding the Calendar View

The Calendar view is a very powerful feature that brings the award-winning look and feel of Organizer to Lotus Notes. It enables you to view your appointments through a calendar metaphor, making it easy to manage your schedule. Because this is such a powerful new feature, it warrants its own section, "Navigating Through the Calendar View," which is later in this chapter. Figure 21.2 displays the Calendar view.

Notice the new calendar-related action buttons on the Action bar. Each of these buttons enables you to change the views of your calendar to display as much data as needed to suit your personal preferences—from two days at a time to up to a month.

Figure 21.2.

*The Calendar view,
displaying a week of
calendar entries.*

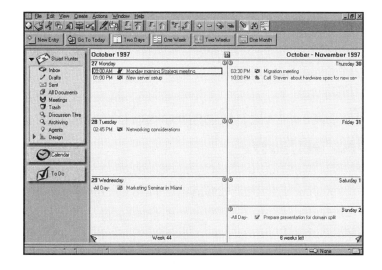

Task 21.1.3: Understanding the All Documents View

By now, the *All Documents* view is probably old hat to you, but it can be used for C & S, as well, because it displays your appointments (see Figure 21.3). Because it does not discriminate toward the documents it displays, however, it can be somewhat overwhelming. In addition Calendar Entries display the date they were created in the *All Documents* view, not the date for which the entry was set. In Figure 21.3, you can see that all the Calendar Entries were created on the same day but you have no idea as to when the events actually take place.

Figure 21.3.

*The All Documents view
displays special icons for
calendar entries.*

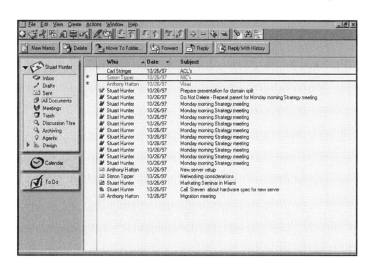

21

As you can see, there are many different types of documents displayed in this view. Lotus did, however, add several new icons to the view to indicate that a document is an appointment.

After you learn how to use the views, you can quickly find your appointments and begin to edit and delete them.

Task 21.2: Responding to a Meeting Invitation

If you receive an invitation to a meeting in your email, there are several ways that you can respond to it. Figure 21.4 shows a Meeting Invitation similar to one you might receive.

Figure 21.4.

A Meeting Invitation.

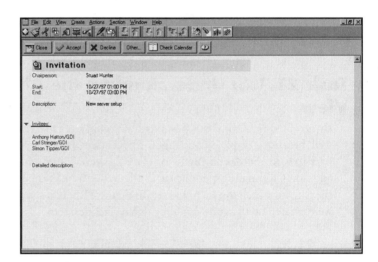

You have the following choices:

- ☐ *Accept*   If you choose to accept the invitation, click the *Accept* button or choose Actions, Accept. An entry is added to your Calendar and an acceptance is sent back to the person who invited you.

- ☐ *Decline*   If you choose to decline the invitation, click the *Decline* button or choose Actions, Decline. The invitation is marked as such in your mail file and no entry is made in your Calendar. The person who invited you is automatically informed that you have declined.

- ☐ *Other/Delegate*   If you click the *Other* button or choose, Actions, Other, you can select from a variety of actions such as Delegate, which enables you to select another person to attend the meeting on your behalf.

- *Other/Propose Alternative Time/Location* This option brings up an additional section where you can choose an alternative date, time, or location for the meeting if the original is not convenient. This counter proposal is mailed back to the chairperson.

- *Other/Pencil In* You can tentatively accept the invitation. An entry is made in your Calendar with the Pencil In field checked. The chairperson is told that you have penciled in the invitation.

- *Check Calendar* If you want, you can quickly look at your Calendar before deciding on your actions; clicking this button displays your standard Calendar view. Press Escape to return to the invitation.

Task 21.3: Navigating Through the Calendar View

As mentioned earlier, the new Calendar view is an incredible feature that can display your schedule graphically. Each view looks similar to an actual piece of paper, and you can navigate through the calendar by clicking the page's dog-eared edges. To get a copy of your schedule, you also can print the view (this is covered in the next section).

You can configure the Calendar view to display data in several ways. The view can consist of two days, one week, two weeks, or one month at a time.

The two days at a time view displays the most detailed information and looks quite similar to a page from a Franklin planner. It includes the appointment's time of day and a description of the appointment. Figure 21.5 shows the two-day Calendar view.

Figure 21.5.

The two-day Calendar view displays detailed information about your schedule.

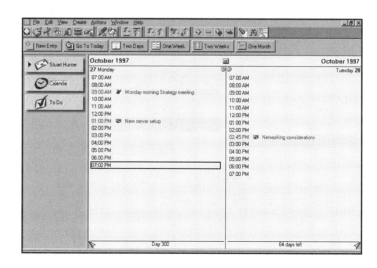

This view is easy to use. When opened, it defaults to today and tomorrow. To view the preceding or the following day, simply click the page's upturned edges to move through your schedule one day at a time. You'll also notice a small, white calendar icon, which you can click to display a calendar control that enables you to move through your schedule in much bigger chunks. In addition, the bottom of each page displays the day as a sequential number in the year (1–365), as well as the number of days left in the current year. Notice the small clock icon that appears on each day. If you click this, it displays the time slots for the day with arrows to help you scroll through them. If you right-click any day, a menu enables you to jump to today's date, change the Calendar view to display one of the other time periods, and show the time slots for the day.

To access any existing scheduling information, simply double-click the entry to open the appointment. If you want to add a new appointment, find an open time and double-click it to launch a new Appointment form. Alternatively, you can choose Create, Calendar Entry.

The one-week version of the Calendar view works exactly like the two-day view, except that is displays slightly less detail (see Figure 21.6). This version shows only the description for any appointments that you have scheduled within a given week. By default, it displays the current week. At the bottom, you see the week number (1– 52) and the number of weeks left in the year.

Figure 21.6.

Get a handle on your week with the one-week view of your Calendar.

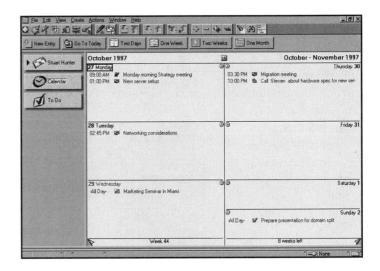

The Calendar view's two-week version also works exactly like the other views but displays even more of your schedule with less detail (see Figure 21.7). Each of the two pages displays a week's worth of your data and defaults to the current week and the following week. The week number (1–52) and the number of weeks left in the year for each of the two weeks display at the bottom of each page.

Figure 21.7.

The two-week version of the Calendar view can be useful to see the current week's schedule and to plan for the next week.

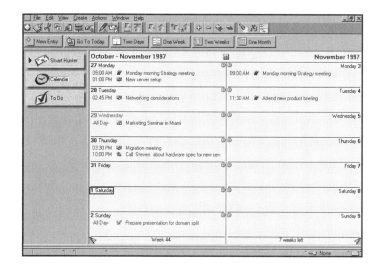

The one-month version of Calendar view is probably the most useful for a quick, one-stop shopping view of your schedule (see Figure 21.8). It displays an entire month of your schedule at one time with minimal detail. For each day that you have a scheduled appointment, Notes displays an icon (the same one used in the standard views) to indicate your appointment. At the bottom of the view, Notes displays the number of the month (1–12) and the number of months left in the year.

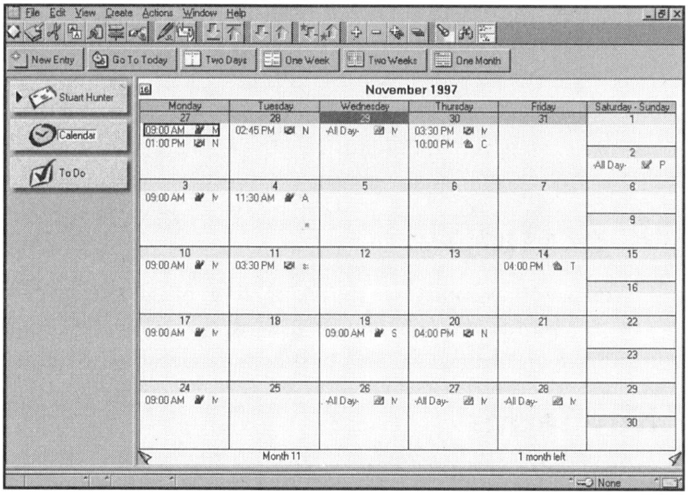

Figure 21.8.

The one-month version displays your schedule on the "macro" level, displaying very little detailed information.

21

Task 21.4: Printing Calendars

If you need a printed calendar to carry around with you, Notes prints the calendar, using whatever calendar view you choose. This did not work in Notes R4.5 but has been fixed in R4.6.

First, choose the Calendar Style you want to print (two day, one week, two week, or one month). Choose File, Print. If you want to print out the Calendar Style you previously selected, press Enter or click OK.

If you only want to print your calendar for a specific number of days, use the date controls in the *Print selected days* section of the Print dialog to control the start and end days (see Figure 21.9). If you override this setting, then regardless of the Calendar Style you previously selected, you will receive a line-by-line listing of your calendar entries.

Figure 21.9.

Choosing the Calendar print range.

Workshop

You have now completed the second hour of Calendaring and Scheduling information. The C & S feature of Notes is one of its most useful and important functions as groupware. Make sure you understand these hours completely, so you can maximize your usage of C & S.

Key Terms

Review the following term:

☐ *Delegation* Enabling someone else to access your calendar (or mail) to make and receive appointments on your behalf.

Common Questions

Q I want to be able to see all of one kind of appointment at a time. Is that possible?

A You can create folders to store your schedule items, making them easier to work with. For example, you can create an Anniversaries folder for quick and easy viewing of your anniversaries or a High Priority Appointments folder to store the appointments that are very important.

Preview of the Next Hour

Prepare to learn about another exciting feature of Notes—the next Hour takes you through accessing the World Wide Web directly from Lotus Notes.

21

Hour 22

Understanding the Web Navigators

You can browse the World Wide Web (or a corporate intranet) either by entering a Uniform Resource Locator (URL) into a dialog box or by clicking a URL link in a Notes or web document. Whether the server or client does the actual browsing (and whether browsing occurs at all), depends on a setting in your current Location document. This setting enables you to choose whether to use the server version, the personal version, or no browser.

Goals for This Hour

The Web Navigator is Notes' built-in web browser. The browser includes a companion Notes database that stores the web pages that the browser retrieves. Actually, two versions of Web Navigator exist: the server version and the personal version. In the server version, the browser and the database, named Web Navigator, both reside on a Notes server (although you can put a replica copy of the database on your workstation). The server on which the browser and database reside is sometimes called the InterNotes server. In the personal version, the browser and the database (the Personal Web Navigator) both reside on the Notes client.

This hour will teach you the following:

- ☐ How to set up the Personal Web Navigator
- ☐ How to search the web with the Web Navigators
- ☐ How to share web pages with Notes users
- ☐ How to store and use documents in the Web Navigators

Task 22.1: Working with Web Navigators

When you enter an URL in Notes or click an URL in a Notes document or a web document in Notes, the result depends on the choices that you have made in your current Location document. There you can choose to browse indirectly through a Notes server, directly from your Notes client (optionally tying in Internet Explorer to perform the actual browsing), from a third-party web browser, or not at all.

If you choose to browse with the Server Web Navigator, your copy of Notes forwards the URL to your designated Notes server. A server task, Web Retriever, forwards the URL to the destination server. If the destination server returns a page, Web Retriever converts it to Notes format. Then the database server task stores it in the Server Web Navigator database and forwards a copy to you, which your copy of Notes displays on your screen. Figure 22.1 shows how this process works.

Figure 22.1.

When you use the Server Web Navigator, your Notes server retrieves pages for you.

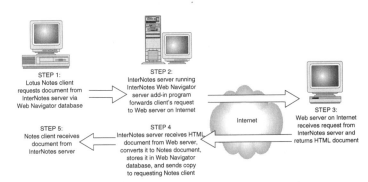

If you choose to browse with the Personal Web Navigator using Notes itself as the Internet browser, your own copy of Notes sends the URL to the computer named in it. If the other computer responds by returning a web page to you, Notes converts the web page to Notes format, stores it in the Personal Web Navigator database, and displays it onscreen. Figure 22.2 shows how this process works.

Figure 22.2.

When you use the Personal Web Navigator, your own computer retrieves web pages directly, without intervention by a Notes server.

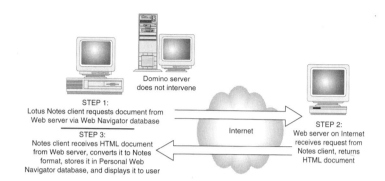

22

Actually, when you ask for a page, Notes might not forward the URL to another computer at all. If you ask for a page that Web Navigator has retrieved recently, Notes might simply return to you the copy sitting in its database. This is one of the advantages of using Notes to browse the web. You can quickly download a whole series of web pages into your Web Navigator database without spending much time in them. Then you can disconnect and read the pages more carefully offline, at your leisure, without accumulating connection charges.

If you choose to browse with the Personal Web Navigator using Notes with Internet Explorer as the Internet browser, the process is similar to that of using the Personal Web Navigator with Notes as the browser. The difference is that when an URL is retrieved, Internet Explorer stores it in its own cache, which is then mirrored in the Personal Web Navigator. If you are working offline, when you open a document from the Personal Web Navigator, the page is actually retrieved from the Internet Explorer cache. In this case, be careful when purging your Internet Explorer cache, or you might receive an error when trying to open a page in your Personal Web Navigator.

When you browse the web, Notes works a little differently than it usually does. When you open standard Notes documents, each document appears in its own window. However, when you browse with the Web Navigator, your web pages all appear in the same window. Lotus designed Notes to browse this way because it can only open nine subwindows at most. When you browse the web, you tend to open so many web documents so quickly that if Notes opened a window for each one, you would quickly reach the maximum number of windows and then would have to stop and close a window whenever you wanted to jump to a new one.

Task 22.2: Setting Up the Personal Web Navigator

To set up the Personal Web Navigator, follow these steps:

1. Make sure that you meet the system requirements in addition to those for running Notes on your system. (The following section covers these system requirements.)

2. Select a Location document that specifies From Notes Workstation in the Retrieve/ Open Pages field (see the next note for more information). All of the Location documents that come with a standard installation of Notes default to From InterNotes Server, so you must change the field before you can use the Personal Web Navigator. The Notes administrator can set this up before or after installing Notes on your computer, or you can do it yourself at any time.

> Don't be confused by the term InterNotes server. In this situation, it means a Notes server (that you specify in the InterNotes Server field of your Location document) that is running the Web Retriever task. It is a holdover from the days before Domino, when Lotus first built HTML capabilities into Notes. The product was called InterNotes Web Publisher, and it could take Notes databases and create HTML documents from them.

3. Open an URL (either from the menu by choosing File, Open URL or from a Notes document by clicking an embedded URL that appears underlined in green). When you open an URL, Notes creates the Personal Web Navigator database. The database, which has the default name of PERWEB.NSF, is based on the PERWEB46.NTF design template. It receives and stores all pages that the Personal Web Navigator retrieves.

Task 22.2.1: Meeting the System Requirements for the Personal Web Navigator

In addition to meeting the requirements for the Notes client itself, your system also must have the following things in order to meet the system requirements for the Personal Web Navigator:

- ☐ A connection to the Internet or intranet
- ☐ Transmission Control Protocol/Internet Protocol (TCP/IP) running on your workstation
- ☐ Lots of free hard disk space

For the first requirement, you must have a connection. There are three types of Internet connections:

- ☐ A direct connection to an Internet service provider (ISP) through your local area network (LAN) or a leased telephone line
- ☐ A direct connection to an ISP by modem
- ☐ An indirect connection to an ISP, through a proxy server to which you will probably connect by LAN

If you are connected to your company's LAN, you will probably connect to the Internet across the LAN—either directly to an ISP or indirectly through a proxy server. If you are at home or in a hotel room, you connect directly to an ISP using your modem.

If you are connecting to your company's intranet, you connect directly across the LAN if you are in the office. If you are out of the office, you might connect directly by modem or indirectly by proxy server. Your Notes administrator can assist with connecting to your company's intranet.

In any event, to meet the second requirement, you must have the TCP/IP protocol stack in your computer's memory to use the Personal Web Navigator. The TCP/IP protocol stack is the hallmark of the Internet and intranets. Without this protocol, you cannot access the Internet or your intranet. Your administrator can tell you whether or not you have the TCP/IP stack.

The third requirement, lots of disk space, is necessary because you tend to accumulate web pages quickly when you surf the web, and your Personal Web Navigator database is likely to become very large. No minimum amount of disk space is specified for running the Personal Web Navigator. But remember this axiom: You can never have too much disk space (or random-access memory [RAM], processing power, video resolution, network bandwidth, and so on).

Task 22.2.2: Setting Up a Location Document for the Personal Web Navigator

To browse with the Personal Web Navigator, you must use a Location document that specifies From Notes Workstation in the Retrieve/Open Pages field.

To access the Location document, click the location on your status bar and select Edit Current. Click the button in the Retrieve/Open Pages field, and the Select Keywords dialog box appears (see Figure 22.3).

Figure 22.3.

Clicking the button in the Retrieve/Open Pages field displays the Select Keywords dialog box.

If you will be using a proxy server to reach the Internet, you can also enter this information on the Location document. Check with your Notes administrator for assistance.

You can specify in the Location document what actions Notes should take after receiving a web page that includes a Java applet. A Java applet is a program and, therefore, could potentially damage your software and data. In particular, it could make network connections to other hosts and give them access to your system and data. Notes enables you to list trusted hosts—computers from which you are reasonably sure you will never receive damaging Java applets—and to specify the degree of access to your computer's resources you will permit to Java applets from both trusted and untrusted hosts. Figure 22.4 shows the Advanced section (expanded) of the Location document, with fields for entering Java preferences. To see this section, scroll down your Location document.

Figure 22.4.

The bottom portion of the Location document, with the Advanced section expanded. The Select Keywords dialog box shows the choices available in the Network Access for Trusted Hosts field of the default Java Applet Security section.

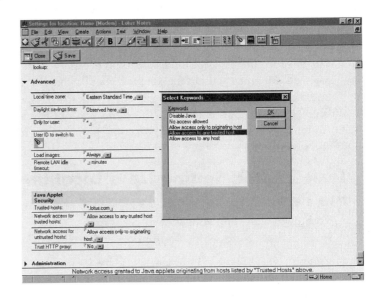

The Network Access for Trusted Hosts field offers the following five choices. The Network Access for Untrusted Hosts field offers only the first three of these choices.

☐ *Disable Java* Tells Notes not to run Java applets.

☐ *No Access Allowed* Tells Notes to prevent a Java applet from exposing your computer's resources to any computer.

☐ *Allow Access Only to Originating Host* Tells Notes to permit a Java applet to expose your computer's resources only to the computer from which it obtained the Java applet.

☐ *Allow Access to Any Trusted Host* Tells Notes to permit a Java applet to expose your computer's resources to any computer in your list of trusted hosts. (This setting is the default.)

☐ *Allow Access to Any Host* Tells Notes to permit a Java applet to expose your computer's resources to any other computer.

22

If the Notes administrator did not have the opportunity or foresight to set up the Location document using a User Setup Profile document, either the administrator or the user must make changes to the appropriate Location documents. In addition to the Retrieve/Open Pages field, the proxy server fields, and the Java security fields that were duplicated in the User Profile Setup document, the following field might affect your web browsing:

☐ *Internet Browser*   Choose your web browser here. The default setting is Notes, but you can choose to have Notes display web pages in another web browser whenever you open an URL.

Task 22.2.3: Configuring the Web Retriever

In this section of the Location document, you control several aspects of the Personal Web Navigator's behavior. The settings include the following:

☐ *Web Navigator Database*   This setting holds the filename of the Personal Web Navigator database. If you ever decide to rename or change the database's location, enter its new path name here.

☐ *Concurrent Retrievers*   This setting specifies the number of retriever processes that can reside in memory concurrently. This field is relevant only if you choose From Notes Workstation in the Retrieve/Open pages field. You can use the commands from the Window menu to view concurrent retrievals.

☐ *Retriever Log Level*   By default, Notes logs retrieval activity to your Notes log. This information might be useful to your Notes administrator. However, you do not need to do anything with this field, so you can skip it.

☐ *Update Cache*   When you have a constant connection to a web server, this field instructs the Navigator to update or refresh web documents. The field applies only when you open a stored page in the database.

The default setting is Never. The first time that the Web Navigator receives a request for a page, it gets the request from the designated web server. The server stores the page in the Web Navigator database and displays a copy to you. Thereafter, whenever you request that page, the Web Navigator delivers the cached copy of the page instead of retrieving it anew from the web server. With the default setting (Never), Web Navigator never checks with the web server to see whether the page has been updated since it was first retrieved.

However, you can change this setting to Once Per Session or Every Time. If you choose Once Per Session, the Web Retriever does not check with the web server if you ask for the same page again in the same browsing session, but it does check with the web server if you ask for the page again in a future browsing session. If you choose Every Time, each time that you request a cached page, the Web Retriever queries the originating web server to see whether it has a new version of the document; if not, it delivers the page's cached copy.

☐ *Trust HTTP Proxy*   This field is relevant only if you access the Internet through a Hypertext Transport Protocol (HTTP) proxy server. If you are using a proxy server, check with your Notes administrator for information on completing this field.

Task 22.2.4: Creating the Personal Web Navigator Database

The last step of setting up the Personal Web Navigator is to create the Personal Web Navigator database. You don't have to do this yourself. Instead, all you have to do is retrieve a web document, and Notes automatically creates the database for you the first time. To use this method, you can either choose File, Open URL or click an URL embedded in any Notes document. You will recognize the embedded URL because it looks like an URL (such as http://www.lotus.com) and is underlined in green. If your Notes workspace has the Personal Web Navigator icon, you don't need to perform this step.

If an URL in your Notes document is not underlined in green and Notes doesn't try to retrieve the document when you click an URL, you probably haven't enabled automatic conversion of URLs to Notes hotspots (which enables you to click the URL to open the page). To do so, choose File, Tools, User Preferences from the Notes menu. In the Advanced Options field of the User Preferences dialog box, select the Make Internet URLs (http://......) into Hotspots check box. Then click OK to accept the change. The next time that you see an URL in a Notes document, it should look and act like a Notes hotspot. Note that URLs do not appear underlined when a document is in Edit mode.

To retrieve your first web document, the Personal Web Navigator first creates the Personal Web Navigator database in your computer's Notes data directory. If the navigator retrieves the document successfully, it puts the page into the new database. The Personal Web Navigator database includes a configuration document, Internet Options, that you can use to fine-tune the way that the database works. The default settings in the Internet Options document are usually acceptable, so you might never have to change them.

Task 22.3: Setting Internet Options in the Personal Web Navigator Database

You have now finished setting up the Personal Web Navigator. As long as you are connected to the Internet or your company's intranet, you can retrieve as many web documents as you want. However, the first time that you open the freshly created Personal Web Navigator database, a dialog box appears that enables you to review and modify the Internet Options document. Anytime after that, you can review and change the Internet Options document by opening the Personal Web Navigator database and choosing Actions, Internet Options. Figure 22.5, which represents three screens, shows the Internet Options document.

Figure 22.5.

Complete the Internet Options document to select search, startup, and collaboration options for the Personal Web Navigator.

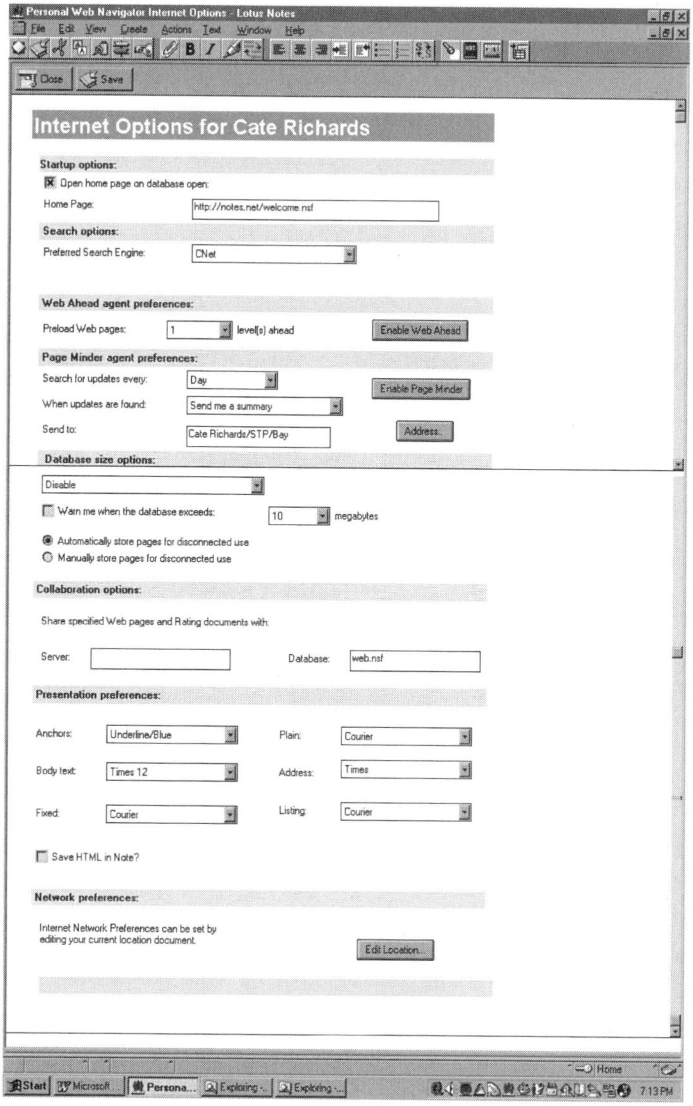

When creating the Personal Web Navigator database, Notes sets up the Internet Options document according to its defaults. As previously mentioned, these defaults are usually acceptable, so you might never have to change any of them.

The Internet Options document consists of eight sections:

- ☐ Startup Options
- ☐ Search Options
- ☐ Web Ahead Agent Preferences
- ☐ Page Minder Agent Preferences
- ☐ Database Size Options
- ☐ Collaboration Options
- ☐ Presentation Preferences
- ☐ Network Preferences

The following sections describe these eight sections of the Internet Options document in detail.

Task 22.3.1: Startup Options

In the Startup Options section, you can specify what happens when you open the Personal Web Navigator database. By default, the database opens to a standard Notes three-pane interface with a list of views in the upper-left corner, a list of the documents in the currently selected view in the lower-left corner, and the currently selected document previewed on the right. If you prefer, you can open to a home page instead. To do so, you edit this section's two fields:

1. Select the check box labeled Open Home Page on Database Open.
2. In the Home Page text box, enter the URL of the home page to which you want to open. The field's default is **www.notes.net**, which is a public site run by Iris Associates (the developers of Notes).

Task 22.3.2: Search Options

A popular method for locating information on the web is to use a search engine to search indexes of documents. In the Search Options section, you can choose a default from several popular search engines. The default setting is CNet, but you can select AltaVista, Excite, Yahoo!, or Lycos, or you can enter the name of any other search engine that you prefer. The search engine that you choose will not search your Web Navigator database; Notes' own search engine performs that search.

Task 22.3.3: Web Ahead Agent Preferences

Web Ahead is a Notes agent that automatically retrieves into the Personal Web Navigator database all the pages pointed to by URLs on a given page. In the Preload Web Pages field, you can choose to retrieve pages one, two, three, or four levels ahead of the current page. In other words, you can tell Notes whether to pull in just those pages pointed to by URLs on the current page, or all those pages plus all the pages pointed to by the second-, third-, or fourth-level pages. (You better have plenty of free disk space if you plan to choose level four.)

Therefore, instead of manually (and tediously) retrieving all the pages and having to wait for their arrival, you can start the agent and then return later to browse at your own pace (not the web's) through the copies of the pages waiting in your database. To use this agent, you first must enable it by following these steps:

1. Choose File, Tools, User Preferences to open the User Preferences dialog box.
2. Select the Enable Scheduled Local Agents check box. Then click OK to close the User Preferences dialog box.
3. Open the Internet Options document in the Personal Web Navigator database. Click the Enable Web Ahead button. If Notes prompts you to specify the server on which to run Web Ahead, choose Local. Click OK.

To use the Web Ahead agent, simply drag a page into the Web Ahead folder. The agent handles the rest automatically and runs on its scheduled basis.

Task 22.3.4: Page Minder Agent Preferences

Page Minder is an agent that watches for updates to chosen web pages and notifies you when it finds them. The agent runs only when your Notes workstation is running, but it can keep you up-to-date on important events effortlessly. You enable Page Minder the same way that you enable the Web Ahead agent:

1. Choose File, Tools, User Preferences to open the User Preferences dialog box.
2. Select the Enable Scheduled Local Agents check box in the User Preferences dialog box. Click OK to close the dialog box.
3. Open the Internet Options document and click the Enable Page Minder button. If Notes asks which server is to run the agent, select Local.
4. Click OK.
5. Set any of the other options in the Internet Options document. Then save and close the document.

The Page Minder Agent Preferences section includes the following fields:

☐ *Search for Updates Every*   You can choose to search every hour, every four hours, every day, or every week. The default is every day.

☐ *When Updates Are Found*   By default, the agent mails you a summary notifying you that the page has changed. In this field, you can tell Notes to put the actual page in your mail instead.

☐ *Send To*   By default, this field lists you as the addressee for change notices. However, you can specify another addressee.

To run the Page Minder agent, simply drag any page to the Page Minder folder in the Personal Web Navigator database. The Page Minder agent then watches for changes to that page.

Task 22.3.5: Database Size Options

With the pages that all these agents are retrieving from all over the Internet in addition to the web pages you are retrieving yourself, you can imagine how quickly your Personal Web Navigator database eats up disk space. To keep this under control, you can set up automatic purging of old files in the database. By default, Notes disables this feature.

However, in the Database Size Options section, you can change the setting to either Reduce Full Pages to Links If Not Read Within or Remove Pages from Database If Not Read Within and then set a time limit. You can specify 30, 60, or 90 days. When reducing full pages to links, Notes purges the pages from the database but retains their URLs. You still see the purged pages' URLs in the Personal Web Navigator database, and if you click one, Personal Web Navigator retrieves it for you.

You can also have Notes warn you when the Personal Web Navigator database exceeds 5MB, 10MB, 25MB, or 50MB.

Task 22.3.6: Collaboration Options

One drawback of using the Personal Web Navigator instead of the Server Web Navigator is that you cannot benefit from other users' browsing experience. The Server Web Navigator database holds not only your pages, but also those of other users browsing through it. When a user finds a page particularly useful, beneficial, or just plain cool (or for that matter, really bad), he or she can rate the page. The Server Web Navigator averages the ratings that different users give to a page. Over time, this rating system can help you make use of other users' experiences and opinions.

Although the Personal Web Navigator doesn't provide this advantage, you can give other users the benefit of your experiences by sharing with them the web pages that you have found as well as your ratings of those pages. To do so, enter the name of a Notes server and a Server Web Navigator database in the two fields of the Collaboration Options section. Then, when you encounter a page that you especially want to bring to other users' attention, click the Share button on the Action bar. Notes displays the dialog box shown in Figure 22.6. In this dialog box, you can choose from two options:

☐ *Copy Page to Shared Web Navigator Database*   This copies the page to the database specified in the fields of the Internet Options document.

☐ *Create Rating in Shared Web Navigator Database*   This displays a rating form in the dialog box. You can give the document a rating from one (poor) to five (great), select a category for it, write your comments, and click OK. Notes forwards the page to the Server Web Navigator database and also creates a Rating document.

Figure 22.6.

This dialog box enables you to share web pages with other users. You can even share your opinion of a web page.

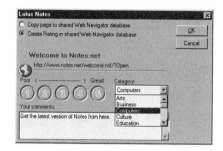

Task 22.3.7: Presentation Preferences

Web documents consist of plain text and embedded codes. The codes are part of the Internet protocol Hypertext Markup Language (HTML), and they define the document's formatting. Web browsers interpret the codes and replace them with formatting so that you see a formatted document, not a bunch of inscrutable codes. The webmaster can affect how Web Navigator interprets the codes by altering the contents of the following fields:

☐ *Anchors*   Anchors are the URL links that appear on HTML pages. By default, anchors are blue and underlined, but you can change their appearance.

☐ *Body Text*   The font setting for body text defaults to 11-point Times. You can change the type size to 10- or 12-point and the typeface to Helvetica or Courier.

☐ *Fixed*   This field controls the typeface used within code pairs that begin with the codes <CODE>, <KBD>, <SAMPLE>, and <TT>. The default is Courier.

☐ *Plain*   This field controls the typeface used within code pairs that begin with the codes <PLAINTEXT>, <PRE>, and <EXAMPLE>. The default is Courier.

☐ *Address*   This specifies the typeface used within the <ADDRESS> code pair. The default is Times.

☐ *Listing*   This field names the typeface used within the <LISTING> code pair. The default is Courier.

☐ *Save HTML in Note*   This option tells Notes to convert HTML documents to Notes format and then save them in this database. By default, Notes discards the HTML source code; however, when you select this check box, the server saves the HTML source code in the field labeled HTMLSource.

Task 22.4: Using the Personal Web Navigator

Lotus introduced the Personal Web Navigator to respond to the need for users to surf the Internet when they might not have an InterNotes server handy. The Personal Web navigator is intended primarily to meet the needs of individuals, not groups. For this reason, its interface is not as fancy as the Server Web Navigator's. The Personal Web Navigator opens to the standard Notes split screen (see Figure 22.7). It provides tools that enable a Notes user to gather information on the web and keep up with changes in the information.

Figure 22.7.

The Personal Web Navigator displays the preview pane by default.

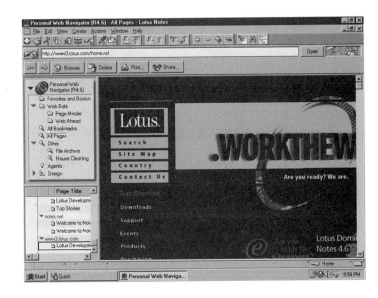

The default list of views and folders includes the following:

- ☐ All Documents is a view that lists all the web pages in the database.

- ☐ Bookmarks is a folder in which you can save your favorite web pages for quick access later. To add a page to the Bookmarks folder, drag and drop the page onto this folder. When you're on the web, add pages to the Bookmarks folder by clicking the Move to Folder action button, selecting Bookmarks as the folder, and clicking Add.

- ☐ Page Minder is a folder in which you can place web pages for which you want the Page Minder agent to periodically check the original sites for updates. If a page has been updated since you downloaded it, the agent notifies you. See the section "Page Minder Agent Preferences," earlier in this chapter, for more details.

☐ Web Ahead is a folder in which you can place a web page for which you want the Web Ahead agent to retrieve (in the background) all pages the particular web page points to. Depending on how you have configured the agent, it might also retrieve all the pages the retrieved pages point to (called the second level of pages), all the pages the second-level pages point to (called the third level of pages), and all the pages the third-level pages point to (called the fourth level). Web Ahead makes it easy to fill up a hard disk quickly. See the section "Web Ahead Agent Preferences," earlier in this chapter, for more details.

☐ File Archive is a view that displays all file attachments and their sizes.

☐ House Cleaning is a view that displays web pages sorted by size so that you can decide which ones to reduce to their URLs.

☐ Web Tours is a view that displays all the web tour documents you've made.

Task 22.4.1: The Personal Web Navigator's Action Bar

The Personal Web Navigator has both View and Form action bars. They are nearly identical but are different from the action bars that appear in the Server Web Navigator. Like the Server Web Navigator's action bars, these action bars emulate those of web browsers. Figure 22.8 shows the Form Action bar (used when displaying a web document full screen), and Table 22.1 describes each button in order from left to right.

Figure 22.8.

The Form Action bar that's available when you're viewing a web page in the Personal Web Navigator emulates those in web browsers.

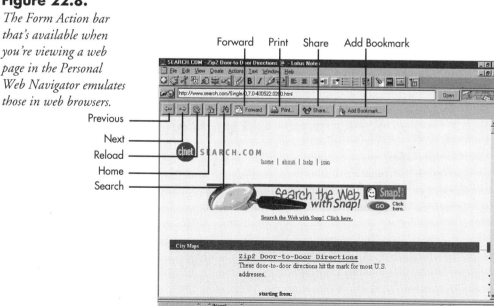

Table 22.1. Buttons on the Personal Web Navigator's Form action bar.

Button	Description
Previous	Moves to the previous page in the History list.
Next	Moves to the next page in the History list.
Reload	Reloads the current web page from the Internet server.
Home	Moves to the page that you defined in the Internet Options document as your home web page.
Search	Searches for pages on the web using the Internet search engine that you specified in Internet Options.
Forward	Emails the web page.
Print	Prints the current page.
Share	Shares the web page according to the specifications that you made in the Internet Options document. When you click this button, a dialog box opens, in which you can choose to forward the page to someone, copy it to the Server Web Navigator database, or rate the page and copy it as well as your rating to the Server Web Navigator database.

If you choose to use Notes with Internet Explorer as your web browser, the Action bar that appears when you are viewing a web page is slightly different. Two extra buttons might appear: A red Stop button appears that enables you to stop the retrieval of the current web page, and a Keep Page button appears if you specified in the Internet Options document that you wanted to store web pages manually.

Task 22.4.2: The Personal Web Navigator's Search Bar

The search bar works the same way in the Personal Web Navigator database as it does in the Server Web Navigator database. See the upcoming task entitled "The Server Web Navigator's Search Bar" for details about its use.

Task 22.5: Searching the World Wide Web with the Personal Web Navigator

22

The Personal Web Navigator enables you to select your preferred search tool, but using a search tool in the Personal Web Navigator isn't quite as intuitive as it is in the Server Web Navigator. To access a search tool, you can either enter the URL or set a preferred search tool in your Internet Options document. To set a preferred search tool, follow these steps:

1. From the workspace, select the Personal Web Navigator and choose Actions, Internet Options.

2. From the Search Options section's Preferred Search Engine list, select the search engine you want to use. If you select CNet, AltaVista, Excite, Lycos, or Yahoo!, save and close this document. If you select Other, a new text box appears in which you must enter an URL (see Figure 22.9). Then save and close this document.

Figure 22.9.

When you select Other from the Preferred Search Engine list, the Internet Options document displays a new text box in which you enter the URL of your preferred search engine.

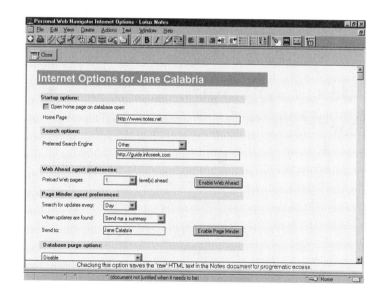

To use the search engine that you just selected, follow these steps:

1. Open the Personal Web Navigator.

2. Click the Search button on the Action bar. The Web Navigator retrieves the search engine web page.

3. Enter your search criteria.

> You can perform searches on some web pages. An indexed web page
> will indicate that it is indexed. Visit **http://www.sec.gov/cgi-bin/
> srch-edgar** for an example of an indexed web page.

Once you have retrieved a web page, you can search for occurrences of the text you are looking
for on the page by using Edit, Find/Replace.

Task 22.6: Saving Bookmarks in the Personal Web Navigator

To add an open page to the Bookmarks folder while using the Personal Web Navigator, click
the Action bar's Move to Folder button. In the Move to Folder dialog box, select the
Bookmarks folder and click Add.

To add a page to the My Bookmarks folder from the database's view pane, drag and drop the
page onto the My Bookmarks Navigator button or the Folder icon.

Task 22.7: Setting Up the Server Web Navigator

The Server Web Navigator resides on the Notes server and, as a shared database, is configured
and made available by the Notes administrator or the database manager. Check your
Location document for Office to confirm that the Retrieve/Open Pages field is set to From
InterNotes Server and that you have the correct server name entered in the InterNotes Server
field.

> If you intend to use both the Personal and the Server Web Navigator, you
> will want to create multiple Location documents to specify the use of
> multiple Web Navigator databases. Consult with your Notes administrator
> when setting up to use both navigators.

Task 22.8: Using the Server Web Navigator

22

When you first open the Server Web Navigator, you will probably see the Home Navigator (see Figure 22.10). The interface consists of a bunch of hotspots that you can click to perform such actions as loading a web page, opening another navigator, or opening a dialog box. For example, one hotspot, Our Home, takes you to the Notes Network Information Center (NotesNIC) home page—unless someone customized the Web Navigator database, in which case the hotspot might take you to your own company's home page.

All the hotspots in the Home Navigator's Sampler section take you to another navigator. The name of the navigator varies depending on the hotspot you click. Each navigator looks similar, however, displaying hotspots that open three of the more popular web search engines. In each navigator, the right pane is a view that displays the documents in the Web Navigator database that fall in the chosen category. Therefore, you can browse the database for documents of the chosen type, or you can search the web for other related documents. Figure 22.11 shows the Entertainment hotspot's navigator.

Figure 22.10.

The Server Web Navigator features a flashy interface. Click one of the icons and see where it leads you.

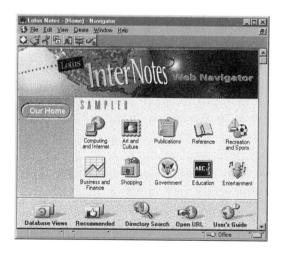

Figure 22.11.

The Entertainment Navigator appears when you click the Entertainment hotspot in the Home Navigator's Sampler section.

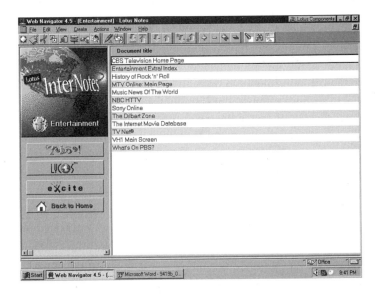

The icons along the bottom of the Home Navigator have the following functions:

- ☐ Database Views opens the View Navigator, which lists various views of the web pages already stored in the database.

- ☐ Recommended opens the Recommended Navigator. This navigator contains web pages that you rate for other users of the Server Web Navigator. When you come across a web page that you want to comment on, you can create a rating document for the page, and the Recommended Navigator rates the document by web page title. The navigator also displays scores and comments by users who have rated the pages.

- ☐ Directory Search displays a search form that enables you to perform searches with Internet search engines.

- ☐ Open URL displays a dialog box in which you can open a web page by entering its URL.

- ☐ User's Guide opens the online Web Navigator User's Guide database.

When you click Database Views in the Home Navigator, the View Navigator opens. In this navigator, each hotspot opens a particular view of the Web Navigator database's contents. Table 22.2 describes the buttons available in the View Navigator.

22

Table 22.2. The View Navigator buttons.

Button	Function
My Bookmarks	Opens pages saved in your Bookmarks folder. To add a page to the Bookmarks folder, drag and drop the page onto this button (or click My Bookmarks, select My Bookmarks in the Move to Folder dialog box, and then click Add).
Folders	Opens a standard Folders Navigator.
All Documents	Displays all the web pages stored in this database.
By Host	Displays all web pages sorted by their host site.
File Archive	Displays all file attachments and their sizes.
Web Tours	Displays all the saved web tours, which are saved histories that you can share with other users.
Recommended	Opens the Recommended Navigator.
Back to Home	Returns to the Home Navigator.

Task 22.8.1: The Server Web Navigator's Action Bar

When you open a document stored in the Web Navigator database, an action bar appears. It is unlike the action bars in other Notes databases (except the Personal Web Navigator database). Rather, it emulates the action bars that you see in such web browsers as Mosaic, Netscape Navigator, and Microsoft's Internet Explorer. Figure 22.12 shows the Server Web Navigator's Action bar, which helps you browse the web. Table 22.3 describes the action bar's buttons in order from left to right.

Figure 22.12.

The Server Web Navigator's Action bar helps you browse the web.

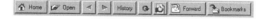

Table 22.3. Buttons on the Server Web Navigator's Action bar.

Button	Function
Home	Returns to the Home Page Navigator.
Open	Opens the Open URL dialog box.
Previous	Moves to the previous page in the History file.

continues

Table 22.3. continued

Button	Function
Next	Moves to the next page in the History file.
History	Opens the History dialog box to save pages to the History file or goes to other pages listed in the History file.
Reload	Reloads the current web page from the Internet server.
Recommend	Opens the dialog box in which you enter your rating of the current web page.
Forward	Emails the web page.
Bookmarks	Stores the current web page in the Bookmarks folder.

Task 22.7.2: The Server Web Navigator's Search Bar

The Notes search bar is actually a dual-purpose tool: You can use it to enter an URL and retrieve a web page, or you can search the Web Navigator database for text that you enter in the search bar. You toggle between the two modes by clicking the search bar's leftmost button.

In the Web Navigator databases, the search bar appears only when a web document is open. In other databases, the search bar appears only when you are in a view—not when a document is open. If you don't see the search bar, choose View, Search Bar.

The two versions of the search bar can be quite confusing. Make sure that the proper icon is showing for the type of search that you want to perform. Figure 22.13 shows the search bar in Open URL mode, and Figure 22.14 shows the bar in Text Search mode.

When you want to retrieve a web page, you might need to click the Search icon to switch to Open URL mode.

When you want to search for text within the pages of the database, you might need to click the Open URL button to switch to Text Search mode first (see Table 22.4). You can search for text only if your database is full text indexed. Otherwise, the search bar's first button is Create Index. Click this button to open the Properties for Database dialog box. In the dialog box's Full Text panel, you can set options and then begin creating the index. If you create an index for a local database, you will have to wait for Notes to create it. If the database is large, you might as well take a coffee break.

Figure 22.13.

The Search Bar in Open URL mode. Note which icon appears on the left and note the button labels on the right (as compared with Figure 22.14).

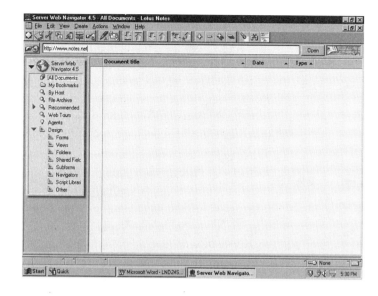

22

Figure 22.14.

The search bar in Text Search mode. Note which button appears on the left.

Table 22.4. The buttons on the search bar for Text Search mode.

Button	Description
Text Search	Sets the search bar to search for text in the database.
Text	Specifies the words or phrases for which you are searching.
Create Index	Creates the index. This button appears only if the database is not already indexed.
Add Condition	Displays the Search Builder dialog box, which is where you do most of your work when building a search query. The Create Index button changes into the Add Condition button after you create the index.
Search	Activates the search.
Reset	Clears the search results from the view pane. The query that produced the search remains in the search bar so that you can edit it.
Search Menu	Drops down a menu of search options.

Task 22.9: Searching the World Wide Web with the Server Web Navigator

To access the search tools in the Server Web Navigator, follow these steps:

1. Open the Server Web Navigator database.
2. Click the Directory Search icon (see Figure 22.15). The Internet Directory Search screen appears.

Figure 22.15.

Click the Server Web Navigator home page's Directory Search icon to access the Internet Directory Search screen.

3. In the text box, enter the topic for which you want to search, as shown in Figure 22.16.

Figure 22.16.

The Internet Directory Search screen provides a text box in which you enter your search topic.

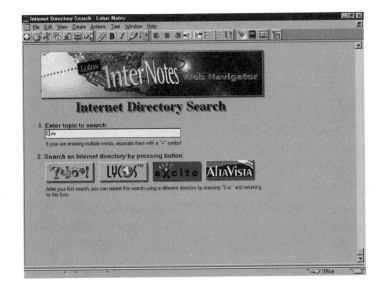

22

4. Click the search tool that you want to use (CNet, Yahoo!, Lycos, Excite, or AltaVista). The Server Web Navigator takes you to your requested site and displays your search's results. Figure 22.17 shows the results of searching Yahoo! for Elvis.

5. Scroll down the Yahoo! page to find some of the links to Elvis sightings, as shown in Figure 22.18.

6. Scroll through the Elvis list. When you find a page that you want to read, double-click the underlined text.

Figure 22.17.

Yahoo! finds Elvis.

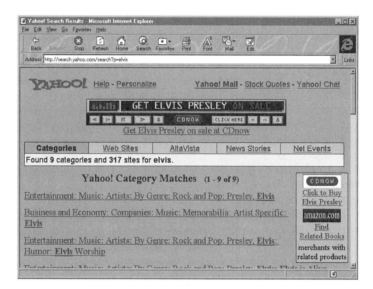

Figure 22.18.

Farther down the Yahoo! page, you can find a list of links.

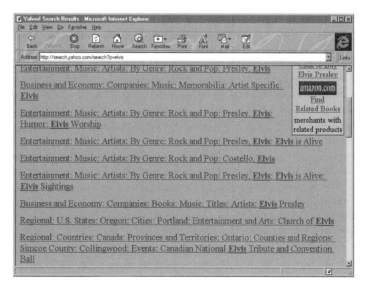

Task 22.10: Saving Bookmarks in the Server Web Navigator

To add an open page to the My Bookmarks folder while using the Server Web Navigator, click the Action bar's Folder button. Then select the Bookmarks folder and click Add.

To add a page to the My Bookmarks folder from the database's view pane, drag and drop the page onto the Bookmarks folder icon in the navigation pane.

Workshop

As more and more information becomes available from the web, you can appreciate how useful it is to be able to access and share that information from inside Notes. With Page Minder and Web Ahead, you can quickly download a large number of web pages to your Personal Web Navigator database for reading offline, and you can be informed when those pages are changed on the web.

You have learned how to access the web from both the Personal Web Navigator and the Server Web Navigator, how to search for documents on the web, and how to bookmark your findings. Here are some of the terms you should be familiar with and some common questions you may have.

Key Terms

Review the following list of terms:

- *URL (Uniform Resource Locator)*   This is the Internet *address* of a web page and it is what you type into the Open URL box or a link you click in another web page to take you to the desired web page.

- *Proxy server*   Sometimes a company directs all web page requests from users to another computer that handles all the retrievals. In this way, the company can monitor usage and filter out any requests for pages that they don't want you to have. The Server Web Navigator works in this way; its web page retrieval is handled by a Notes server.

- *Cache*   This is a common function of proxy servers that also exists in the Personal and Server Web Navigators. If several people all want to access the same web page, it is wasteful to go out to the Internet every time to retrieve it. Instead of doing that, when a web page is retrieved, it is stored in a cache for a defined period of time and subsequent requests for the same page will be served from the cache. If you suspect that the cached page is out of date, you can choose to reload it from the Internet in either the Personal Web Navigator or the Server Web Navigator.

☐ *Search engine* These are special web sites whose sole purpose is to help you find information you want on the Internet. They have special software that scours the Internet for content and then indexes the information, making it easy for you to locate just the information you are looking for.

Common Questions

Q I want to download a file from an FTP site. Can I do this with the Personal and Server Web Navigators?

A Yes. Both navigators support the FTP protocol. However, you enter the address with FTP instead of HTTP, such as **ftp://ftp.lotus.com**. See Hour 20 for more information on downloading files from the web.

Q Occasionally I am told that my web browser does not support frames that are required to view a web page. What can I do?

A It is true that the Personal and Server Web Navigators currently do not support frames. However, they may in the future. For now, if you have a TCP/IP connection, you can use Notes and Internet Explorer (recommended), Internet Explorer on its own, or Netscape Navigator to view pages with frames.

Preview of the Next Hour

Building on what you have learned here, in the next hour, you will learn how to download files from the web, how to share web pages with friends and colleagues, and how to view Java applets.

Hour 23

Working Smart with the Web Navigators

Goals for This Hour

The Web Navigator is the Notes built-in web browser. The browser includes a companion Notes database that stores the web pages that the browser retrieves. Actually, two versions of Web Navigator exist: the *server version* and the *personal version*. In the server version, the browser and the database, named Web Navigator, both reside on a Notes server (although you can put a replica copy of the database on your workstation). The server on which the browser and database reside is called the InterNotes server. In the personal version, the browser and the database (the Personal Web Navigator) both reside on the Notes client. This hour shows you the following:

☐ *How to set up the InterNotes Personal Web Navigator* You go through all the steps and examine all the configuration options.

☐ *How to search the web with the Server and Personal Web Navigators and how to share web pages with Notes users* Step-by-step, you examine all the different ways to locate web documents in both versions of the Web Navigator.

☐ *How to store documents and use stored documents in the Server and Personal Web Navigators*   You see how the Web Navigators convert web documents to Notes documents saved in Notes databases so that you can refer back to them.

☐ *How to share web pages with Notes users*   You examine tools that automate the sharing of your web search efforts with others.

> By editing your Location document, you can opt to use Microsoft Internet Explorer or Netscape Navigator in place of the Notes web browser. This is advantageous because these browsers support multiple frames and other newer features available only in the 4.0 versions.

Task 23.1: Downloading Files from the Web

When you need to retrieve files from a web page, double-click the filename listed in the web page and click the web page's download option or follow the page's instructions for downloading. Just before the download screen appears, the Attachment properties box opens, as shown in Figure 23.1.

Figure 23.1.

The Attachment proper-ties box.

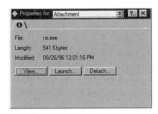

Click the Detach button. The Save Attachment dialog box opens, as shown in Figure 23.2. Select a drive, directory, and filename to download the file. Choose the Detach button.

Figure 23.2.

In the Save Attachment dialog box, you select the drive, directory, and filename to download the web page.

Task 23.2: Recommending Web Pages in the Server Web Navigator

The Server Web Navigator enables you to recommend useful or interesting web pages to other Notes users within your company. Because the Server Web Navigator is a shared database, when you recommend a page, anyone who can access the Server Web Navigator database can see your recommendations and you can see his.

To recommend a web page while using the Server Web Navigator, follow these steps:

1. Open the web page that you want to recommend.
2. Click the Action bar's Recommend button. A dialog box appears, as shown in Figure 23.3.

Figure 23.3.

In the Recommend dialog box, you can rate and comment on a given web page.

3. Select a rating from 1 (poor) to 5 (great) for this page.
4. In the Your Comments text field, enter your comments about this page.
5. Select a category for your recommendation. Categories include such subjects as Arts, Education, and Science. Your Notes administrator or database manager might have customized your category list. Scroll through the drop-down list of categories to investigate the choices provided.
6. Click OK to save this recommendation.

Task 23.3: Recommending or Sharing a Document in the Personal Web Navigator

To use the Personal Web Navigator to recommend a web page, you first must supply your Notes server's name in your Internet Options document. You also must be connected to your Notes server. You cannot recommend pages when working remotely.

To recommend a web page when using the Personal Web Navigator, follow these steps:

1. Open the Personal Web Navigator.

2. Click a document in the Navigator pane or open a document.

3. Click the Action bar's Share button. A dialog box appears that differs from the one that appears in the Server Web Navigator (see Figure 23.4). This dialog box provides the following options:

   ☐ *Copy Page to Shared Web Navigator Database* sends a copy of the web page to the Server Web Navigator's All Documents view.

   ☐ *Create Rating in Shared Web Navigator Database* prompts you to create a rating as you would in the Server Web Navigator database and sends the page with its rating to the Server Web Navigator's Recommend view.

4. Choose OK to send this document and close the dialog box.

Figure 23.4.

The Share Options dialog box opens when you click the Action bar's Share button in the Personal Web Navigator.

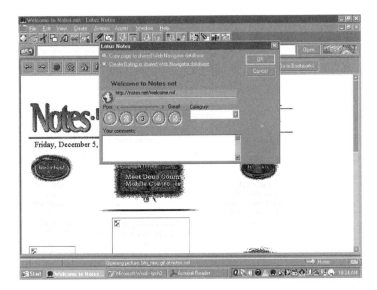

Task 23.4: Viewing Recommended Web Pages

To view the web pages that you and others have recommended in the Server Web Navigator, follow these steps:

1. Open the Server Web Navigator.

2. Click the Recommended button in the navigator's home page. The Recommended Navigator appears on the screen's left side. The navigator enables you to view the recommended web pages' contents in three ways:

- ☐ *By Category* lists the classifications chosen when web page ratings were created. This view is useful for finding pages by topic.
- ☐ *By Reviewer* sorts the contents by the person who rated the web page.
- ☐ *Top Ten* shows the 10 pages with the highest cumulative ratings.

Task 23.5: Forwarding Web Pages

You can email a web page to other Notes users from any view in your Personal Web Navigator or from an open document in the Server Web Navigator. When you click the Action bar's Forward button, Notes displays the Forward Options dialog box. You can choose to forward just the bookmark, which consists of the URL, or the whole web page. If you select to forward the whole web page, Notes opens a mail memo. The web page appears in the memo's body, and Notes automatically fills the subject line with the web page's title. Figure 23.5 shows a web page ready to be forwarded. Add your comments and click the Action bar's Send button.

Figure 23.5.

Clicking the Action bar's Forward button generates a mail memo with the web page in the body field.

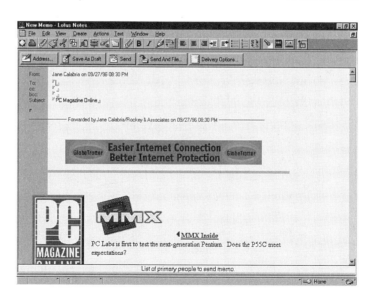

Task 23.6: Viewing Java Applets

Java is a programming language that enables you to build small applications called applets. You can embed applets within a web page by including them in an HTML code with the <APPLET> tag. Embedded applets can run from a browser. Notes temporarily copies the <APPLET> tag into your PC's RAM. The Java interpreter that ships with Notes then runs the Java applet. Java applets are very popular and can run animated pictures and voice clips. Lotus Notes supports running Java applets on your Windows 95 and Windows NT machines.

Allowing Java applets to play on your PC, however, raises questions of security. Because these applets are actual programs, they can harm your PC. Worse, they can expose your PC's resources and, by extension, the rest of your network to an outside computer. They pose a real security threat.

Lotus Notes enables you to decide whether or not you want to enable Java applets and from whom (which host) you will receive Java applets. Additionally, Notes does not permit any outside host access to any of your system resources (files, environment variables, password files, and so on). For example, if you feel confident that Lotus Corporation isn't going to send you any viruses, you might decide to trust the Lotus host. On the other hand, Elvis in Bulgaria might not be as trustworthy, so you can decide to put him on your untrusted list and thus disallow him from sending you applets.

To set the Java security for your workstation, modify the Java Applet Security section located in your the current Location document. See Hour 22, "Understanding the Web Navigators," for more details on Location documents. There are four settings in the Java Security Section:

- ☐ *Trusted hosts*   The field in which you list those hosts that you will allow Java applications to run from.
- ☐ *Network access for trusted hosts*   Enables you to set the amount of access granted to a trusted host.
- ☐ *Network access for untrusted hosts*   Enables you to deny access to untrusted hosts or to give them access.
- ☐ *Trust HTTP proxy*   Enables an HTTP Proxy, if one exists, to decide which hosts are trusted and untrusted.

With Java applets, the program's URL is embedded in the page. When you retrieve a page, your browser sees the Java applet's URL, downloads the applet, and executes it.

If you don't enable applets, you can still see the web pages minus the applets. If you are using the Server Web Navigator, check with your Notes administrator to see whether your system enables Java applets.

Task 23.7: Viewing HTML Code

Sometimes you want to know how a developer created a web site. The use of colors, formatting, and graphics can help entice people to your site. In this section, you learn how to view the HTML code behind web pages so that when you want to find out more about the page's design, you can view the page's HTML code and glean some ideas for your own web site.

If you are using the Server Web Navigator, ask your Notes administrator whether the option has been set for HTML code. If you are using the Personal Web Navigator, edit your Internet Options document by selecting the Save HTML in Note? check box in the Presentation Preferences section.

By default, when Notes converts a retrieved HTML page to Notes format, it discards the HTML source code. After you enable the Save HTML in Notes option, Notes saves the HTML source code of newly retrieved pages in a hidden field called HTMLSource. You can view the HTML source code only in the Document Properties box of a web page. Reading within that confined space is a little difficult, however. To make reading easier, copy the HTML source code from the Document Properties box to a text editor or a text field in a Notes document.

To view HTML code, follow these steps:

1. Select the web page in either the Server or Personal Web Navigator.
2. Choose File, Document Properties.

3. Click the Fields tab.

4. Select the check box Save HTML in Note? in the left column to see the HTML code in the right column.

Viewing HTML Source Code in Notes Documents in a Usable Form

You might think that Lotus would provide a form that displays the HTML source code in a field. Lotus has not yet done so, however, and you cannot create such a form. The HTMLSource field is of data type HTML, which is not a data type that you can choose when you create a field in a form. So, even if you create a form with a field in it called HTMLSource and switch to that form when viewing a document, the HTML source code does not appear in that field.

What you can do is select the contents of the HTMLSource field in the Document Properties box, copy the selected text to the Clipboard, and paste it into a text editor or a text field in a Notes document.

Task 23.8: Retrieving Multiple Web Pages Simultaneously

If you have a fast PC and Internet connection, you can use the Persoanl Web Navigator to retrieve up to six web pages at the same time. To retrieve multiple web pages, follow these steps:

1. Edit your Location document by clicking the location on the status bar and selecting Edit Current.

2. In the Concurrent Retrievals field, select the number of pages that you want to retrieve simultaneously.

3. Save your changes and close the document.

After editing your Location document, you can retrieve several web pages at one time. For each web page that you want to open, choose File, Open URL. The Personal Web Navigator opens a new window each time you choose the Open URL command. To see the pages, choose Window and then move from page to page within the Window menu or choose Window, Cascade or Window, Tile to see all your web pages.

Task 23.9: Viewing the Most Current Version of a Web Page

When you visit a web site, you want current information, not last week's news. Web pages are updated constantly, so a web page stored in your database might be out of date a day later. On the other hand, opening a web page from the Notes database is much faster than opening a web page on the web. How can you balance the advantages of opening pages from the web or the database?

First, consider the web page's contents. The web pages that you retrieved on the history of chocolate in America are unlikely to change. On the other hand, the Chocolate Lovers home page that leads you to the history of chocolate might change daily—and you don't want to miss the daily chocolate chuckles! If you want to see the Chocolate Lovers home page, you can type the URL in the Open URL dialog box, or you can select the Chocolate Lovers home page in your InterNotes Web Navigator database and click the Action bar's Reload button. This ensures that you get the page from the Internet server, not from the Notes database.

Second, you can tell the Web Navigator how often it should refresh stored web pages. With a constant Internet connection, you can use a cache option to instruct the Web Navigator to update or refresh stored web documents. These options apply when you open a page stored in the database. If pages are stored in the database but not opened by anyone, Notes does not update or refresh the page. You can set the cache options to reload a web page from Internet server when you open it from the Web Navigator database. To find out which caching options are set for your Server Web Navigator, check with your Notes administrator, who is the only person who can set caching options for the Server Web Navigator. Your Notes administrator might have the caching options set to Never. If so, when you open a document from the Web Navigator database, be certain to open it by reloading it if you need to see the most current version of the page.

You set the caching options for your Personal Web Navigator. If you're dialing into an ISP, the caching options that you set apply only while you are connected to the ISP. Obviously, when you're working offline, Notes can't access the Internet to update the pages. Remember, updating occurs only when you open a page in the database; don't assume that simply because you've dialed into an ISP, every page in your database is current since the last time that you dialed in.

To set your Personal Web Navigator's cache options, follow these steps:

1. Edit your Location document by clicking the location on the status bar and selecting Edit Current.

23

2. In the Update Cache field, choose one of the following options:

☐ *Never* specifies that Notes never refreshes web pages. This setting is the default. If you select Never, you must click the Action bar's Reload button to refresh your Web page or select the Action bar's Reload from Internet Server button when you type a URL in the Open URL dialog box.

☐ *Once Per Session* specifies that Notes refreshes a web page when you first open it from the database, but not again during your session.

☐ *Every Time* specifies that Notes refreshes a web page every time you open it from the database during a session.

3. Save your changes and close the document.

Task 23.10: Managing Your Database Size

With the Personal Web Navigator, web surfing can result in disk space drowning! Remember that each page is cached into your database. To control your database's size, you should set deletion options for your database in the Internet Options document. After you set the deletion options, Notes executes the deletion each time you open the database.

To control the size of your database, follow these steps:

1. Open the Personal Web Navigator and choose Actions, Internet Options. The Internet Options document opens. Scroll down to the Database size options section.

2. In the Database size options section's drop-down list box, select one of these options:

☐ *Reduce Full Pages to Links If Not Read Within ___ Days* specifies the number of days a web page should be stored as a full document. If you choose 10 days, for example, on the eleventh day the navigator reduces the document to a URL.

☐ *Remove Pages from Database If Not Read Within ___ Days* indicates the number of days that you want to store a web page that you haven't viewed. If you choose 10 days, on the eleventh day the navigator deletes the page.

☐ *Disable*, the default setting, specifies that the navigator never purges anything from the database.

☐ If you have chosen one of the first two options, you can click the Enable Housekeeping button to enable the process.

You also can keep track of the database's overall size by asking Notes to notify you if the database exceeds a certain size. If you specify that you want notification when the database exceeds 100MB, Notes displays a message box when the database grows beyond that limit. To specify the size limit, open your Internet Options document, scroll to the Database size options section, select the Warn Me When the Database Exceeds check box, and enter your limit (in megabytes) in the adjacent scroll list.

23

Workshop

By now, you should have a pretty thorough understanding of the many ways to utilize the Personal and Server Web Navigator that comes with Notes. Following, you will find some of the key terms and common questions that people working with the web navigators encounter.

Key Terms

Review the following list of terms:

- [ ] *Caching option* Dictates how often the stored web pages in the navigator are refreshed. You can change these options only in the Personal Web Navigator. The Notes Administrator must change the Server Navigators settings.

- [ ] *Personal Web Navigator* Created and managed by each Notes user. You can set your own options in and keep your bookmarks private.

- [ ] *Server Web Navigator* Located on the InterNotes server, this is shared with all allowed Notes users and is administrated by the system administrator.

- [ ] *Java applets* Special programs created by web designers that run in a web browser. These applets can cause security problems, so it is important to be selective about whose applets will run on your computer.

- [ ] *Internet Options Documents* Can be set within the Personal Web Navigator to options such as preferred search engine and how notes should control the size of your database.

Common Questions

Q Do I have to be connected to view my favorite web pages?

A No, by setting the Personal Web Navigator to retrieve multiple pages, you can refresh your pages and then view them on the road because they will be saved in the database.

Q I set up a Personal Web Navigator, but I cannot load any web pages.

A Make sure that your internal network is running TCP/IP; otherwise, you must connect via modem to an ISP.

Preview of the Next Hour

Now that you understand the basics of working with the Web Navigators, you move to a new subject in the next couple of hours: working remotely. Because of the amount of business travel undertaken today, access to information from a remote location is extremely important. Notes is structured to be extremely helpful in that respect, and Hour 24, "Working Remotely," gets you started.

Hour 24

Working Remotely

Goals for This Hour

When you connect to a Notes server through a LAN, you can connect your PC—whether it is a desktop or a laptop—with cables directly from the LAN to one or more servers. You have direct, continuous, high-speed access to databases on the servers in your network.

This hour's lesson assumes that your Notes Administrator assisted you in setting up your workstation to work off the network—in other words, remotely. If you are not sure whether or not you are configured correctly for working remotely, contact your Notes Administrator before continuing with this hour's lesson.

Notes works quite differently, however, when you work remotely. When you set up Notes on your remote PC, you must use a modem to connect to a Notes server through a telephone line connection. You create replica copies of all the databases that you want to use and store them on your PC's hard disk (unless you are working strictly through Interactive Connection, discussed later in this hour). You also control the times when information passes between you and others on the network because you must initiate the call to the server to begin the communication process. The speed at which you communicate with the server is typically much slower, as well. As mentioned previously, you work with replica copies of Notes databases, which are identical copies of databases located on a server. You exchange information with the server through a process called *replication*, which is the process of updating replica copies, or replicas, of a database. After you create a replica of a server database on your hard drive, you work in that copy and then dial the server to exchange new, modified, and deleted documents in the databases.

For example, when you replicate a single database with a server, your computer tries to find a replica of that database on the server by matching the Replica ID of your database. If a match is found, it tries to establish the last time the database replicated with that server by analyzing the replication history. If they have replicated before, your computer pulls down any new or modified documents since the last replication and sends up any new or modified documents that you have created since that time. If there is no replication history, your computer does a document-by-document comparison, looking for documents you don't have, pulling them down to your computer, and pushing up to the server any documents you have that the server doesn't. When this is done, replication is over. The date and time of this replication is recorded in your database (and on the server's replica) to be used the next time you replicate.

Here are some of the things you can expect to learn during this hour:

☐ Replicating a database
☐ Setting database encryption
☐ Using the Replicator page
☐ Understanding background replication
☐ Working with the Interactive Connection Method
☐ Configuring your PC to track free time remotely

Task 24.1: Replicating a Database

To work with a replica of a database (one stored on your hard drive), it is helpful to understand how to distinguish a local copy of a Notes database from a server copy. The icon for a database's local copy includes the name Local with the database title, whereas a server icon displays the server name. To verify which databases are local and which are on the server, choose View and make sure that the Show Server Names option is selected. If a server name is present below the database's title, the icon represents a server copy of the database; otherwise, the icon represents a local database. If you double-click a server copy's icon when you are working disconnected from the server, Notes prompts you to call a server to open the database. Double-clicking a local database icon opens the database from your hard drive when you are working remotely. Figure 24.1 shows examples of network and local database icons for the same database.

Figure 24.1.

This workspace displays several examples of local and network database icons.

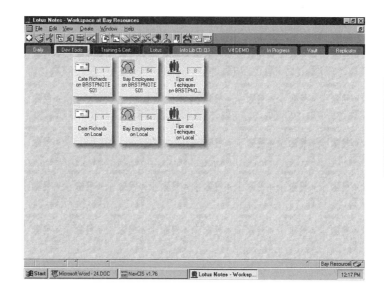

24

If your workspace stacks database icons (that is, if you chose View, Stack Replica Icons), click the icon indicator in the database icon's right corner to view a list that indicates the location that each database references. If Local is one of the options in that list, your hard drive has a local copy of the database. The drop-down list box might also include multiple server names if you have added the same network copy of the database icon from multiple servers, as shown in Figure 24.2.

Figure 24.2.

This menu shows an example of stacked icons referencing multiple servers.

Having multiple database icons for the same database that is stored on multiple servers is common for many remote users and is often convenient for updating purposes. All of an organization's servers might include a database that users access frequently (such as the Database Catalog) to make it easier for users to access the database from the network or when calling in from a remote location.

To replicate a database, follow these steps:

1. Prepare a first-time replica of a database (known as a replica "stub").

2. Choose appropriate replica options.

3. Verify access levels.

4. Replicate the database.

The following sections discuss these steps in detail.

Task 24.2: Preparing a Replica of a Database

Before you use the replication method, you must prepare a replica icon of each database that you plan to use. Replicas of server databases are duplicates of the server databases; the Replica ID that they share differentiates them from all other databases. When you exchange or access a Notes database, Notes looks at the Replica ID, not the name of the database, to determine what database you are trying to access. If the numbers don't match, Notes does not access the server's copy of the database during replication.

If you do not create replicas of databases when you work remotely, your databases cannot exchange information with the server. Don't confuse creating replicas of a database (choosing File, Replication, New Replica) with creating copies (choosing File, Database, New Copy). Copies of databases contain all the database's design and documents but not the same Replica ID—which is what the Notes server looks for when exchanging information with a database. If the Replica IDs between your database and the server do not match, you cannot replicate the database.

To create a replica of a database, follow these steps:

1. Select the database icon that you want to use to create a replica. You might have to connect to the server and add the database icons that you want to use to create replicas. You learn more about dialing the server shortly.

2. Choose File, Replication, New Replica to display the New Replica dialog box (see Figure 24.3).

3. In the Server list box, select the server on which you want to store the replica database—in this case, Local.

Figure 24.3.

The New Replica dialog box enables you to create replicas.

4. In the Title text box, Notes enters the network title of the database that you selected.

5. In the File Name text box, type the database's filename, including the path under which you want your hard drive or floppy disk to store it. By default, Notes enters the filename as it is stored on the server.

Make sure to name replicas of any databases as they're named on the server—unless you are making a replica copy of the Public Address Book in which the filename is identical on the server and your hard drive (in this case, change the name to something else you can remember, such as NAMES2.NSF). Although this practice isn't mandatory, naming databases this way helps eliminate confusion. If you highlight a copy of a database for which you want to make a replica, Notes automatically fills in the appropriate server and filenames for you when you choose File, Replication, New Replica.

Although it is not required, if you are making a replica of your Mail database, for consistency, always give the replica the same name as the original database on the server, including any subdirectory names (for example, MAIL\CRICHARD). Otherwise, Notes might not be able to find your Mail database if you later switch from On Server mail (onsite) to Local mail (offsite) settings in the Location document.

6. Select either or both of the following options:

☐ The *Copy Access Control List* option copies the original database's access control list (ACL) to the new replica. You should select this option; otherwise, Notes lists you as the database's manager but does not list servers, which can create problems when you try to replicate later.

☐ The *Create Full Text Index* for Searching option automatically creates a full-text index when you make the database's replica so that the Full Text Search option is immediately available. If you do not select this option, you can always create an index later. Before selecting this option, remember that creating an index can take some time, depending on your database's size.

7. Choose the Immediately option to immediately create a replica of the database that Notes initializes and fills with the contents (or a subset) of the original database or choose Next Scheduled Replication to create a replica stub of the database that Notes fills with the contents the first time you perform a replication.

> Choose the Next Scheduled Replication option if you plan to make several replica copies of databases or you expect that the initial replication of the database will be lengthy. You can then replicate with the server once to fill all the database shells at the same time.

8. Choose Encryption, Size Limit, or Replication Settings if you want your replica database to use any of these features. The following section discusses each of these options.

9. Choose OK to create the replica database.

> If your workspace doesn't display a copy of the network database icon when you want to make a replica copy to take on the road, the database isn't available on your workstation. Before following the preceding steps to make a replica copy, choose File, Database, Open to add the database icon to your workspace. If you are working remotely and do not have a copy of the icon, choose File, Mobile, Call Server and call as described later in this chapter, or choose File, Replication, New Replica and select the name of the server on which the database is located. Notes prompts you to call the server. After you connect with the server, the Choose Database dialog box opens. Select the database that you want to replicate and click Select. Notes displays the New Replica dialog box with the relevant information entered for you. To create your replica, complete the settings, as mentioned in the preceding steps.

Task 24.3: Setting Database Encryption Options

You can set the security of your local database so that only a user with your Notes ID and password can open it. To do so, follow these steps:

1. Choose the Encryption button in the New Replica dialog box. The Encryption dialog box appears (see Figure 24.4).

Figure 24.4.

In the Encryption dialog box, choose settings that determine how Notes encrypts your database.

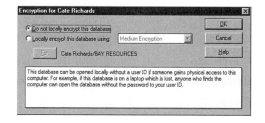

2. Choose the option Locally Encrypt This Database Using.

3. Select Simple, Medium, or Strong Encryption from the drop-down list box. With Simple Encryption, you can open the database much more quickly than you can with Medium or Strong encryption. Unless you must carry a higher level of security on the database, select Simple. Note that databases secured with Medium or Strong encryption cannot be compressed with disk compression utilities.

4. Choose OK to return to the New Replica dialog box.

Notes uses the public portion of your Notes ID encryption key to secure this database from other users accessing it without your Notes ID and password. Keep in mind, however, that if you are sharing a public workstation and encrypt a database locally that others also need to use, they cannot access the database with their IDs. Needless to say if you lose your ID file or it becomes corrupt, then you, too, will not be able to access the database.

Task 24.4: Identifying a Size Limit

You can specify the maximum size for this database by choosing the Size Limit button in the New Replica dialog box. The Size Limit dialog box appears (see Figure 24.5).

Figure 24.5.

In the Size Limit dialog box, you can set a local data-base's size limit.

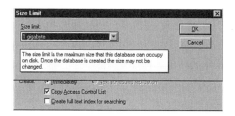

Size limits are set in gigabytes, so you most likely can leave the default (one gigabyte) as your entry. Your remote PC probably cannot host databases larger than one gigabyte anyway. Choose OK to exit and save your selection.

Task 24.5: Choosing Replication Settings

To conserve space, speed up replication time, control what you send to the server, or specify any other settings that affect the way a replica database replicates with servers, choose the New Replica dialog box's Replication Settings button while creating a new replica of a database. You also can modify replication settings later by highlighting a replica database and choosing File, Replication, Settings to display the Replication Settings dialog box shown in Figure 24.6.

Figure 24.6.

In the Replication Settings dialog box, you can control different aspects of the replication process.

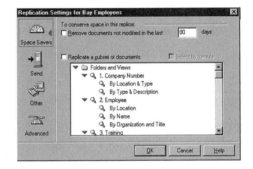

To set or change replication settings for a database, perform the following steps:

1. Select the database for which you want to change replication settings.

2. Select the File Replications Settings button if you are creating a new replica or choose File, Replication, Settings while highlighting an existing replica database icon to display the Replication Settings dialog box, as shown in Figure 24.6.

3. Choose all options that meet your needs and then choose OK.

The Replication Settings dialog box offers four panels in which you specify all replication settings for the database; the following sections describe the options available in each panel.

Task 24.5.1: Saving Space

The first panel to appear when you open the Replication Settings dialog box is the Space Savers panel. This is the panel shown in Figure 24.6. You can select either of the following options:

☐ *Remove Documents Not Modified in the Last __ Days*   Purges documents that have not been edited within the specified time period. If your database has documents meeting the criteria specified in this option, Notes prompts you each time you open the database until you choose Yes to remove the documents, change the number of days, or disable this option. The purging process removes from this replica all references to the deletion stub that Notes can copy to other replicas of the database. This option is a great way to save space. Selecting this option in your remote copy of the database does not remove documents from the database's server copy.

☐ *Replicate a Subset of Documents*—Enables you to specify the criteria that define the specific documents that you receive from the server during replication. You can select particular views or folders of documents to replicate from the list shown or specify a formula to use to limit the documents that you replicate with the server. For example, there might be a view called "New Prospects" in a Sales tracking database. You might choose just to receive any documents in that view by clicking it.

Task 24.5.2: Limiting What You Send to the Server

Just as you can limit what information you receive from the server, you also can limit the information that you send to the server. To do so, select the Send icon in the Replication Settings dialog box. The Send panel of the Replication Settings dialog box appears (see Figure 24.7).

Figure 24.7.

In the Replication Settings dialog box's Send panel, you can limit the information that you send to the server.

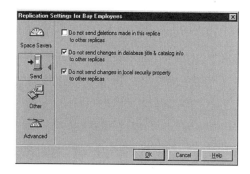

You can make any of the following selections:

☐ *Do Not Send Deletions Made in This Replica to Other Replicas*   When you select this option, you can delete documents from your local copy of the database without worrying about passing those deletions on to other replicas on the server. This option is handy if you cannot define a particular selective replication setting (such as the date created, the author name, or the subject matter) to limit the documents in your local database and you need to reduce the size of the database that you are storing locally. Your deletions do not pass on to the server. This option is also handy if you accidentally delete documents from a local copy and do not want to risk passing those deletions to the server. If you have the correct access to delete documents from the database's server copy, you can delete all instances of a particular document unless you select this option.

☐ *Do Not Send Changes in Database Title & Catalog Info to Other Replicas*   Select this option if you want to change the title of the database's local replica and update the catalog information without having the change replicate to the server copy of the database. Applications managers or designers primarily use this setting so that they can work with their applications locally. You must have at least designer-level access on the database's server copy to change database titles on the server copy and catalog information.

☐ *Do Not Send Changes in Local Security Property to Other Replicas*   Select this option if you want to change access control information for this database replica without changing the access control information in other replicas. Applications managers or designers primarily use this setting so that they can work with their applications locally. You must have manager-level access to change access control settings on the server copy of the database.

Task 24.5.3: Working with Other Replication Settings

You can temporarily disable replication, assign replication priority, limit documents received during replication according to a specified date, or identify a CD-ROM publishing date. Select the Other icon in the Replication Settings dialog box to display the Other panel shown in Figure 24.8.

Figure 24.8.

Open the Replication Settings dialog box's Other panel to control replication further.

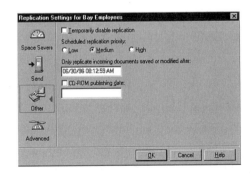

Select from any of these options:

☐ *Temporarily Disable Replication*   When you choose this option, Notes doesn't include the selected database in any replications with other replicas, even if you select the database when scheduling a replication. This option is ideal if you think your application might be corrupted and you want to avoid passing corrupt data to another copy of the database. You also can use this option to disable a database that changes infrequently so that the server doesn't spend time trying to read it during a scheduled replication. You can deselect this option later when you want to begin replication again.

☐ *Scheduled Replication Priority* You can choose Low, Medium, or High to indicate the level at which this database replicates during scheduled replications. Notes provides options that enable you to choose to replicate only databases with a particular priority setting during a session. The Replicator enables you to replicate only High priority databases as a way to limit the number of databases replicated during a scheduled replication. This is particularly useful if you are in a hurry and want to receive information only from databases that you have indicated as being highly important.

☐ *Only Replicate Incoming Documents Saved or Modified After* In this text box, you enter the cutoff date to limit the documents to replicate. You can minimize the number of documents that you replicate to only those created or edited on or after the specified date to reduce the amount of hard disk space used and the length of replication time. This setting is ideal if you want only the latest information from a database while working remotely, particularly if you typically access this database frequently while you are connected to the network.

> This option is a great feature to use if a high volume of documents is being added to a database and you go on vacation. You can specify that Notes replicate only a small subset of the documents rather than everything (which can take a long time).

☐ *CD-ROM Publishing Date* If you create a CD-ROM in which you publish a replica of your database, this option tells Notes to specify the replica's publishing date. The recipient of the CD-ROM copy of the database can then copy the CD-ROM file to his or her local drive (or server) and then replicate with the original database without having to perform a full replication—Notes need only replicate those documents created after the publishing date.

Task 24.5.4: Working with Advanced Replication Options

If you want really sophisticated replication strategies, select the Advanced icon in the Replication Settings dialog box to open the Advanced panel shown in Figure 24.9. The options in this dialog box are beyond this book's scope, but they enable you to replicate with a much finer granularity, such as deciding whether to replicate agents, forms, views, and changes to the ACL.

Figure 24.9.

The Replication Settings dialog box's Advanced panel contains more replication options.

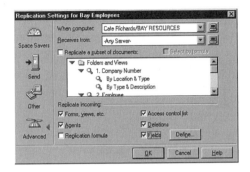

Task 24.6: Setting Up the Replicator

Notes 4.6 provides a feature called the Replicator. With the Replicator, you can use a single command to replicate multiple databases with different servers. You also can do other work while Notes replicates in the background.

To display the Replicator, click your workspace's Replicator tab. When you switch to the Replicator, the workspace appears, as shown in Figure 24.10.

Figure 24.10.

The Replicator enables you to manage the replication of your local databases in one place.

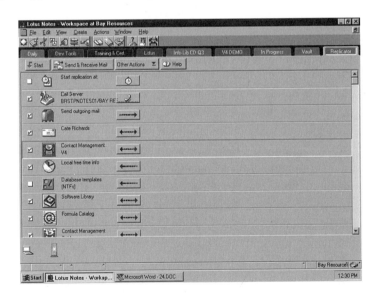

When you use Notes away from the office, the Replicator automatically can call each server with which you want to replicate. If you're using a passthru server or a remote LAN server, Replicator can make a single call and replicate all of your local databases at one time, even if they're on different servers. Using the Replicator, you also can customize replication based on the location from which you are working. Replicator also provides additional ways to replicate; for example, you can assign high priority to selected databases and replicate only those high-priority databases. The following sections describe the Replicator.

Task 24.6.1: Understanding the Replicator Page

The Replicator is always the last page on your workspace; you cannot delete it. The Replicator automatically contains the following types of entries:

☐ *Database*   The Replicator contains a database entry for each local replica that you have unless you deleted the entry from the Replicator page (see Figure 24.11). When you add replicas of databases to your workstation, Notes automatically adds them to the Replicator. To remove replicas of databases that you do not want on your Replicator, highlight the database entry and press Delete. Choose Yes to confirm that you want to remove the entry. If you are not using scheduled replication, to replicate you must click the Start button manually, as described in "Replicating Databases with the Replicator" later in this chapter.

24

Figure 24.11.

Database icons on the Replicator tab represent local replica copies of databases. The example icon here shows the Database icon for a database titled Contact Management V4.

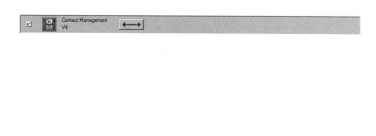

☐ *Start Replication At*   Use this entry to specify a replication schedule and enable scheduled replication. The replication schedule used depends on the location that you are using and the settings that you made in the current Location's document. If you want to modify the time in which you start replication, click the clock icon displayed on the Start Replication At entry; Notes then opens your current Location document (see Figure 24.12). After you have made any necessary changes, press Esc and choose Yes to save your changes. If you are not using scheduled replication, this option is blank. To replicate, you must click the Start button manually, as described in "Replicating Databases with the Replicator" later in this chapter.

Figure 24.12.

The Start Replication At entry is always first in the Replicator. You cannot delete this entry.

☐ *Database Templates* Use this entry to replicate any design templates you have (see Figure 24.13).

Figure 24.13.

You cannot delete the Database Templates entry, which refreshes any database templates that you have on your computer; however, you can uncheck it.

☐ *Send Outgoing Mail* Use this entry to send all pending messages from your Outgoing Mail database, MAIL.BOX (see Figure 24.14).

Figure 24.14.

You cannot delete the Send Outgoing Mail entry, which sends all pending messages from the Outgoing Mail database.

You also can create the following types of entries for mobile locations (such as Home and Travel):

☐ *Call Server* When you create a Call Server entry, you specify the server that you want to call. The Replicator then uses the information from the Server Connection record, along with any special location prefix and suffix numbers that you might have defined, when dialing (see Figure 24.15).

Figure 24.15.

You can use a Call Server entry to connect to a server.

☐ *Hangup*   You can use a Hangup entry to end a connection with a server (see Figure 24.16).

Figure 24.16.

The Hangup entry tells Notes to end a call with the current server.

To set up the Replicator, perform any of the tasks described in the following sections.

Task 24.6.2: Moving a Replicator Entry

Except for the Start Replication At entry, which always comes first, you can arrange Replicator entries in any order you want. For example, you might want to group Replicator entries according to the server on which you want to replicate so that the Replicator has to call that server only one time to exchange all databases in common. To move a Replicator entry, follow these steps:

1. Click and hold the left mouse button over the entry that you want to move. Be careful not to drag over the actual button, or you might start that button's procedure!

2. Drag the entry to its new position.

3. Release the left mouse button.

Task 24.6.3: Creating a Replicator Entry

You can create entries that automatically connect and disconnect from servers when you replicate over a modem. You can create a Call Server entry or Hangup entry, as explained in the following steps.

As previously mentioned, the Replicator automatically adds Database entries when you create replicas of databases. If you have deleted a database replication entry and want to restore it to the Replicator, however, switch to the workspace page that has the database's replica and click the replica's icon. Hold down the left mouse button and drag the icon to the Replicator tab. Release the mouse button when the mouse cursor is positioned over the tab. Notes restores the Database entry to the Replicator.

24

To make a Call Server entry, perform the following steps:

1. If necessary, switch to the location where you use your modem to connect to the Notes servers.

2. In the Replicator page, click where you want to position the Call Server entry. Notes places the Call Server entry directly above the entry that you click.

3. Choose Create, Call Entry. By default, Notes creates the entry for your Home server.

4. If you want to create a Call Server entry to a server other than your Home server, click the new Call Server entry's action button (the icon displays a small, yellow phone). Select the server that you want to call and then choose OK.

When creating Call Server entries, keep the following tips in mind:

☐ If you have set up a server connection for a passthru server or a remote LAN server, create a single Call Server entry for this server on the Replicator page. When you do so, the Replicator can make just one phone call to replicate with all the servers. Ask your Notes administrator about passthru and remote LAN server connections particular to your company.

☐ When calling a server, the Replicator stays connected to the server until it reaches another Call Server entry or a Hangup entry. You don't need to create a Hangup entry for each Call Server entry, just the last one.

☐ If you create two or more Call Server entries next to each other, the Replicator tries each call in turn. After connecting to the server, the Replicator skips to the first entry that is not a Call Server entry.

☐ You can replicate over a modem without Call Server entries. If you haven't created Call Server entries, the Replicator tries to call the last server with which the first Database entry replicated.

You can create a Hangup entry so that the Replicator automatically disconnects from a server when you replicate over a modem. To create a Hangup entry, follow these steps:

1. In the Replicator page, click where you want the Hangup entry. Notes adds the Hangup entry immediately above the entry that you click.

2. Choose Create, Hangup Entry. Notes adds a new Hangup entry to the Replicator directly above the entry that you clicked.

If you want to make the Hangup entry the last entry in the list, click and hold the left mouse button over the Hangup entry and drag it to the last position. Remember, you need only one Hangup entry, even if you have more than one Call Server entry. After reaching a new Call Server entry, the Replicator automatically hangs up the current call.

Task 24.6.4: Specifying Replicator Options

Replicator entries contain action buttons that you can use to specify Replicator options. Table 24.1 describes the options available.

Table 24.1. Replicator page action buttons.

Icon	Description
	You can click the clock action button on a Start Replication At entry to specify a replication schedule for the current location. The current location document opens in Edit mode so that you can make any changes that you want. Press Esc and then choose Yes to save your new settings.
	You can click any Call Server entry action button to specify a different server to call. Select the server from the pop-up list that appears when you click this action button. In this list, Notes displays the servers for which you already have defined phone numbers.
	You can click the arrow action buttons on a Database entry to specify whether you want to send or receive documents from a server. If you select the Receive Documents from Server option, you can reduce the time that replication takes by also selecting to receive full documents, document summaries, and the first 40K of rich text only or document summaries only.

By choosing the option Receive Summary and 40KB of Rich Text when you click the arrow action buttons on a Database entry, you shorten a document only by removing bitmaps and other large objects and all attachments from the document copies that the server sends. When you select this option, Notes retrieves only the document summary (which consists of basic document information, such as author and subject) and the first 40KB of information. Notes removes the large objects and attachments from the copies that you receive, not from the documents stored on the server. This option helps reduce long exchange times and saves valuable disk space by keeping file size low. If you later decide that you want to get the information that you excluded during replication, you can deselect this option or work interactively in the server copy of the database to review the entire document.

Keep the following points in mind when using this option:

☐ When you open a shortened document, Notes displays (TRUNCATED) in the title bar as part of the document's title.

24

☐ You cannot categorize or edit shortened documents.

☐ Agents do not work on shortened documents.

☐ Notes does not send shortened documents to another replica unless you have chosen for the replica the option Receive Summary and 40KB of Rich Text only.

☐ If you elect to shorten documents, you can retrieve the entire document by choosing Actions, Retrieve Entire Document while reading the document. Notes dials the server and retrieves the rest of the document for you to review.

> If you find errors in your replication with a server and are either not receiving or not sending documents during a session, check whether the arrow action button is set to send (the arrow is pointing rightward), receive (the arrow is pointing to the left), or send and receive (a double-headed arrow is pointing both ways). Make changes as necessary.
>
> If you are still having difficulty, check the access control to make sure that both you and the server with which you are replicating have the appropriate access level for the database. Finally, make sure your database is a replica of the database located on the server, not just a plain copy.

Task 24.6.5: Deleting a Replicator Entry

You easily can delete Replicator entries by clicking the entry that you want to remove and pressing the Delete key. Choose Yes to confirm the deletion.

Task 24.7: Replicating with the Server

When you are ready to replicate with the server—either to fill the database replica shells (database replicas that have not yet been replicated for the first time) that you might have created in the previous section or to exchange information with the server on an ongoing basis—you must plug your modem into your PC and connect the modem to the telephone jack. You can either carry your own telephone cable with you when working remote or unplug the cable from the connection in back of the phone (if possible) and plug it into your modem jack. Make sure the other end of the cable is plugged into the telephone jack in the wall.

You should take a telephone cable with you. In the United States, the telephone jack connector is commonly referred to as an RJ-11; you might need to verify the appropriate cable connector that you need when working internationally, because it varies by country. If you need to dial manually (that is, dial through an operator to get an outside line), if the closest phone cable is permanently attached to the phone, or if you are trying to use a damaged phone cable, you will be thankful that you have a spare. You can then plug your cable into the wall socket, attach it to your modem, and plug the telephone into your modem (if you have a second jack in your modem).

Some phones have data ports located in the back of the phone. If you have such a phone, run a telephone cable from your modem to the back of the phone, rather than directly to the jack. You need a second cable in this case. If possible, running the telephone cable directly from your modem into the wall jack is preferable. This setup makes replication much smoother.

Task 24.8: Performing a Replication

You can replicate information between the server and one (or many) of the replica databases located on your workspace. When you perform an exchange (replication), you dial the server, send and receive database information, and hang up. There are two ways to replicate with a server:

☐ Replicate selected databases in the foreground.

☐ Replicate selected databases with the Replicator.

This section describes both options.

Task 24.8.1: Replicating in the Foreground

You can replicate a database with a server in the foreground, by following these steps:

1. Select the database that you want to replicate.

2. Choose File, Replication, Replicate or click the File Replication Replicate SmartIcon. The Replicate dialog box appears (see Figure 24.17).

Figure 24.17.

The Replicate dialog box appears when you replicate in the foreground.

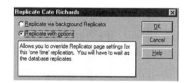

3. Choose the option Replicate with Options and then choose OK. The Replicate dialog box displays new settings, as shown in Figure 24.18.

Figure 24.18.

You can choose addi-
tional settings in this
Replicate dialog box.

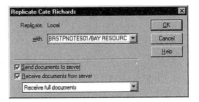

4. Select a different server with which to replicate by clicking the down arrow next to the With drop-down list box, if necessary.

5. Select one or both of the following:

  ☐ Send Documents to Server.

  ☐ Receive Documents from Server. If you select this option, you can specify whether you want to receive full documents, document summaries, the first 40KB of rich text only, or document summaries only.

6. Choose OK. Notes prompts you for permission to dial the server that you selected. Choose Yes to begin the replication.

When you use the Replicate with Options setting to replicate databases, Notes calls the server and performs the replication in the foreground; before you can continue working, you must wait until the replication finishes. If you want to continue working while Notes replicates, use the Replicator (background replication), as discussed in the following section.

> If you work onsite and offsite, you can decrease the amount of time required to perform remote database exchanges. While you are still connected onsite to the server, perform a database exchange for all your local replicas, as described earlier. You leave the office with the most recent database information and decrease the amount of time needed to perform a remote replication because you don't need to send and receive as many documents. Database replication with the server is also much faster over the network.

Task 24.8.2: Replicating Databases with the Replicator

You can use the Replicator to replicate databases in the background. With Notes replicating in the background, you can continue to do other work. If your current location is set up for scheduled replication, you don't need to do anything to have the Replicator begin background replication when the replication settings criteria are met. If your modem is connected to a phone line, Notes begins calling the first server identified on the Replicator page and replicates information until it handles the last replication entry. You also can tell Notes to begin a replication sequence whenever you want by clicking the Start button at the top of the Replicator page.

Watch the bottom of the Replicator page to determine the status of each database as it replicates (see Figure 24.19). Notes communicates to you each step in the replication process, as well as the estimated time that it will take for the replication of each database to complete. Notice that a hand points to each entry on the Replicator page as the entry becomes active.

If you click the Next button, Notes stops replicating the current database and moves to the next entry. Click Stop if you want to end the current replication completely. Notes stops replicating the current database and ignores the remaining entries on the Replicator page but does not hang up the connection. If you want to hang up manually, choose File, Mobile, Hang Up; highlight the Port you want to disconnect and select Hang Up.

24

If you switch between working offsite and onsite, keep in mind that any information that you enter into your local replicas doesn't appear on the server copy of the database when you return to the office, unless you perform a database exchange after your last entry. To update the server copy of the database, perform a background replication as soon as you reconnect to the network.

Figure 24.19.

When you use the Replicator to replicate databases, the Replicator page provides several indications of the replication's progress.

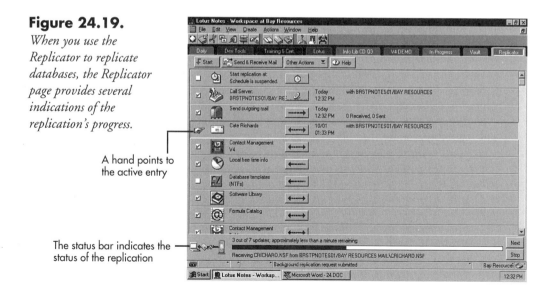

A hand points to the active entry

The status bar indicates the status of the replication

Task 24.8.3: Performing Some Special Actions with the Replicator

Often, when working remotely, you might want to replicate mail, replicate only one database, replicate only selected databases or with a selected server, or replicate high-priority databases only. The Send & Receive Mail Only and the Other Actions buttons enable you to perform the following actions during replication:

☐ Click the Send & Receive Mail Only button if you want to replicate mail only during a particular replication (or select it from the Mail section of the status bar). Notes immediately calls your Home/Mail server and exchanges Mail databases. It also transfers all the mail that you might have created and stored in your Outgoing Mail database.

☐ Click the Other Actions button. A drop-down menu opens. Select Replicate High Priority Databases from the menu to begin replicating only those databases whose replication settings indicate high priority (see the section "Working with Other Replication Settings," earlier in this chapter, for information on setting database priorities).

☐ Select the databases that you want to replicate by clicking the check boxes next to their entries. Click Select Other Actions, select Replicate with Server from the drop-down menu, and then select the server with which you want to replicate. Choose OK to begin the replication. Notes calls only that server to replicate with. Keep in mind that if the databases that you select do not have replicas on that particular server and you are not calling a passthru server, Notes does not update your databases.

☐ Select the database that you want to replicate by clicking its entry in the Replicator page. Click Other Actions and select Replicate Selected Database Only from the drop-down menu. Notes calls the server and replicates only that database.

☐ Select any database that you want to replicate by clicking the check box next to its entry (also make sure that you deselect the check boxes for the entries that you don't want to replicate). Click Other Actions and select Replicate Selected Databases Only from the drop-down menu. Notes calls and replicates only the selected databases.

☐ To send your outgoing mail only, click Other Actions and then select Send Outgoing Mail from the drop-down menu. Notes calls your server and transfers only your outgoing mail to the server. You will not receive any updates or send any updates to other server databases.

Task 24.8.4: Monitoring Replication History

After you replicate using the Replicator, you see how many documents that you sent and received logged directly onto each database entry that you selected for replication. However, you might want to see the history of past replications to see who replicated with a particular database and when. To see this history, move to the regular workspace page, highlight the database in which you are interested, and choose File, Replication, History. The Replication History dialog box appears (see Figure 24.20).

Figure 24.20.

You can view a database's replication history in the Replication History dialog box.

You can copy the information to the clipboard to paste into a report (by choosing the Copy button), clear the history (by choosing Clear if you have at least Designer access), or change the way that you view the information by server name (by choosing Server Name) or by date (by choosing Date). Choose Done when you are ready to exit the Replication History dialog box. This technique is ideal for database managers who need to review database activity.

Task 24.9: Using the Interactive Connection Method

An interactive connection establishes a direct link between your remote station and the server, requiring a constant telephone connection. Although your PC connects to the server by telephone lines rather than LAN cables, you can use the databases stored on the server and receive the most up-to-date information in the databases just as though you were working onsite. You receive mail directly from the mail router, and the mail that you send transfers through the mail router directly to the specified recipient as soon as you send the mail.

Interactive connections, however, tie up the server for a longer period of time, resulting in higher phone costs. Plan to use an interactive connection only when you work with a very large database and don't have the resources to install the database on your remote PC or when you are adding a database so that you can create a replica of it. An interactive connection also can be useful if you don't use the database frequently. However, working with databases interactively is much slower than utilizing the replication method.

24

If you use an interactive connection, save documents often. Otherwise, if your connection with the server discontinues before you complete and save an entry, you might lose the information. If you lose the connection, keep the document open on your desktop until you can reestablish the connection. Save the file when you reconnect with the server.

To work interactively, you first must call the server. After you are connected, you can work in the databases on that server as though you were connected on a LAN.

 If the databases you are using are on different servers, you must repeat this process for each server after you finish working with one, unless you are connecting to a passthru server. Contact your Notes Administrator if you are not sure how your Notes server connections are set up.

To call the server, follow these steps:

1. Choose File, Mobile, Call Server or click the File Mobile Call Server SmartIcon. The Call Server dialog box appears (see Figure 24.21).

Figure 24.21.

In the Call Server dialog box, you can call the server directly.

2. Select a server from the server list. The servers listed are the ones for which you have Connection documents in your Personal Name and Address Book.

3. Specify any prefix or suffix options that you want to use.

4. Choose Auto Dial to have the computer dial the server immediately, or choose Manual Dial if you want Notes to prompt you to pick up the phone to dial manually.

5. Choose File, Mobile, Hangup when you are through working with the server.

If you are unsuccessful connecting to the server, Notes prompts you with the appropriate message. Try to dial the server again. If you are still having trouble connecting remotely, contact your Notes Administrator.

If you plan to use NotesMail interactively (connected to the server) and want to route the memos immediately when you send them, select a location that is set up for On Server mail. Select the location indicator in the status bar and then select Edit Current to determine your mail file location setup. Use your network copy of your Mail database while working interactively.

You now are connected to the server and can open any database on the server to which you have been granted access. (Your connection is just like a network connection at this point, only slower and less reliable.) If the server's database icon isn't already on your desktop (the icon displays the server's name if you chose View, Show Server Names), you can add it. If you have stacked your replica icons, click the icon for the database that you want to use, and in the drop-down list, highlight the name of the server to which you have just connected.

24

When you use the interactive connection method, you might lose your connection to the server on several occasions. Usually, an interruption in the phone line causes this problem, but you might also have this problem if you don't perform an activity for a long time (such as when you are reading a long document) and the Hangup If Idle For time expires. If this problem occurs too frequently, contact your Notes Administrator for assistance in adjusting your Hangup If Idle setting.

Task 24.10: Setting Up Calendaring and Scheduling to Check Free Time When Working Remotely

You can set up Notes to check the free time available for selected individuals in your company while you are working remotely. In Hour 20, "Working with Notes Calendaring and Scheduling," you learned how to schedule appointments and check on the free time for each person you were inviting to a meeting. However, when you are working remotely, you typically do not have access to each user's free time unless you tell Notes to replicate the user's information to your remote workstation.

When Notes 4.6 was installed on your workstation, a database entry for checking free time was automatically entered on your Replicator page (you learn more about this feature in the next hour's lesson), as displayed in Figure 24.22. When you click the replicator arrow (the blue arrow next to the database icon), Notes might prompt you to call the server to check free time. To set up free time, however, you need not call the server, so select No if prompted. The Local free time settings dialog box appears, as shown in Figure 24.23.

Figure 24.22.

Notes 4.6 automatically adds the Local Free Time Info replication entry to your workspace. Place a check mark next to its icon if you want to poll the server for free time information when you replicate.

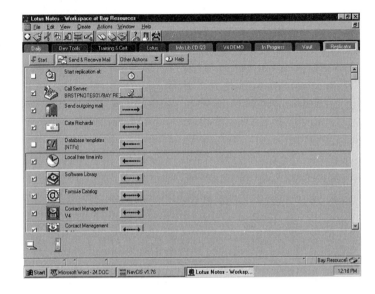

Figure 24.23.

You can tell Notes whose free time schedules you want to maintain while working remotely.

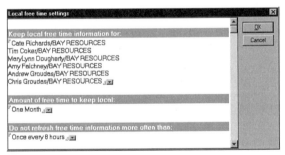

Specify the following settings in the Local free time settings dialog box:

☐ Type or select the user names for which you want to replicate free time schedules. Make sure that this list includes your name. To select the user names (which is recommended), click the down arrow next to the Keep local free time information for field to open the Name & Address Books to which you have access.

☐ Select the amount of free time that you want to keep local. For example, if you want to keep as much as a month's worth of free time information for scheduling purposes, select One Month from the selection list in the Amount of free time to keep local section.

☐ In the Do not refresh free time information more often than section's list box, select the length of time that you want Notes to wait before checking for free time again with the server. For example, select Once every 8 hours if you want Notes to check for free time only once during the working day.

Choose OK to save your settings. You have now configured Notes to keep track of the free time for the selected users.

> Keep in mind that keeping track of users' free time takes up space on your hard drive and increases the amount of time that it takes to replicate with the server. Set up only those users for whom it is important to keep track of free time; otherwise, you might find yourself short on disk space pretty quickly! Also, limit the amount of time that you want to keep the free time information to reduce further the amount of drive space used. Finally, limit the number of times that you poll the server to check free time in order to eliminate several calls to the server while you are working remotely.

24

Workshop

During this hour, you learned how to perform replication with a server. You learned how replication is based on Replica ID's and time of last replication and you understand the ways in which you can control what is replicated.

Here are some of the words this hour introduced you to and some common questions you might have.

Key Terms

Review the following list of terms:

☐ *Replication*   The process of synchronizing the content of databases sharing a common Replica ID.

☐ *Replica stub*   An empty replica of a database containing no documents or design elements (forms or views). During the next replication, the documents and design elements will be replicated and the stub will "fill out" to become a standard Notes database.

☐ *Truncated document*   A document that has been limited in size to avoid long replication times when downloading documents with large file attachments.

Common Questions

Q **I have replicated with the server, but I did not receive documents I can see in the server replica in my local replica. What can I do?**

A Replicas can get out of sync for a variety of reasons. The first thing to do with most replication problems is to clear the replication history in your local replica of the database. That way, the next time you replicate, a document-by-document comparison takes place. This lengthens your replication time substantially if you are replicating a large database.

Q **When dialing in to my server, I hear the modem connecting, but I never receive the "Connected at" message on my status bar, and no replication takes place. What's the problem?**

A You might have a bad phone connection and Notes is struggling to connect at the speed you have set for your modem. Try gradually reducing your modem speed.

INDEX